Bean Cooking Times at a Glance

For instructions on cooking beans, see pages 184–187.

Approximate Minutes Under High Pressure

Beans (1 Cup Dry)	Soaked Natural Pressure Release*	Soaked Quick-Release	Unsoaked Quick-Release	Yield in Cups
Adzuki	2–3	5–9	14–20	2½
Anasazi	1–2	4–7	20–22	2¼
Black (turtle)	3–6	5–9	18–25	2
Black-eyed peas	—	—	10–11	2¼
Cannellini	5–8	9–12	22–25	2
Chickpeas (garbanzos)	9–14	13–18	30–40	2½
Christmas Lima	4–6	8–10	16–18	1¼
Cranberry (borlotto)	5–8	9–12	30–34	2¼
Fava†	8–14	12–18	22–28	2
Flageolet	6–10	10–14	17–22	2
Great Northern	4–8	8–12	25–30	2¼
Lentils (brown)	—	—	8–10	2
Lentils (French)	—	—	10–12	2
Lentils (red)	—	—	4–6	2
Lima (large)‡	1–3	4–7	12–16	2
Lima (baby)	2–3	5–7	12–15	2½
Mung	—	—	10–12	2
Navy (pea)	3–4	6–8	16–25	2
Peas (split, green or yellow)	—	—	6–10	2
Peas (whole, green)	4–6	8–10	16–18	2
Pigeon peas (gandules)	2–5	6–9	20–25	3
Pinto	1–3	4–6	22–25	2¼
Red kidney	5–8	10–12	20–25	2
Scarlet Runner	8–10	12–14	17–20	1¼
Soy beans (beige)‡	5–8	9–12	28–35	2¼
Soy beans (black)‡	16–18	20–22	35–40	2½

NOTE: Do not fill the cooker more than halfway. Owners of jiggle-top cookers should add 1 tablespoon of oil per cup of dried beans to control foaming.

*Use the timing in this column if you intend to let the pressure come down naturally, about 10 minutes. This is the preferred technique.

†Skins remain leathery after cooking and must be removed before serving unless the beans are puréed.

‡Requires 2 tablespoons of oil per cup of dried beans. Add ½ teaspoon salt when soaking/cooking large limas and black soy beans. Remove any floating bean skins before cooking.

GREAT
VEGETARIAN
COOKING
UNDER
PRESSURE

GREAT VEGETARIAN COOKING UNDER PRESSURE

TWO-HOUR TASTE IN TEN MINUTES

Lorna J. Sass

William Morrow and Company, Inc. / *New York*

Library of Congress Cataloging-in-Publication Data

Sass, Lorna J.
    Great vegetarian cooking under pressure / Lorna J. Sass.
        p.   cm.
    Includes bibliographical references and index.
    ISBN 0-688-12326-0
    1. Pressure Cookery.   2. Vegetarian cookery.   I. Title.
TX840.P7S363   1994
641.5'636—dc20   94-10054
                                              CIP

Printed in the United States of America

First Edition

7 8 9 10

BOOK DESIGN BY RICHARD ORIOLO

For My Mother

who introduced me to the
magical world of pressure cooking
and to the wondrous world of food

ACKNOWLEDGMENTS

his book has been enriched by the efforts and creative energies of many generous friends and colleagues.

First and foremost, I would like to express my sincere gratitude to the pressure cooker elves—that loosely knit group of pressured cooks around the country—who retested my recipes and whose suggestions for improving taste and clarifying instructions are sprinkled throughout the book.

Heartfelt thanks to Pat Baird, Maryann Bolles, Ann Brady, Barbara Breuer, Kay Bushnell, Marian Cahir, Joyce Curwin, Marilyn Einhorn, Carolyn Adams Griffith-Hampson, Michele Lunt, Marissa La Magna, Maryann Mayo, Virginia Messina, Elizabeth Moffett, John Niblett, Margaret Polischeck, Eleanor Sass, Sandra Shapiro, Beth Adams Smith, Kate Schumann, Marjorie Thomas, and Steve Weinberg.

A few people deserve the lofty status of "super elves" because they tested dozens of recipes and kept asking for more. They are Johnna Albi, Judy Bloom, Joan Carlton, Arlene Ciroula, Gloria Drayer, Elizabeth Germain, and Roberta Chopp Rothschild.

And special appreciation for:

Pat Baird, whose culinary virtuosity graces many pages of this book, and whose support and encouragement always provide a safe harbor;

Judy Bloom, who lifted my spirits and improved many of the dishes in this book immeasurably during our Monday recipe development sessions;

Phyllis Wender, my literary agent, whose generosity and friendship extend well beyond business hours;

Arlene Ciroula, who offered valuable suggestions on the introductory material;

Ann Bramson, my editor at William Morrow, whose enthusiasm for pressure cooking runs a close second to my own;

Deborah Weiss Geline, who allows the buck to stop at her desk with such grace and good cheer;

Pamela Lyons, whose attention and copyediting pencil are impressively sharp;

Dennis Hunsicker and Christian Dorbandt, who cheerfully "cat-sat" during my escapes from the city.

CONTENTS

INTRODUCTION

I was first introduced to the irresistible pleasures of pressure cooking in 1986. While on a trip to India, my mother had been very impressed by the magnificent curries and dals that she watched being turned out of the pressure cooker in a flash.

My mom wanted to replicate these dishes with the same speed and convenience back home. Thinking she wouldn't be able to locate a pressure cooker in this country (they had fallen out of fashion during the late fifties, probably due to America's fascination with TV dinners and other convenience foods), she carted back a rather tinny, old-fashioned jiggle-top model and began producing full-flavored lentil soups in seven minutes and chickpea curries in under half an hour.

I was very impressed with the soul-satisfying results, and wondered why in our very busy lives we weren't all using pressure cookers. I soon found out: The very mention of pressure cooking induced fear and trembling. Each time I brought up the subject among friends and colleagues, I heard a litany of "Tales of the Jiggle-Top," replete with gruesome details of Aunt Tillie's split pea soup on the ceiling.

Since I had no such trauma in my family history, I remained undaunted. After cooking hundreds of different dishes in a variety of pressure cookers, I became convinced that the newly designed pots now on the market were perfectly safe. In 1989 I published *Cooking Under Pressure* and have since received many enthusiastic letters from the converted.

Over the past few years, more and more people have become committed to lowering the fat and cholesterol in their diets. Because the pressure cooker creates such full-flavored foods with little to no fat, it is the ideal ally in fulfilling such a goal. And since this powerhouse-of-a-pot performs some of its most impressive magic with vegetables, beans, and grains, I decided to focus an entire volume on vegetarian cooking.

Pressure cooking is the pressured cook's best way to beat the clock. It's the only satisfactory reply I've found to the questions that plague health-conscious Americans: How am I going to eat healthy food without spending lots of time in the kitchen? How can I achieve two-hour taste in ten minutes?

The answer: Cook under pressure.

Happy cooking!

Lorna J. Sass
New York City

If you need information on purchasing a pressure cooker or would like to share your recipes for the next edition of this book, I'd be happy to hear from you. (Please be sure to enclose a self-addressed stamped envelope if requesting a response.) Write to me c/o Cooking Under Pressure, P.O. Box 704, New York, N.Y. 10024.

GREAT
VEGETARIAN
COOKING
UNDER
PRESSURE

PRESSURE COOKING PERFECTED

Welcome to the world of pressure cooking, an inviting place that offers you twice the flavor in one third (or less) the time.

If you are a newcomer to this land and find yourself experiencing appliance phobia, I guarantee that you'll be over it the moment you taste your first pressure-cooked risotto (5 minutes) or lentil soup (7 minutes). By the time you've made Zucchini Bisque (4 minutes) and Coconut Rice Pudding (13 minutes), you'll wonder how you ever managed without a pressure cooker.

Once you've locked the lid in place and brought up the pressure, you can't look inside the pot and stir or fiddle. Your kitchen will be filled with tantalizing aromas and you'll be aching to see what's going on inside, but you just can't.

This dramatic tension is happily short-lived and your patience handsomely and tastefully rewarded with delicious food that's ready to eat in the time it has taken you to set the table.

After all my years of cooking under pressure, there's still something about the process that feels just a bit like magic.

More Versatility: The design of the stationary pressure rod eliminates concerns about clogging the vent and makes it possible to cook beans and grains without careful monitoring or the addition of oil.

User-Friendliness: It's easier to tell when you've reached high pressure, or if the pressure has dropped because the heat is too low.

Serenity: The new cookers are quiet. There is no chug-chug racket and little to no hissing.

Better Construction: Most are made of high-quality stainless steel and have a copper or aluminum sandwich in the bottom for even cooking. (This is especially important to prevent scorching when using high heat to bring the ingredients up to high pressure.)

Stove-top Release Option: Each model offers a stove-top option for releasing pressure. Most jiggle-top cookers must be carried to the sink and placed under cold running water.

Less Liquid: Some models require less than 1 cup of liquid to bring the cooker up to high pressure. This is not a major concern, but does provide more versatility.

PRESSURE COOKER BASICS

How the Pressure Cooker Works The pressure cooker performs its impressive wizardry by cooking foods (with some added liquid) in a tightly sealed pot at a temperature higher than the standard boiling point. When the cooker is set over high heat, steam pressure builds and the internal temperature rises, increasing the boiling point from the standard 212 degrees to 250 degrees Fahrenheit. Under high pressure, the fiber in food is tenderized and flavors mingle in record time.

Since there has to be sufficient room inside the pot for the steam pressure to build, pressure cookers are filled anywhere from halfway to three quarters of total capacity, depending upon the type of ingredient and the manufacturer's specifications.

A New Generation of Safe Pressure Cookers

The growing interest in pressure cooking over the last decade has in part been a response to a new and improved style of pressure cooker. Introduced to this country from Europe during the mid-eighties, this sophisticated appliance—what I refer to as a second-generation pressure cooker—has a stationary pressure regulator rather than a removable jiggle-top. Among the popular jiggle-tops are brands such as T-Fal, Presto, and Mirro. Some manufacturers of second-generation cookers include Kuhn-Rikon, Magefesa, Zepter, and Cuisinarts.

Most cookers now on the market (both first-generation jiggle-tops and second-generation models) have one or more backup mechanisms that prevent the buildup of excess pressure and are therefore quite safe to use. However, second-generation cookers provide a number of advantages worth considering.

What Size Cooker Should I Buy?

For those investing in their first cooker, I usually recommend a 6- or an 8-quart model. This may seem rather large, but keep in mind that the pressure cooker cannot be more than three quarters full (only halfway full when cooking beans) since there has to be sufficient room inside the pot for the steam pressure to build. A 6-quart cooker is an ideal size for cooking soups and stews; an 8-quart is preferred if you like to cook in quantity and make stocks.

If you really get into pressure cooking, there will be many times when you'll want to cook two dishes at once, perhaps a bean stew and a grain pilaf. For a second cooker, I recommend a 2½- or a 4-quart, which are ideal for cooking grains (especially risotto) and most vegetables.

Please note that European cookers are sized by liters. A 2-liter cooker is roughly 2½ quarts. A 3½-liter cooker holds about 4 quarts, and so on.

Accessories

A *timer* is essential to successful pressure cooking. Many foods are not harmed by an extra minute or two of intense cooking, but some are ruined. Use a timer and relax.

If your stove has a built-in timer, you're all set. If you need to purchase one, I recommend a digital timer. Mine can handle three settings at once, which proves very handy when cooking more than one dish.

It's also critical to own a *Flame Tamer* (heat diffuser) that is set under the cooker to prevent scorching when cooking dry pilafs or concentrated ingredients that contain a high percentage of natural sugar. It is an inexpensive item available at any well-stocked housewares store. When I feel that a Flame Tamer is needed in the recipe, I call for it in the instructions. (For more on the Flame Tamer, see page 6.)

A very useful item is a 1½- or 2-quart *soufflé dish* or a Corning Ware, Pyrex, or other type of *heatproof casserole* that fits into the cooker with at least ½ inch to spare around the diameter.

For making steamed pudding-cakes, you'll need a 1-quart *Bundt pan* (a traditional baking pan with a central funnel). These are available at many specialty food stores and by mail-order at a good price from Zabar's (see Mail-Order Sources).

ALSO USEFUL

Kitchen Scale: This comes in very handy for weighing vegetables (and also envelopes, which saves trips to the post office and leaves me more time to cook).

Mini-chopper: I am in love with my mini-chopper, a veritable workhorse for mincing cloves of garlic and knobs of ginger.

Spice Grinder: I use my mini-chopper as a spice grinder, but you can use a coffee grinder that you dedicate to spices only.

Good Vegetable Peeler: I use an old-fashioned peeler for removing citrus peel, but the Swiss Kuhn-Rikon peeler for other tasks. The latter is inexpensive and available through Williams-Sonoma and other retailers.

Nutmeg Grater: This very inexpensive item affords you the enhanced scent and flavor of freshly grated nutmeg. Quite a treat.

Can I Use My Old Cooker?

Chances are that many of you already own a first-generation, jiggle-top pressure cooker and would prefer not to invest in a new model at this moment. (If you really get into the swing of things, I suspect that you'll decide to treat yourself to one before too long.) Some of you may opt for a jiggle-top because it is more readily available and about half the price.

Although the majority of recipes in this book have been tested in second-generation cookers, you can certainly prepare them in jiggle-top models.

Before beginning to cook with a jiggle-top, however, please read on.

If your cooker hasn't been used in a while, it may need a new gasket (the rubber ring that fits inside the lid). Check the gasket by placing 2 cups of water in the cooker and seeing if the pressure comes up without any difficulty. If water drips down the sides of the pot or the pressure doesn't rise, replace the gasket (available in well-stocked housewares departments, hardware stores, or through the manufacturer). Use only the gasket that is designed specifically for your cooker.

When cooking foods that create foam— like beans, grains, and cranberries—be sure to adhere to special recipe instructions offered to jiggle-top users. Since preparing such foods is frequently cautioned against in manufacturers' manuals, you must remain present in the kitchen while they are cooking.

If any loud hissing occurs, interrupt the cooking process immediately. Quick-release the pressure under cold running water. Check the vent for any bits of food that may have clogged it, and clean the lid thoroughly. Return to high pressure and continue cooking. If problems persist, add a tablespoon of oil to control foaming.

Jiggle-top cookers tend to lose more liquid in the form of vented steam during the cooking process. If you consistently experience dry results or scorching when preparing grain pilafs or other types of dishes, increase the liquid by 1/4-cup increments until you discover the right formula for your cooker.

If your appliance has a thin bottom, get into the habit of using a Flame Tamer (page 6) to avoid scorching. Cooking time under pressure should not be affected.

Caring for the Cooker

Pressure cookers require little maintenance beyond what is normally required for any other piece of cookware. However, here are a few helpful cleaning and storage tips:

Remove and Clean the Gasket: Most manufacturers recommend doing this after each use. To preserve the life of your gasket, allow it to air-dry thoroughly before setting it back in the lid.

Clean the Vent/Valve Area: Glance at this area each time you're washing the lid. If needed, scrub the area with a soapy toothbrush. From time to time (particularly if your cooker is not functioning properly), disengage the pieces that comprise the pressure regulator and wash them. Look for detailed instructions in your owner's manual.

Clean the Bottom: If the bottom is scorched or if food is stubbornly sticking to it, bring about 2 cups of water to the boil in the cooker. Sprinkle in a scouring cleanser such as Bon Ami and let the cooker sit for a few hours or overnight. At this point, you won't need much elbow grease to scrub it clean.

Storage: Lean the lid against the side of the cooker or store it upside down in the pot. If the gasket isn't thoroughly dry, drape it loosely on top of the lid. (If you lock the lid in place for storage, you'll prevent the gasket from drying out properly, and the next time you open the cooker, you'll be greeted by a strong whiff of the last dish you prepared.)

THE LANGUAGE OF PRESSURE COOKING

Here are the phrases you will commonly encounter in the recipes, roughly in order of appearance. By reading through them, you'll have a clear picture of the simple step-by-step process involved.

Use Manufacturer's Recommended Liquid Minimum: Almost all pressure cookers require some added liquid to create steam pressure. Most cookers require ½ to 1 cup. (A few cookers function beautifully with no added liquid, relying only on the liquid released from the ingredients.)

If your instruction booklet doesn't provide this information, you can call the manufacturer or test your cooker by trying to bring it up to pressure with ¼ cup of water. If you are not successful, try it with ½ cup of water and so on, until you determine the minimum required.

Keep in mind that certain ingredients—such as onions, tomatoes, celery, and mushrooms—release liquid as they are brought up to pressure. This liquid can be calculated as part of the total requirement. (I figure every 2 cups of chopped vegetables will release about ¼ cup of liquid.)

Place the Rack in the Cooker: Most cookers come with a rack or basket that sits in the bottom and is used primarily for steaming vegetables. In some recipes, the rack is used to raise a casserole dish off the bottom.

If your appliance doesn't come with either, you can substitute an ordinary steaming basket when cooking vegetables or a metal trivet when using a casserole. (A makeshift trivet can be created by forming aluminum foil into a log and shaping the log into a ring that fits in the cooker.)

Do not use the rack unless it is specifically called for in the recipe.

Lock the Lid in Place: This is a simple matter of nesting the lid into the pot and then turning it until the pot and lid handles line up. Some cookers have an additional locking mechanism that involves pushing a small lever into place. Check the instruction booklet for specifics.

Cookers are designed so that if the lid is not properly locked, the pressure won't rise.

Set the Cooker on a Heated Flame Tamer: A Flame Tamer is an inexpensive heat-diffusing device that is set under the cooker, directly on the burner. It is highly recommended if your cooker has a thin bottom and you experience scorching. I also find it useful when cooking grain pilafs, which require relatively little liquid and have a tendency to stick to the bottom of the pot. Flame Tamers are readily available in housewares stores.

To use one, heat the Flame Tamer for 1 minute over high heat. Set the cooker on the Flame Tamer and bring it up to pressure. (This will take a few minutes longer than if the cooker were directly over the flame, but the extra time should not critically affect the final product. I do not use a Flame

Tamer when preparing quick-cooking vegetables.) Once the cooker is up to pressure, lower the heat to maintain high pressure.

Remove the cooker from the Flame Tamer before quick-releasing the pressure or letting it come down naturally. Allow the Flame Tamer to cool before attempting to move it.

Over High Heat, Bring to High Pressure: High pressure is achieved as rapidly as possible by setting the cooker over maximum heat. Depending on the quantity and type of food you are cooking and the size of the cooker, it can take from 30 seconds to 20 minutes to bring the pressure up to high. This process can be speeded up considerably by starting with boiling (rather than cold or room temperature) liquid.

Lower the Heat Just Enough to Maintain High Pressure: It is a cardinal rule that once high pressure is reached, the heat must be lowered; otherwise the pressure will continue to rise, causing loud hissing sounds. After using your cooker a few times, you'll have a good idea of the amount of heat required to maintain high pressure. For most cookers, a flame akin to simmering is just about right.

If the pressure starts to fall, assume you've lowered the heat too much. If this happens, bring the pressure back up over high heat and lower the heat again. A slight drop in pressure for a brief period will not normally affect the timing or the quality of the finished product.

Under High Pressure: Check your manufacturer's instruction booklet for details on how to determine when high pressure has been reached. For second-generation cookers, it is indicated by a line on the stationary pressure rod. For jiggle-top cookers, high pressure is generally signaled by a gentle rocking of the pressure regulator.

Although some cookers offer a choice of settings, all recipes in this book have been tested under high pressure (13 to 15 pounds).

Unless otherwise noted, cooking time is calculated from the moment high pressure is reached. For example, above each recipe is a phrase such as "3 minutes high pressure." This means that as soon as the cooker reaches high pressure, you set the timer, lower the heat, and cook under high pressure for 3 minutes.

Total Cooking Time: This term is used exclusively for quick-cooking vegetables. Since such vegetables can so easily be

overcooked, the timer is set the moment the lid is locked into place and the flame is turned on. For example, "3 minutes total cooking time" means that you should release any pressure that has built up—whether or not high pressure has been reached—exactly 3 minutes after the pot is set on the heat. After quick-releasing the pressure, remove the lid immediately.

Use a Quick-Release Method: When the timer goes off, bring down the pressure by placing the cooker under cold running water. (I usually tilt the cooker about 45 degrees and run the water down one side of the cover; this directs water away from the pressure regulator.) Recipes for preparing vegetables and other quick-cooking foods normally require the quick-release method.

Second-generation cookers offer a quick-release option that can be executed without moving the pot from the stove. After turning off the heat (and moving the cooker to another burner, if using an electric stove), you manipulate a lever or button to release the pressure in a steady stream.

I'm sure that many cooks find this alternative handy, but I don't enjoy the steam bath it gives my kitchen and rarely use it. If the stove-top method causes sputtering at the vent, bring down the pressure under cold running water instead.

Allow the Pressure to Come Down Naturally: When the timer goes off, turn off the heat and let the cooker sit until the pressure drops of its own accord. (Move the cooker to a cool burner if using an electric stove.) Depending on the quantity and type of food in the pot, this can take from 3 to 20 minutes. The food continues to cook as the pressure drops. (I calculate a 10-minute natural pressure release to be the equivalent of 4 minutes of cooking under pressure.)

Some recipes call for a partial natural pressure release. For example, when a recipe says to "let the pressure come down naturally for 10 minutes," keep the lid in place for as long as indicated, whether or not the pressure has already dropped. Release any remaining pressure before attempting to remove the lid.

When overcooking is not a danger, some recipes offer you the option of quick or natural pressure release. If time permits, choose the natural pressure release. I believe that flavors and textures benefit from this approach. It is a gentler way to bring down the pressure—an advantage when cooking beans (which otherwise tend to "lose their skins") and grains, for which steaming is a crucial part of the cooking process.

Replace (But Do Not Lock) the Lid and Let Cook for a Few More Minutes in the Residual Heat: If delicate foods such as fresh vegetables are slightly underdone after the pressure is released, set the lid in place but do not lock it, and let the food cook in the heat that remains in the pot, without applying any additional heat.

With the Aid of a Foil Strip: To move a heatproof casserole both into and out of the pressure cooker, cut a piece of aluminum foil measuring 2 feet long by 1 foot wide (the width of standard foil) and double it twice lengthwise. Center the casserole on the strip, grasp each end of the strip, lift and then gently lower the casserole into the cooker. Loosely fold the ends of the foil strip over the top of the casserole. After cooking, air-dry the strip and save it for future use.

BEFORE YOU BEGIN, READ THIS

HIGH-ALTITUDE COOKING

The pressure cooker is a great boon for those living at high altitudes, where the boiling point of water is lower and foods can take dramatically longer to cook. As a general rule of thumb, if you live more than 2,000 feet above sea level, increase cooking time by 10 percent for every additional 2,000 feet.

General Tips and Techniques

Cooker Size: Quantities in the recipes that follow are calculated for preparation in a 6-quart cooker.

If you own an 8-quart cooker, feel free to follow the recipes as is. However, since the larger cooker will take slightly longer to come up to pressure, reduce cooking time under pressure by 1 to 2 minutes when preparing quick-cooking ingredients.

Most of the recipes will also work just fine in a 4-quart cooker. However, when making soups and stews, be sure that the ingredients don't fill the cooker beyond the manufacturer's recommended fill line. (Usually one half full for beans and two thirds to three quarters full for other types of ingredients.)

Cooking Times: Since personal taste and the performance of ingredients and cookers vary, cooking times are of necessity approximate. I have always tried to lean in the direction of undercooking since it's a simple matter to either bring the pressure back up (if the food needs quite a bit more cooking) or finish off the dish by stove-top simmering (if it is just short of done).

Browning: Many recipes call for an initial browning of garlic and/or onions. Before or just after adding the liquid, make sure that no bits of food are sticking to the bottom of the cooker. If you neglect this detail, the intense heat used to bring up the pressure might cause them to burn, detracting from the good taste of the finished dish.

Toasting Spices: Some recipes start by asking you to sizzle whole spices in heated oil. This procedure toasts them and intensifies their flavor but you must work rapidly to achieve good results. Heat the oil very briefly, and take care that it does not reach smoking point at any time during this process. If the spices are about to burn, turn off the heat and immediately add the next ingredient (usually onions or water), stirring constantly, to cool down the pot quickly. If you find the process of toasting spices troublesome, skip it. Alternatively, dry roast the spices in a heavy cast-iron skillet (see recipe for curry powder, page 20) and transfer them to the cooker.

Veggie Prep: Often the ingredients list will specify the size and shape of vegetables. These guidelines are calculated in relation to the cooking time; however, they are not intended to make you nervous or compulsive. For example, if a recipe calls for potatoes cut into 1-inch chunks, it's fine if the pieces are slightly unequal in size as long as they are roughly about an inch. For ready reference, I use the area between the tip of my thumb and the first knuckle to calculate 1 inch.

Coarsely Chopping an Onion: If you are taking more than a minute to peel and coarsely chop an onion, you are being too exacting. First slice off the root and top and peel the onion. Then cut it in half through the middle. Turn it cut side down on a chopping board and make four to five slices across. Holding the slices together, turn the onion the other way and make four to five slices across. Repeat with the other half.

Ingredients List: Ingredients are listed in order of use. A dotted line divides those ingredients that are cooked under pressure from those that are added after the dish is cooked.

Freezing Leftovers

Although I take special pleasure in eating freshly prepared food, I'm happy to report that with few exceptions pressure-cooked foods freeze beautifully. It's therefore a bonus to have leftovers that can be kept on hand for a homemade dinner down the road. Store them in convenient serving sizes and either defrost overnight in the refrigerator or more rapidly at room temperature. Quicker still, pop them into the microwave.

Here are a few pointers to keep in mind:

Soups freeze the best of any category. After heating, perk up the flavor with a bit of vinegar or lemon juice. Thin with stock or water if needed.

Beans may be frozen at any stage, either after they are soaked and drained or once they have been fully cooked (either plain or in a soup or stew). Beans that have been frozen will generally not retain their shape.

Grains and Grain Dishes may be frozen, but they dry out considerably during a sojourn in the freezer. For best flavor and texture, rehydrate defrosted grains by steaming them over boiling water.

Vegetables and Vegetable Stews lose some texture when frozen, but maintain reasonably good taste.

Adapting Recipes for the Pressure Cooker

Once you get accustomed to speed-cooking, it's hard to wait around for an hour or two as your favorite soup simmers to perfection. While there are no hard-and-fast rules, I can offer a few guidelines for adapting favorite recipes to the pressure cooker.

Choose only stove-top recipes. Opt for those that combine most ingredients at the beginning. Soup recipes are the easiest to translate, and I offer more details in this category on page 32 .

In general, for any recipe, cut the cooking time down to approximately one third. For more precise timing, check the cooking charts and similar recipes in this book. If in doubt, always err on the side of undercooking.

Since relatively little liquid is lost during cooking, it's a good idea to reduce the liquid in soup and stew recipes by about 20 percent. For grain dishes, however, you'll do better by checking the proportions I use in this book.

Plan to use one and a half times the quantity of herbs and spices since the pressure cooker mellows their intensity.

Tips for Cooking on an Electric Stove Top

Pressure cooking on an electric stove top definitely presents special challenges because the coils create such intense (and frequently uneven) heat and respond so slowly to adjustments in temperature. Here are some thoughts to keep in mind:

Your best weapon is to have a second-generation cooker that has a copper or aluminum sandwich in the bottom.

Use a Flame Tamer (page 6) to diffuse the heat. Heat the Flame Tamer over a burner set to the highest setting before you place the cooker on it. This will facilitate bringing the cooker to high pressure quickly.

Lower the heat a minute or so before the cooker actually reaches high pressure to accommodate the time delay. Alternatively, after reaching high pressure, transfer the cooker to a burner pre-set to low (or whatever you've determined to be the appropriate temperature for maintaining high pressure).

Transfer the cooker to a cool burner when you use the natural pressure release.

Since all of the recipes in this book have been tested on gas burners, you may need to make minor adjustments in the timing.

THE PRESSURED COOK'S PANTRY

A rmed with a pressure cooker and a well-stocked larder, you are poised to send forth a healthy and soul-satisfying meal at a moment's notice. To make such delicious spontaneity a part of your life, you need to have some basic ingredients plus a good selection of herbs, spices, and condiments within arm's reach.

This goal is easily accomplished since the majority of essential ingredients may be kept for months on end. A small number of items need to be replenished weekly. Here's a quick reference list, plus some tips on ideal storage conditions. For further information on selection and storage, see the introductions to the bean and grain chapters.

SHOPPING TIP

Bring a 1-cup measure with you when shopping from bulk bins. Buy just the amount you need for a recipe to avoid getting stuck with odd bits of leftover beans and grains.

Fresh herbs will keep well for a week or more if you place stems or roots in a glass of water and wrap a plastic bag over the leaves.

If ginger is not readily available, buy a very large knob and freeze it whole in a heavy-duty zippered bag.

In the Refrigerator

ALWAYS: garlic, carrots, celery, lemons, fresh ginger, fresh parsley, raisins, one or two types of olives.

FREQUENTLY: parsnips, cabbage, leeks, plum tomatoes (once fully ripe), fresh dill, basil, or coriander, dried chestnuts, dried currants, maple syrup.

In the Freezer

ALWAYS: brown rice (short-grain, long-grain, and basmati), quinoa, whole-wheat couscous, corn grits, frozen corn kernels, peas, chopped spinach.

FREQUENTLY: hulled or pearl barley, coarse bulgur, millet, sesame seeds, walnuts, coconut (dried, grated, unsweetened), frozen lima beans, artichoke hearts.

All whole grains, seeds, nuts, and whole-grain flours should be stored in the freezer to avoid rancidity. I find the most convenient storage containers to be heavy-duty zippered bags. Label the date of purchase and use within 4 months.

On the Countertop

ALWAYS: onions, winter squash (in season).

FREQUENTLY: avocados, tomatoes (until ripe; then refrigerate).

In Drawers or Cabinets

ALWAYS: lentils, split peas, two or three types of dried beans, two or three types of pasta, white basmati rice, potatoes, dried mushrooms, canned beans, canned peeled plum tomatoes, instant vegetable stock.

FREQUENTLY: arborio rice (for risotto), extra-long-grain white rice, one or two types of dried sea vegetables, sun-dried tomatoes, store-bought spaghetti sauce and salsa, apple juice.

Oils, Condiments, and Seasonings

ALWAYS: apple cider vinegar, balsamic vinegar, tamari soy sauce, olive oil, canola oil, safflower oil, toasted (Oriental) sesame oil, tomato paste (in a tube), a wide range of seasonings, including these personal favorites:

Dried Herbs: oregano, rosemary, thyme, sage, dill, bay leaves, tarragon.

Spices: black pepper, chili powder, curry powder, whole cumin seeds, whole coriander seeds, ground cinnamon, whole fennel seeds, whole nutmeg, saffron, sweet paprika, ground ginger, crushed red pepper flakes, small whole red chili peppers, ground turmeric.

FREQUENTLY: sherry wine vinegar, umeboshi plum vinegar.

STORAGE TIP

Store potatoes up to 3 weeks in a cool, dark place that is well ventilated. Avoid refrigerating potatoes, which causes them to darken when cooked.

STORAGE TIPS

Store all oils in the refrigerator to maintain maximum freshness and to avoid rancidity.

Store all herbs and spices away from heat and light. If possible, buy them in small quantities and replenish every 6 months. Store saffron in a well-sealed container in the refrigerator.

COOKING TIP

Because cooking under pressure involves intense heat, recipes require larger amounts of herbs and spices than you might normally be accustomed to using. Whenever possible, buy whole spices and grind them as needed in a mini-chopper or coffee grinder set aside for this purpose. The flavor will be much more vibrant.

A Short Glossary of Ingredients

Here is some background information on a variety of ingredients you'll encounter in the recipes. You will also find instructions for preparing a few items—such as roasted garlic and roasted bell peppers—that may not already be in your repertoire.

Annatto Oil: This infused oil, used in Latin American cooking, has a golden color and a subtle taste. It is available at Hispanic markets but is easy to prepare at home. Heat 1 tablespoon of annatto seeds in ¼ cup of olive or canola oil and simmer over low heat for 5 minutes. Cool, then pour through a fine-meshed strainer. Discard seeds. Refrigerate oil until needed.

Arborio Rice: A short-grained "chubby" rice with a high starch content, this is the rice of choice for making classic Italian risotto and a terrific alternative for rice pudding. If you can't find arborio in your supermarket, try an Italian grocer or a gourmet shop, or order by mail (see Mail-Order Sources). Other varieties of white rice will not result in as creamy a final product, though some people find the results quite pleasant.

Beans: For detailed information, see pages 181 to 188.

Bell Peppers (Sweet Peppers): Red peppers, my personal favorite, are green peppers that have been left on the vine to ripen and sweeten further. Chopped, raw peppers add color to bean and grain dishes, and they are especially tasty when roasted. Select firm peppers without blemishes or soft spots. Peppers should be naturally glossy, not waxed. Store in a plastic bag in the refrigerator for up to 4 days. Prepare for cooking by halving from bottom to stem and plucking out stem, seeds, and large white membranes.

Chestnuts: The good news is that despite their rich taste and texture, chestnuts are remarkably low in fat. (Alas they are rather high in calories.) Fresh chestnuts are wonderful during the fall. Dried chestnuts are available year-round and make a superb smoky-sweet addition to soups, grains, and stews. They are sold already peeled and last for a year or two under refrigeration. Usually I soak chestnuts in water so that I can chop them before cooking. Dried chestnuts are available in health food stores and in some gourmet shops, but do not confuse dried chestnuts with the canned or bottled peeled chestnuts; the latter are much more expensive.

TO SPEED-SOAK DRIED CHESTNUTS

Set the chestnuts and just enough water to cover in the cooker. Lock the lid in place. Over high heat, bring to high pressure. Reduce the heat just enough to maintain high pressure and cook for 2 minutes. Allow the pressure to come down naturally for 10 minutes. Remove the lid, tilting it away from you to allow any excess steam to escape. Proceed as directed in recipe.

ROASTED BELL PEPPERS

It's amazingly quick and simple to roast peppers, and they add wonderful flavor to salads and sauces. You can even do four at a time if your eye-hand coordination is good.

Set 1 washed and dried pepper per flame on the grid covering the gas burner. Turn the flame to high and roast until the pepper is completely blackened and charred on the underside. Give the pepper a quarter-turn with a pair of long tongs (avoid long-handled forks or skewers, which prick the pepper and release juices) and continue to roast until the pepper is charred all around. This process will take 4 to 5 minutes. Alternatively, you may set the peppers under the broiler on a tray and turn as needed.

Place the charred pepper(s) in a brown paper bag (make sure there are no live embers), fold over the top, and let steam for 15 minutes. Peel off the charred skin as you dunk the pepper up and down in a bowl of water. Rinse the peeled pepper.

Halve the pepper and remove the seeds. (Do this on a platter to catch any juices.) Cut into strips and proceed as directed in individual recipes.

Extra roasted peppers can be refrigerated in a small jar, tossed with a clove of crushed garlic (if desired) and covered with a thin layer of olive oil. They will last about a week. Roasted peppers can also be puréed in a food processor or blender for use as a garnish or sauce. Two large roasted peppers yield about 1 cup of purée.

Chili Peppers: Chili peppers are a world unto themselves, with more than two hundred varieties available. They come both fresh and dried and range from mild to scorchingly hot. To make matters more complicated, there is considerable variation of "heat" within any given type, so it's always a gamble.

The real burn of the chili resides in the seeds and surrounding membrane; by removing them you tone down its potency. Wear rubber gloves when working with chili peppers, and keep your hands away from your eyes. Select firm, plump, unblemished fresh chili peppers. Store them in the refrigerator for up to 5 days.

An excellent mail-order source for high-quality dried chili peppers is Los Chileros de Nuevo Mexico (see Mail-Order Sources).

Chili Powder: A blend of ground chilies (from mild to hot), oregano, cumin seeds, garlic, and sometimes salt. Taste before using and make sure your blend isn't stale or bitter. If it's old and the flavor has faded, you may need to add more than is called for in the recipe. Best yet, try making your own to assure freshness and maximum flavor (see page 18).

MILD CHILI POWDER

Rather than include garlic powder in my homemade mixture, I opt to use fresh garlic in recipes that call for chili powder. *Makes about ⅓ cup*

3 to 4 dried ancho chilies (wear rubber gloves when handling chili peppers)

1½ tablespoons whole cumin seeds

2 teaspoons dried oregano leaves

1 teaspoon whole coriander seeds

1 teaspoon ground cinnamon

1 teaspoon unsweetened cocoa powder (optional)

In a toaster oven, roast the ancho chilies at 350 degrees until they darken slightly or puff up, about 2 minutes. (Pay strict attention, as the chilies transform from roasted to burned in a flash.) With a small scissors, snip off the stems and open the peppers to release and discard the seeds. Snip the peppers into bits and grind them to a powder in a spice grinder. Transfer to a small, wide-mouthed glass jar.

Grind the cumin, oregano, and coriander and blend this mixture plus the cinnamon and cocoa (if using) with the chili powder. Transfer to a glass jar, cover, and refrigerate until needed, up to 3 months.

Chipotle Peppers: A personal favorite, this dried and smoked jalapeño adds relatively mild heat and delightful smokiness. To prepare it for cooking, snip or cut off the stem and tear open (wear rubber gloves). Remove the seeds and snip or tear the pepper into bits. Include a few of the seeds if you're having the Fire Alarm Chili Club over for dinner. See Chili Peppers.

Coconut Milk: This luscious cooking liquid adds richness and complex taste. Unfortunately, it is high in saturated fat, so is best used with discretion. Recipes in this book have all been tested with coconut milk extracted from rehydrated dried, grated, unsweetened coconut. (For optimum freshness, store dried coconut in the freezer.) This approach is convenient and economical and enables you to avoid the preservatives in most canned coconut. Some health food stores now carry a preservative-free canned coconut milk, and a low-fat version is becoming more readily available.

Coriander (Leaf): The fresh herb (also known as cilantro and Chinese parsley) looks a bit like flat-leafed Italian parsley but its leaves are broader, lacier, and not as long. If in doubt, rub a leaf and sniff. It's difficult to describe coriander's distinct aroma, but you will certainly be able to distinguish it from parsley. The roots (thoroughly cleaned) are full of flavor and may be used in cooked dishes. The leaves are best raw.

COCONUT MILK

Makes about 2 cups

2¼ cups boiling water
¾ cup dried, grated,
   unsweetened coconut

In the jar of a blender, pour the boiling water over the coconut. Let the mixture cool for 2 to 3 minutes. Hold the cover securely in place and blend for 1 minute. Let sit for 5 to 10 minutes. Blend an additional 30 seconds.

Strain through a fine-meshed strainer, pressing with the back of a spoon to extract all of the liquid. Discard the coconut pulp.

Refrigerate for 1 week or freeze for up to 3 months.

NOTE: This recipe could theoretically be doubled or tripled, but I find that the jar of my blender will not accommodate larger quantities—and I prefer the blender to the food processor for this task.

Coriander's taste is unique: adored by many, detested by others. I belong to the former group, and find that almost any savory dish can be transformed from dull to delicious with a generous smattering of it. (If you belong to the latter group and think it tastes a lot like soap, feel free to substitute fresh parsley to taste.) Store fresh coriander in the refrigerator, stems down, in a glass of water. Cover the leaves with a plastic bag. It will last up to a week this way, although its flavor will diminish daily. I have tried dried coriander and don't find it a satisfactory substitute for fresh. Do not be tempted to substitute coriander seeds for the leaves.

Coriander Seed: The spice tastes nothing like the leaf, although it comes from the same plant. A small, round, tan ribbed seed with a flavor reminiscent of citrus, coriander is an important ingredient in curry powder and adds a slightly sweet and aromatic quality to baked goods. For optimum taste, purchase the whole seeds and grind as needed.

Currants, Dried (Zante Currants): The seedless, raisinlike dried fruit of the Zante grape. Currants are smaller and less sweet than raisins, making them a nice alternative in grain and vegetable dishes as well as baked goods. An equal amount of raisins may be substituted in recipes calling for currants.

Curry Powder: A blend of spices that varies considerably in taste and "heat" from one producer to the next. Most curry powders include cumin, coriander, and mustard seeds, fenugreek, red chilies, black peppercorns, and turmeric. I prefer to

MILD CURRY POWDER

Use these quantities as a rule of thumb, and adjust to taste. *Makes about ¾ cup*

- 4 tablespoons whole coriander seeds
- 2 tablespoons whole cumin seeds
- 4 teaspoons whole fennel seeds
- 2 teaspoons white mustard seeds
- ½ teaspoon white peppercorns
- 3 whole cloves
- 3 tablespoons ground turmeric
- 4 teaspoons ground ginger
- 1 teaspoon ground cinnamon
- ¼ teaspoon ground nutmeg
- **Pinch of ground cayenne pepper**

In a small bowl, combine the coriander, cumin, fennel, mustard, peppercorns, and cloves.

Heat a large nonstick or heavy iron skillet. Pour the whole spices into the skillet and dry roast them over medium heat, stirring constantly, until they darken slightly or become aromatic, about 20 to 30 seconds.

(Take care not to burn the spices, which can happen from one second to the next.) *Immediately* transfer them back to the bowl and continue to stir them to release excess heat.

Once the spices have cooled slightly, grind them to a fine powder in a spice grinder. Blend in the remaining ground spices.

Transfer to a glass jar, cover, and refrigerate until needed, up to 3 months.

ROASTED GARLIC

- 1 large, firm head of garlic
- 1 teaspoon olive oil (optional)

Remove as much of the outer papery skin covering the head as will come off easily. Brush the garlic liberally with olive oil, if desired.

Set in a small shallow baking dish in a toaster oven and roast at 375 degrees until the outside is lightly browned and the innermost cloves are soft, about 20 minutes.

Refrigerate the roasted garlic in a sealed container for up to 2 weeks.

use a mild curry powder and add some cayenne or crushed red pepper flakes to taste. Be sure to taste your curry powder before using it; any bitterness indicates that it's time to toss it.

Delicata Squash: A cucumber-shaped winter squash with bright yellow skin and green or rust stripes. Its flesh is creamy and dense.

Garlic: I'm one of those cooks who can't imagine life without garlic, and when I discovered roasted garlic I thought I'd died and gone to heaven. Roasted garlic has become one of my favorite seasonings. It's a snap to prepare and is preferable to the overwhelming taste of raw garlic in uncooked dressings and sauces.

Ginger: Second only to garlic, this fragrant root plays a dramatic role in my kitchen. Look for a plump piece of ginger with smooth skin; the freshly broken off tip should emit a delightfully fresh and pungent fragrance and feel moist to the touch. Choose young ginger with thin skin; older ginger tends to be quite fibrous. Store uncovered ginger in the butterkeeper of your refrigerator for 2 to 3 weeks. Should a section get moldy, simply cut away the affected part. If fresh ginger is not always available, buy a large piece when you have access and freeze it in a tightly sealed plastic bag for up to 3 months. (There is some loss of flavor and texture, so use a bit more.) Slice off pieces as needed.

To prepare for cooking, you can peel the section needed, but I prefer to scrub the skin with a vegetable brush and rub one end of the whole piece against a fine grater until I have the amount that I need. Alternatively, I mince small pieces of ginger in a mini-chopper.

Grains: For detailed information, see pages 115–120.

Hijiki: A jet-black sea vegetable that resembles angel hair pasta. When rehydrated, the strands quadruple in size. Hijiki is usually soaked and drained before cooking, a process that diminishes its briny flavor.

Kabocha Squash: A type of winter squash that closely resembles the buttercup in appearance but is starchier, sweeter, and more intensely flavored. It is also known as Hokkaido pumpkin.

Kombu: A sea vegetable sold in broad, dark green, dehydrated strips that expand considerably upon soaking or cooking. Kombu contains glutamic acid, a natural flavor enhancer. Prepare kombu for cooking by rinsing it quickly. Traditionally, the strip is cooked whole and either discarded or chopped finely and stirred back into the dish.

Leeks: These cousins to the onion are easy to cook and absolutely delicious. I think of leeks as two vegetables: the white part, which can be braised on its own or chopped like onions, and the green part, which requires longer cooking and imparts a delicious flavor to stocks, soups, and stews.

Leeks are often quite sandy and require thorough cleaning. Prepare them for cooking by removing any tough or yellowed outer leaves. Unless otherwise directed, cut off all but about an inch of the greens. Trim off and discard the root end. Slice the leek in half lengthwise. Under cold running water, gently separate the layers to wash away any sand. Drain thoroughly. Slice or chop as directed.

Lemongrass: A fetching ingredient from the Southeast Asian kitchen, lemongrass combines a faint lemony flavor with the heat of a mild chili pepper. (In fact, freshly grated lemon peel and a generous pinch of crushed red pepper flakes make a viable substitute.) Fresh lemongrass, a long greenish stalk with a bulb at the bottom, is often available in Asian markets and may be tightly wrapped and frozen for up to 3 months.

Prepare fresh lemongrass for cooking by pulling off the tough outer layer. Cut the bulb and fleshier part of the stalk into 1-inch bits and add to soups and stews. Since lemongrass remains hard after cooking, remove any large pieces before serving. Better yet, before adding it to soups or stews, tie the sliced lemongrass loosely in a small cheesecloth bundle. Follow the same procedure if your dried lemongrass is in coarse bits rather than finely ground.

Lemon Peel and Juice: Also known as zest, the peel is the thin, colored, top layer of skin on a lemon (or other citrus) that contains full-flavored citrus oils. If possible, use organically grown fruit to avoid pesticide residues.

For maximum yield, remove the peel in strips by using a sharp old-fashioned potato peeler. Use a gentle sawing motion to avoid scraping off the white layer of pith underneath, which is bitter. Finely chop the peel by hand or use a mini-chopper. Extra peel is best frozen in strip form, but plan on using one and a half times the amount called for as there will be some loss of flavor.

A less efficient but workable approach is to grate the peel on the finest side of a box grater. Alternatively, use a zester.

After removing the peel, squeeze out the juice within 48 hours (it can be frozen) as the fruit will quickly begin to get moldy. The juice is a marvelous natural flavor enhancer and I frequently suggest adding it just before serving a dish. (The flavor and punch of lemon juice are quickly dissipated.)

Roll the lemon firmly back and forth on the countertop before squeezing to extract the maximum amount of juice. One large lemon yields 3 to 4 tablespoons of juice and 1 tablespoon of finely grated peel.

Liquid Smoke Flavoring: Most supermarkets carry some type of liquid smoke. I use a mesquite smoke flavoring that comes in a spray bottle. A light misting at the end of cooking imparts a very pleasant barbecued flavor.

Mushrooms: It is very convenient to keep dried mushrooms on hand as they add a rich flavor to soups and stews and last indefinitely when stored in a well-sealed container in a cool, dry place. Many supermarkets carry sliced, dried mushrooms in ½-ounce containers.

Some mushrooms require soaking to eliminate any sand and grit. Steep the mushrooms in boiling water in a covered bowl until soft, 15 to 30 minutes. Lift out the soaked mushrooms, rinse carefully, and cut away any gritty sections. Strain the tasty soaking liquid through cheesecloth or a coffee filter and use it as part of the liquid requirement for your dish. See Shiitake and Porcini.

Nori: Paper-thin, square, greenish-brown sheets of a sea vegetable traditionally used for making sushi rolls. When labeled "sushi nori," the sheets have been pretoasted.

Orange Peel: See Lemon Peel.

Plantains: Plantains start out looking like large green bananas, but as they ripen, they become yellow with large black spots. When green-skinned, they are bland and starchy. When the skin becomes completely black, they are very sweet.

Plantains must be cooked. When green, they are used as a potatolike ingredient in soups and stews. When ripe (blackened), they are generally fried. If you buy green plantains, you can let them ripen at room temperature; it may take close to a week for their skins to turn black.

Porcini: These intensely flavored dried Italian boletus mushrooms are found in gourmet shops and Italian groceries. They are usually quite sandy and require soaking. See Mushrooms.

Quinoa: A small seed native to the Andes, quinoa is quick-cooking and very easy to digest. For information on washing and cooking quinoa, see pages 159 and 172.

Rice Milk: A nondairy milk substitute made from brown rice. Rice Dream and EdenRice are popular brands available in health food stores.

Salt: All salts are not created equal. I opt for unrefined sea salt, which is free of additives and contains dozens of the trace minerals destroyed during the processing of ordinary table salt. Unrefined sea salt is usually available in coarse and fine grades. I prefer fine, which is more convenient for use in cooking. Two excellent brands are Lima and Si Salt, both available at health food stores.

TO FRY RIPE PLANTAINS

Peel by cutting shallow incisions down the length at about 1½-inch intervals and pull off the skin. Cut on the diagonal into thin slices and brown the slices on both sides in an oil-brushed cast-iron skillet over medium-high heat. Take care, as they burn easily.

ROASTED SHALLOT CREAM

Created by inventive Manhattan chef Alan Harding, this is a terrific nondairy substitute for sour cream. It also makes a great dip for raw vegetables.

Silken tofu produces a soft and creamy product; firm tofu creates a slightly thicker topping with a bit more texture. *Makes 1 cup*

¼ pound shallots of approximately equal size and shape
1¼ teaspoons olive or safflower oil, divided
¾ cup (6 ounces) mashed silken or firm tofu
2 to 3 teaspoons brown rice vinegar
1 teaspoon maple syrup
½ teaspoon salt

Brush the shallots with ¼ teaspoon of the oil and set them in a pie plate.

Roast them in a 375-degree toaster oven until very soft, 15 to 20 minutes.

When they are cool enough to handle, peel the shallots. In a food processor or blender, combine the shallots with the remaining oil, tofu, 2 teaspoons vinegar, maple syrup, and salt. Process until smooth.

Taste and adjust the seasonings, adding a bit more vinegar, maple syrup, or salt, if needed, to achieve a slightly sweet taste with just a hint of acid.

Use immediately or refrigerate in a tightly sealed container for up to 3 days. Reblend before using, if necessary.

Scallion Greens: Since I find the taste of raw scallion bulbs too strong, I use only the thinly sliced green part for adding at the last minute. I chop the bulbs for use in stir-fries. In some parts of the country, scallions are known as green onions.

Sea Palm: A wiry sea vegetable with a delicious mild taste and a delightfully chewy texture. After rehydrating sea palm, cut off the tough root ends that hold together the fronds. If sea palm is not available in your health food store, you may mail-order it from Gold Mine Natural Food Co. (see Mail-Order Sources).

Sea Vegetables: A category that deserves much more attention in American kitchens, sea vegetables are high in protein and loaded with minerals. They are available dry in health food stores and Asian markets. You may store them indefinitely in a well-sealed container in a cool, dry place. See Hijiki, Kombu, Nori, Sea Palm, Wakame.

Shallots: These diminutive members of the onion family have multiple cloves and are a bit pesky to peel, but their unique mild onion flavor sings gaily in sauces and dips. Select firm shallots that show no signs of sprouting. Store in a paper bag in the refrigerator for up to 1 week.

Shiitake: The king of Oriental mushrooms, shiitake are culti-vated on logs and are rarely sandy. However, they normally require soaking so that the tough, inedible stem can be cut away and the cap cut into slivers. Always use the delicious soaking liquid. Shiitake are readily available in health food stores. See Mushrooms.

Toasted (Oriental) Sesame Oil: An intensely flavored oil ex-tracted from toasted sesame seeds. Since so little goes such a long way, you get a lot of flavor mileage for relatively few fat calories. I use it in combination with soy sauce and toasted sesame seeds to dress steamed vegetables and grains.

Because toasted sesame oil burns easily, avoid using it for sautéing.

Tofu (Bean Curd, Soy Cheese): Tofu is an ancient food made by coagulating soy milk, then draining it and pressing the curds into a cake. It is an inexpensive and versatile form of high-quality protein, rich in calcium and cholesterol free.

Tomatoes: For cooking, I find that plum (Roma) tomatoes of-fer the best flavor and texture. These egg-shaped fruits (the tomato is actually a fruit) have fewer seeds and more flesh per square inch than other varieties. The pressure cooker does a reasonably good job of softening tomato skins in dishes that cook for longer than 10 minutes under high pressure. How-ever, if you have a particular dislike for these skins, peel the tomatoes before cooking.

When fresh tomatoes are not in season, you can substitute canned, peeled tomatoes. Drain them before chopping. (You may use the drained tomato juice instead of an equivalent amount of water called for in the recipe, except when cooking beans.) It's most economical to buy a large can and freeze what you don't use in 1- or 2-cup quantities.

In some cookers, the sugars in tomatoes burn and scorch the bottom. The remedy is to use a Flame Tamer (page 6) and, when possible, to set the tomatoes on top of other ingredients or stir them in after cooking.

Vegetable Stock: A recipe for Basic Vegetable Stock may be found on page 68. However, it's handy to keep an instant broth powder on hand for those moments when you want to make risotto or enrich a soup and have no homemade stock. After a blind tasting of different brands with colleagues, we

TOFU WHIP

This tasty, nondairy alternative to whipped cream may be refrigerated for up to 1 week. The recipe may be halved. *Makes about 2 cups*

 1 pound firm or extra-firm tofu, drained and cut into chunks
 ¼ cup maple syrup
 1 tablespoon vanilla extract
 1 to 2 tablespoons water (optional)

In a food processor or blender, combine all of the ingredients and process until very creamy, adding water if needed to achieve a thickness that approximates whipped cream.

Cover and refrigerate until ready to use. If the mixture separates after refrigeration, reblend it thoroughly before using.

VARIATION

Instead of maple syrup, try 3 to 4 tablespoons of fruit-juice-sweetened preserves and some finely minced citrus peel. Choose the fruit and citrus flavors to complement the dessert.

TO PEEL TOMATOES

Bring a large pot of water to the boil. Submerge the tomatoes in the boiling water for 20 seconds, then immediately transfer them to a bowl of cold water. When cool enough to handle, remove from the water and slip off the skins.

determined that Vogue Vege Base has the best flavor. It is available in many health food stores, or see Mail-Order Sources.

Wakame: A dark green sea vegetable sold in broad strips. After rehydrating, some recipes will suggest that you cut away any stiff midribs.

MENUS FOR MEALS IN MINUTES

THE PRESSURED COOK'S GUIDE TO PLANNING VEGETARIAN MENUS

I know that many people have difficulty planning vegetarian menus because they tell me so. Having grown up with the meat-starch-vegetable triad, cooks often find it quite challenging to switch gears once meat moves from center-plate position or disappears entirely.

The most sensible way to plan a vegetarian meal is to give grains the dominant role (as most of the world's population have done for eons). You are already taking this approach when you serve pasta or risotto for dinner, accompanied by a steamed vegetable or green salad. Stir-fried vegetables with rice is another common vegetarian meal that is served without a second thought in homes throughout the country.

You can think of planning a vegetarian meal by borrowing the Chinese restaurant menu scheme: Choose one from column A and two from column B. Column C is optional.

LEFTOVERS ON PURPOSE

One of the most efficient ways to organize healthful meals is to cook leftovers on purpose. Depending upon the size of your cooker, you can double or triple recipes with the intention of freezing a substantial portion for a meal down the road. Alternatively, a small amount of leftover food can be creatively recycled into a meal eaten the next day.

For example, make a double batch of black beans. Serve a portion of them tossed with a little olive oil and herbs. Next day, create a bean salad, offer the beans rolled up in a tortilla with some avocado slices and salsa, or prepare Caribbean Rice and Beans. Alternatively, freeze leftover beans in 1- or 2-cup quantities for use the following month.

Grain leftovers can also be refrigerated or frozen and then rehydrated by steaming (page 119). Stuff them into sheets of nori for sushi rolls (see page 180), stir them into soups, make them the basis of a stir-fry, or prepare an imaginative grain salad.

Column A	Column B	Column C
GRAINS *(choose one)*	VEGETABLES *(choose two)*	DESSERT *(optional)*
Frequently: Whole grains such as brown rice, quinoa, millet. Alternatively, serve whole-grain bread.	Steamed fresh vegetables in season or a prepared vegetable dish.	This can be a fresh fruit or a cooked dessert such as Brown Rice Pudding or Pumpkin Bread Pudding.
	Beans (plain, cooked with seasonings, or in a soup).	
Occasionally: Refined grains such as white rice, bulgur, risotto, pasta.	Fresh green or raw vegetable salad or coleslaw.	

MENU TIP

Pair up a green and yellow (or orange) vegetable to maximize the meal's nutritional value and visual appeal.

Here are a few possible game plans:
Whole grain (A) with beans (B) and a steamed vegetable (B).
Whole-grain bread (A) with bean soup (B) and coleslaw (B).
Pasta (A) with tomato-vegetable sauce (B) and salad (B).

Those who are concerned about the nutritional requirements for vegetarians may want to consult one of the books listed in the resource section on page 261.

How the Pressure Cooker Fits In

By preparing a dish from column A or B in the pressure cooker, you will be able to set a meal on the table in record time. For example, while a 7-minute lentil soup (B) is cooking under pressure, you can be making white rice or quinoa (A) and a steamed vegetable (B). Alternatively, as you pressure-cook a 5-minute Risotto with Kale and Gremolata (A and B), you can be tossing a green salad (B). Both of these meals will be ready in under half an hour.

Once you've experienced the ease of preparing such dinners, I predict you'll come to the conclusion that it would be nice to have a second cooker. Owning a second cooker opens up an even wider world of quick-dinner possibilities. You can be preparing soup or a vegetable stew in one pot while a grain dish is cooking in another. Or make some rice pudding for dessert while your bean chili is under way.

When planning menus, keep in mind that for aesthetic and textural appeal, it's best to complement the comfort food that comes out of the pressure cooker with dishes that have crunch. See the pages that follow for some specific menu ideas.

Menu Suggestions

In the menus that follow, I've listed recipes to aid you in preparing theme dinners (letters refer to the guide for menu planning described on page 28). After choosing one or two (or more) of the pressure-cooked dishes, plan to round out the menu with a steamed vegetable or salad and perhaps some fresh fruit for dessert.

If you own only one cooker and want to cook a few recipes under pressure, you'll have to transfer finished dishes to another pot for rewarming. In this case, make the grain dish last and serve it straight from the cooker.

THANKSGIVING DINNER

Creamy Apple-Squash Soup (B)
Celery, Corn, and Potato Chowder (B)
Gingered Adzuki-Squash Stew (B)
Fall Harvest Rice Casserole (A)
Maple-Glazed Turnips with Prunes (B)
Revisionist Boston Brown Bread (A)
Pumpkin Bread Pudding (C)

PICNIC FARE

Middle Eastern Potato Salad with Bulgur (A, B)
Georgian Kidney Beans with Walnut-Coriander Sauce (B)
Bean Salsa (B)
Quinoa Salpicón (A)
Double Sesame Grain Salad (A)
Blueberry Pudding-Cake (C)

CURRY IN A HURRY

Curried Split Pea Soup (B)
Split Pea Dal with Apple and Coconut (B)
Cauliflower-Potato Curry (B)
Parsnips with Indian Spices (B)
Chutney Rice (A)
Sun-Dried Tomato Chutney (B)
Coconut Rice Pudding (A, C)

QUICK FIXES

Here is a selection of dishes that cook very quickly and require minimal preparation:

Curried Split Pea Soup

Collard Spaghetti

Coriander Carrots

Potatoes Paprikash

Coconut Rice

Chutney Rice

Risotto with Winter Squash

Quinoa Corn Chili

Baby Limas with Spinach and Dill

Lentils with Squash

Sun-Dried Tomato Chutney

Squash Colombo

Gingered Pear Sauce

SOME OF MY FAVORITE THINGS

Soups: Herb-Scented Lima Bean, New Mexican Pinto Bean, White Bean Gazpacho, Quinoa Vegetable, Oriental Eggplant.

Vegetables: Cauliflower-Potato Curry, Parsnips with Indian Spices, Maple-Glazed Turnips with Prunes, Potatoes Paprikash, Southwest Succotash.

Grains: Triple Fennel Rice, Paella Vegetariana, Risotto with Broccoli Rabe and White Beans, Squash Couscous with Dates, Quinoa Corn Chili.

Beans: Baby Limas with Spinach and Dill, Black Bean Chili, Thai Chickpeas, Indonesian-Style Tempeh, Pasta e Fagioli.

Pickles, Chutneys, and Sauces: Onion Compote, Sun-Dried Tomato Chutney, Squash Colombo, Chunky Eggplant Sauce for Pasta.

Desserts: Fig-Hazelnut Risotto, Pumpkin Bread Pudding, Date-Nut Couscous, Blueberry Pudding-Cake, Pear Pudding-Cake.

AMERICAN CREOLE

Herbed Cauliflower-Tomato Soup (B)
Creole Okra Stew (B)
Louisiana Red Beans (B)
Black-eyed Pea Gumbo (B)
Collard Spaghetti (B)

AMERICAN SOUTHWEST

New Mexican Pinto Bean Soup (B)
Southwest Succotash (B)
Black Bean Chili (B)
Mexican Green Rice with Corn (A)
Quinoa Corn Chili (A)

TIME FOR THAI

Thai-Style Vegetable Curry (B)
White or Brown Basmati Rice (A)
Thai Chickpeas (B)
Potatoes and Onions Thai-Style (B)

MEDITERRANEAN

Split Pea Soup with **Herbes de Provence** *(B)*
Ratatouille Soup (B)
Mushrooms and Leeks with Saffron Rice (A, B)
Triple Fennel Rice (A)
Sweet and Sour Zucchini (B)
Onion Compote (B)

RUSTIC ITALIAN

Chickpea Soup Italiano (B)
Garlic Lovers' Lentil Soup (B)
Risotto with Kale and Gremolata (A, B)
Tuscan White Beans with Sage (B)
Polenta with Dried Mushrooms and Olives (A)

OLD WORLD SUNDAY SUPPER

Double Mushroom Barley Soup (A, B)
Dilled Cabbage Soup with Rice (A, B)
Carrot Tsimmes (B)
Millet Pilaf with Mushrooms, Carrots, and Peas (A, B)
Potatoes Paprikash (B)

SOUPS

It is in the category of soup-making that the pressure cooker performs some of its most impressive kitchen wizardry, providing mellow texture and long-cooked flavor in minimal time. Because they are so quick, filling, and nutritious, soups are a natural for taking center stage on a lunch or dinner menu. For impromptu meals, I always have lentils and split peas on hand since they require no soaking and take less than 10 minutes to pressure-cook. By adding an interesting range of herbs or spices and some onions, carrots, or squash, I can have a hearty main-dish soup ready about fifteen minutes after the idea comes to mind. (See The Pressured Cook's Pantry, pages 13-26, for other basics to keep on hand.)

In classic cooking, stocks often play a major role in creating full-flavored soups, but in my experience the pressure cooker renders them less necessary. The cooker does such a great job intensifying and mingling flavors that you can virtually create the stock and the soup in the pot simultaneously. It is for this reason that you will find many basic stock ingredients—celery, carrots, and onions—built right into most of the soup recipes that follow. On those occasions when I call for stock instead of water, I feel that it is needed for added depth and complexity. In such cases, an instant stock such as Vogue Vege Base is quite acceptable. I've included a few basic stock recipes at the end of the chapter for those cooks who prefer homemade to instant.

General Tips and Techniques

Save considerable time bringing a pot of soup up to pressure by adding water or stock that's already boiling rather than at room temperature.

When making bean soups, always add salt and acid ingredients, such as tomatoes or vinegar, at the end. These ingredients harden bean skins and retard cooking.

I rarely take the time to brown or sweat onions as the first step in making a soup, but you may choose to do so. Brown the onions by stirring them frequently while cooking over medium-high heat. Alternatively, sweat them over low heat, covered, for about 10 minutes. Both processes will bring out sweetness and flavor. (Be sure to scrape up any browned bits stuck to the bottom of the cooker before proceeding.)

A pressure-cooked soup develops more visual and flavor appeal when fresh herbs or a quick-cooking green vegetable like spinach is added at the end of cooking.

If a soup is too thick (or becomes too thick after refrigeration), thin it slightly with water or stock. If it is too thin, purée a cup or two of the solid ingredients and stir them back in.

Adapting Soup Recipes for the Pressure Cooker

Soup recipes are relatively easy to translate from standard stove-top to pressure cooker preparations. Here are some general rules for making adaptations. Depending upon the results of your trial run, you can make refinements as needed.

When pressure cooking, it's not convenient to add ingredients here and there along the way. Recipes that include all of the ingredients at the beginning work best. However, if you wish to add a second batch of ingredients before the soup is done, just bring the pressure down with a quick-release method. Either return the cooker to high pressure or simmer until the added ingredients are cooked.

If your recipe assumes that flavors will be concentrated by simmering without a lid, reduce the initial liquid by a cup or two. You can always thin the soup after it's cooked, if necessary.

Cut the cooking time down to approximately one third of the time suggested in your recipe—or one quarter for a bean soup. Check the charts in this book and recipes using similar ingredients for an approximation of cooking time. First time around, it's best to err on the side of undercooking: You can always bring the pressure back up or simmer the soup until it's done to perfection.

TWELVE-BEAN MIX

Makes 12 cups

Combine 1 cup of each of the following dried beans:

black beans

pinto beans

navy beans

Great Northern beans

red kidney beans

large limas

baby limas

brown or green lentils

chickpeas

green split peas

yellow split peas

black-eyed peas

TWELVE-BEAN SOUP

14 minutes high pressure (approximately),
2 to 3 minutes simmering

This recipe calls for 1½ cups of twelve-bean mix (at left), which I keep on hand in bulk for home use and gift giving (accompanied by the recipe). I am indebted to my literary agent, Phyllis Wender, for this idea.

The mix provides a great excuse to use up odd bits of left-over dried beans and a good opportunity to experiment with boutique beans—or you can use the combination listed to the left. Calculate cooking time (see the bean cooking chart on page 188) for the longest-cooking bean. Quick-cooking beans such as split peas and lentils dissolve into a purée, creating a luscious backdrop for the larger beans.

The soup is substantial enough to be the focal point of a meal, accompanied by a hearty peasant loaf and a crunchy salad or slaw.

In the recipe below, I've cooked the bean mix with typical North African spices. Another approach is to use Mediterranean herbs (see directions following the recipe). *Serves 6 to 8*

> 1½ **cups twelve-bean mix, picked over and rinsed,**
> **soaked overnight in ample water to cover or speed-**
> **soaked (page 185)**
> 1 **tablespoon safflower or canola oil**
> 2 **teaspoons finely minced garlic**
> 2 **cups coarsely chopped onions**
> 5 **cups boiling water**
> 2 **large carrots, halved lengthwise and cut into ½-inch**
> **slices**
> 2 **large bay leaves**
> 1½ **tablespoons ground coriander seeds**
> 2 **to 3 teaspoons dried mint leaves**
> 2 **teaspoons ground cumin seeds**
> 1½ **teaspoons ground caraway seeds**
> ⅛ **teaspoon crushed red pepper flakes**

2 tablespoons tomato paste

Salt and freshly ground pepper to taste

⅓ cup minced fresh parsley

2 to 4 tablespoons balsamic vinegar

Drain and rinse the beans. Remove any loose skins and discard. Set aside.

Heat the oil in the cooker. Cook the garlic over medium-high heat, stirring constantly, until light brown. Immediately add the onions and cook, stirring frequently, for 1 minute. Add the water (stand back to avoid sputtering oil), reserved beans, carrots, bay leaves, coriander, 2 teaspoons mint, cumin, caraway, and red pepper flakes.

Lock the lid in place. Over high heat, bring to high pressure. Lower the heat just enough to maintain high pressure and cook for 14 minutes (or the amount of time needed for the longest-cooking bean). Allow the pressure to come down naturally or use a quick-release method. Remove the lid, tilting it away from you to allow any excess steam to escape.

Remove the bay leaves; stir in the tomato paste and salt and pepper. Simmer for 2 to 3 minutes. Just before serving, stir in the parsley, extra teaspoon of mint, if desired, and vinegar to taste.

Omit the spices and mint and substitute 2 teaspoons dried oregano leaves, 1 teaspoon dried basil leaves, 1 teaspoon sweet paprika, and a pinch of crushed red pepper flakes. Add ½ pound fresh mushrooms, halved (if small) or quartered.

CHICKPEA SOUP ITALIANO

16 minutes high pressure, 2 to 3 minutes simmering

Chickpeas are quite at home with Mediterranean herbs. Pressure cooking accentuates their delightful creaminess and turns them into a quick-cooking bean. A nice menu might include a second course of risotto and a green salad, followed by fresh fruit for dessert. *Serves 6 to 8*

2 cups dried chickpeas, picked over and rinsed, soaked overnight in ample water to cover or speed-soaked (page 185)
5 cups boiling vegetable stock
3 large celery ribs, thinly sliced
3 cups thinly sliced leeks (white and light green parts) or coarsely chopped onions
2 large bay leaves
1½ teaspoons dried oregano leaves
¾ teaspoon dried rosemary leaves
Generous pinch of crushed red pepper flakes

. . . .

2 cups finely chopped fresh or canned (drained) plum tomatoes
⅓ cup minced fresh basil or parsley
1 to 2 teaspoons balsamic or other red wine vinegar
Salt and freshly ground pepper to taste

Drain and rinse the chickpeas. Place them in the cooker together with the stock, celery, leeks, bay leaves, oregano, rosemary, and red pepper flakes.

Lock the lid in place. Over high heat, bring to high pressure. Lower the heat just enough to maintain high pressure and cook for 16 minutes. Allow the pressure to come down naturally (for more tender chickpeas) or use a quick-release method. Remove the lid, tilting it away from you to allow any excess steam to escape. If the chickpeas are not quite done (they should be soft and creamy), return to high pressure for a few more minutes and, if time permits, let the pressure come down naturally.

Remove the bay leaves. With a slotted spoon, transfer about 2 cups of the cooked chickpeas to a food processor or blender, and purée them with 1 cup of the tomatoes. Stir the remaining cup of tomatoes and the purée back into the soup. Stir in the basil, vinegar, and salt and pepper. Simmer until the flavors are mingled, 2 to 3 minutes.

GARLIC LOVERS' LENTIL SOUP

7 minutes high pressure

This soup is very full of flavor. With its bright specks of carrot, red bell pepper, and parsley, it is also about as fetching as a lentil soup can be. The recipe calls for an outrageous amount of garlic, and browning the garlic exaggerates the flavor. You can use less; just don't tell me.

For a nice cold-weather meal, follow the soup with polenta and a steamed vegetable. *Serves 6 to 8*

1 tablespoon olive or canola oil

¼ cup coarsely chopped garlic

2 cups thinly sliced leeks (white and light green parts) or coarsely chopped onions

2 large carrots, halved lengthwise and cut into ¼-inch slices

2 large celery ribs, diced

½ pound fresh mushrooms, halved (if small) or quartered

2 cups dried lentils, picked over and rinsed

6 cups boiling water

1¼ teaspoons dried rosemary leaves

1 teaspoon dried thyme or marjoram leaves

2 large bay leaves

¼ teaspoon crushed red pepper flakes

. . . .

2 large red bell peppers, roasted (page 17), seeded, and diced

½ to ¾ cup minced fresh parsley

2 to 3 teaspoons balsamic vinegar

Salt and freshly ground pepper to taste

continued

VARIATIONS

For a more intense garlic flavor, omit the chopped garlic. After cooking, stir in 5 to 6 large cloves of roasted garlic that have been puréed with 2 tablespoons of the roasted red bell pepper.

Substitute black-eyed peas for the lentils. Increase cooking time to 11 minutes under high pressure.

After the soup is cooked, stir in some chopped kale, Swiss chard, or spinach and simmer until the greens are tender.

Purée the roasted red bell peppers and swirl a dollop of the purée into each portion of soup just before serving.

Use 2 cups of peeled, diced winter squash instead of the carrots.

Heat the oil in the cooker. Cook the garlic over med-high heat, stirring constantly, until it begins to brown. Immediately add the leeks and continue cooking, stirring frequently for another minute. Add the carrots, celery, mushrooms, lentils, boiling water (stand back to avoid sputtering oil), rosemary, thyme, bay leaves, and red pepper flakes.

Lock the lid in place. Over high heat, bring to high pressure. Lower the heat just enough to maintain high pressure and cook for 7 minutes. Allow the pressure to come down naturally or use a quick-release method. Remove the lid, tilting it away from you to allow any excess steam to escape. If the lentils are not quite tender, either return to high pressure for a few more minutes or replace (but do not lock) the lid and simmer until the lentils are done.

Remove the bay leaves. Stir in the roasted red bell peppers, parsley, just enough vinegar to bring up the flavors, and salt and pepper to taste.

ARMENIAN RED LENTIL SOUP WITH APRICOTS

4 minutes high pressure

In this unusual soup, the sweet-tart edge provided by the apricots is complemented by the sourness of lemon juice added at the end. This interesting balance is characteristic of the Armenian kitchen and is guaranteed to expand your flavor horizons in unexpected ways. If you are fond of the approach, you might also enjoy Armenian Vegetable Stew.

This soup is very pretty, with its flecks of bright green parsley and red tomatoes against a mustard-colored backdrop. A recipe in the fine Russian cookbook *Please to the Table*, by Anya von Bremzen and John Welchman (Workman, 1990), motivated me to create this pressure-cooker version.

Corn bread and a colorful salad are nice accompaniments to this soup. ***Serves 4 to 6***

TIPS & TECHNIQUES

Red lentils turn a greenish-yellow when cooked under pressure.

The soup thickens considerably after overnight refrigeration and makes a most unusual sauce. Try it over spinach fettucine or basmati rice.

4 cups water

1 cup coarsely chopped onions

1½ cups dried red lentils, picked over and rinsed

¼ to ⅓ cup (depending on desired sweetness) finely
chopped dried apricots

1 cup coarsely chopped fresh or canned (drained) plum
tomatoes

1 tablespoon safflower or canola oil (optional, except for
owners of jiggle-top cookers)

1 teaspoon dried marjoram or oregano leaves

½ teaspoon dried thyme leaves

. . . .

2 to 3 tablespoons freshly squeezed lemon juice

Salt and freshly ground pepper to taste

2 to 3 tablespoons minced fresh parsley

Begin bringing the water to the boil in the cooker as you
add the onions, lentils, apricots, tomatoes, oil (if needed), marjoram, and thyme.

Lock the lid in place. Over high heat, bring to high pressure. Lower the heat just enough to maintain high pressure
and cook for 4 minutes. Allow the pressure to come down
naturally or use a quick-release method. Remove the lid, tilting
it away from you to allow any excess steam to escape. If the
lentils are not quite tender, replace (but do not lock) the lid
and simmer until they are done.

If the soup is too thick, thin it with a bit of water. Stir in
the lemon juice and salt and pepper. Garnish with a sprinkling
of parsley.

HERB-SCENTED LIMA BEAN SOUP

9 minutes high pressure

Dried large lima beans are a great boon to anyone on a quest for low-fat creaminess. They have very thin skins that virtually dissolve in the pressure cooker, creating soup with an elegance and complex flavor that would suggest a much more labor-intensive dish.

Don't consider the tomato and parsley garnishes optional. They add most welcome color and flavor to the final product. The soup has a lightness that sets it firmly in the first-course category. I like to follow it with a pasta dish. *Serves 4*

1½ cups dried large lima beans, picked over and rinsed, soaked overnight in ample water to cover or speed-soaked (page 185)

1 tablespoon safflower or canola oil

½ cup coarsely chopped onion

3 cups boiling water

1 teaspoon dried chervil leaves (or substitute 1 large celery rib, very finely chopped)

½ teaspoon dried rosemary leaves

½ teaspoon dried sage leaves

. . . .

Salt and freshly ground pepper to taste

1 to 2 teaspoons balsamic vinegar (optional)

2 tablespoons minced fresh parsley

¼ cup seeded and finely chopped fresh plum tomato

Drain and rinse the limas. Remove any loose skins and discard. Set aside.

Heat the oil in the cooker. Cook the onion over medium-high heat, stirring frequently, for 1 minute. Add the water (stand back to avoid sputtering oil), reserved limas, chervil, rosemary, and sage.

Lock the lid in place. Over high heat, bring to high pressure. Lower the heat just enough to maintain high pressure and cook for 9 minutes. Allow the pressure to come down

TIPS & TECHNIQUES

Large lima beans foam considerably when cooking. Owners of jiggle-top cookers should probably avoid this recipe. If you choose to try it, add 1 more tablespoon of oil to reduce the possibility of a bean skin being catapulted into the vent. Don't leave the kitchen while this soup is cooking; turn off the heat and put the cooker under cold running water if you hear any unusual hissing noises.

Don't be tempted to substitute baby limas in this recipe. "Babies" hold on more tightly to their skins and don't result in as creamy a final product.

naturally or use a quick-release method. Remove the lid, tilting it away from you to allow any excess steam to escape.

Stir well as you add salt and pepper. With a fork, mash a few dozen limas against the side of the cooker and stir vigorously to create a thick, creamy texture. Add balsamic vinegar, if desired, to bring out the flavors. Serve in individual bowls, garnished with parsley and tomato.

New Mexican Pinto Bean Soup

8 minutes high pressure

TIPS & TECHNIQUES

If using fresh corn kernels, add the cobs to the soup for extra flavor; remove them before serving. Or cook the soup with an ear of corn that has been hacked into 1-inch slices (in addition to the corn kernels).

The dried chipotle pepper adds just a hint of smokiness and heat. For a hotter version, cook 3 to 4 of the chipotle seeds with the soup. If chipotles are not available, add a bit of liquid smoke flavoring at the end.

This pretty adobe-colored soup flecked with bright ye[llow] corn brings together all of the best flavors of the South-west. I've adapted it for the pressure cooker from a similar preparation in Maggie Oster's imaginative *Recipes from an American Herb Garden* (Macmillan, 1993).

The sophisticated flavor makes this soup ideal for serving guests of any dietary persuasion. (You're in for a wonderful surprise if you haven't already discovered how superbly avocado marries with beans.) Almost a meal in itself, you can serve it as the main dish with warm tortillas or corn chips and a green or grain salad on the side. ***Serves 4 to 6***

1½ cups dried pinto beans, picked over and rinsed, soaked overnight in ample water to cover or speed-soaked (page 185)

1 tablespoon safflower or canola oil

1 teaspoon whole cumin seeds

1 tablespoon finely minced garlic

2 cups coarsely chopped onions

1 large red bell pepper, seeded and diced

1½ to 2 cups fresh or frozen (defrosted) corn kernels

1½ teaspoons dried oregano leaves

1 dried chipotle pepper, stemmed, seeded, and snipped into bits, or 1 to 2 jalapeño peppers, seeded and minced (wear rubber gloves when handling chili peppers), or a generous pinch of crushed red pepper flakes

4 cups boiling water

. . . .

2 tablespoons tomato paste

½ cup minced fresh coriander or parsley

1 to 2 tablespoons freshly squeezed lime juice

Salt and freshly ground pepper to taste

1 ripe but firm avocado, preferably Haas variety, peeled, pitted, and cut into ½-inch dice (sprinkle with lime juice if not adding to the soup immediately)

Drain and rinse the beans. Set aside.

Heat the oil in the cooker. Sizzle the cumin seeds over medium-high heat just until they begin to pop, 5 to 10 seconds. Add the garlic and cook, stirring constantly, until the garlic turns light brown. Immediately add the onion and red bell pepper and cook, stirring frequently, for 1 minute. Add the reserved beans, corn, oregano, chipotle, and water (stand back to avoid sputtering oil).

Lock the lid in place. Over high heat, bring to high pressure. Lower the heat just enough to maintain high pressure and cook for 8 minutes. Allow the pressure to come down naturally or use a quick-release method. Remove the lid, tilting it away from you to allow any excess steam to escape. If the beans are not quite tender, replace (but do not lock) the lid and simmer until they are done.

With a slotted spoon, transfer a generous cupful of the beans to a food processor or blender, and purée with the tomato paste. Stir the mixture into the soup. Add the coriander, lime juice, and salt and pepper. Gently stir in the avocado just before serving.

Split peas foam considerably when cooking, so a tablespoon of oil is needed to reduce the possibility of foam catapulting a piece of food into the vent. I have never had a problem when cooking this recipe in newly designed pots, but do be on the alert for loud hissing noises if you are using a jiggle-top cooker.

This soup is hearty and ready to eat after 6 minutes under pressure; the extra cooking time afforded by the natural pressure release will create more of a puréed texture.

Because their seed coats have been removed, split peas do not hold their shape and are best used for soups, like this one, and purées.

SPLIT PEA SOUP WITH *HERBES DE PROVENCE*

6 minutes high pressure, optional natural pressure release

I consider my cupboard bare when there are no split peas in it. Since they require no soaking, I rely on these tiny quick-cooking morsels for last-minute soups that are hearty and full of flavor. Split peas take kindly to a wide variety of seasonings, as you can see from this and the following recipe.

Mediterranean Vegetable Couscous makes a nice follow-up to this soup. *Serves 4 to 6*

- 1 **tablespoon safflower or canola oil**
- 1 **tablespoon finely minced garlic**
- 2 **cups coarsely chopped onions**
- 1 **teaspoon** *each* **dried basil, oregano, and rosemary leaves**
- 1 **teaspoon whole fennel seeds**
- 1 **large bay leaf**
- 2 **large carrots, halved lengthwise and cut into ¼-inch slices**
- 2 **large celery ribs, diced**
- 6 **cups boiling water**
- 2 **cups dried green split peas, picked over and rinsed**

¼ **cup minced fresh parsley**
Salt to taste

Heat the oil in the cooker. Cook the garlic over medium-high heat, stirring constantly, just until it begins to brown. Immediately add the onions and continue to cook, stirring frequently, for another minute. Stir in the basil, oregano, rosemary, fennel, and bay leaf. Add the carrots, celery, boiling water (stand back to avoid sputtering oil), and split peas.

Lock the lid in place. Over high heat, bring to high pressure. Lower the heat just enough to maintain high pressure and cook for 6 minutes. For a hearty texture, quick-release the pressure by setting the pot under cold running water. For a smoother texture, allow the pressure to come down naturally. Remove the lid, tilting it away from you to allow any excess steam to escape.

Remove the bay leaf. Stir the soup well as you add the parsley and salt to taste. This soup will thicken considerably on standing. Thin as needed with water or stock.

VARIATIONS

Use 2 cups of red lentils instead of split peas. Once they are cooked, their color turns to olive green and their flavor and texture closely resemble split peas. Cooking time remains the same.

Stir in one of the following when you add the parsley:

⅓ **cup chopped oil-packed sun-dried tomatoes**

1 **to 2 cups coarsely chopped fresh plum tomatoes**

¼ **cup snipped dried dulse sea vegetable (adds a slightly briny taste and cheerful flecks of red)**

5 **ounces frozen (defrosted) chopped spinach or corn kernels; simmer until cooked, 2 to 3 minutes**

CURRIED SPLIT PEA SOUP

6 minutes high pressure, optional natural pressure release

I love the flavors of curry and find that they marry especially harmoniously with split peas. I like to doctor curry powders with an extra dose of cumin, fennel, and black mustard seeds. The fresh ginger brings an additional spark of vitality.

This soup makes a nice introduction to any Indian meal. Cauliflower-Potato Curry and Coconut Rice are good choices to complement the soup. *Serves 4 to 6*

1 tablespoon safflower or canola oil

1 teaspoon *each* whole cumin, fennel, and black mustard
   seeds (the last is optional)

1 tablespoon finely minced fresh ginger

1 teaspoon finely minced garlic

2 cups coarsely chopped onions

3 large carrots, halved lengthwise and cut into ½-inch
   slices

6 cups boiling water

2 cups dried green split peas, picked over and rinsed

2 tablespoons mild curry powder

. . . .

Salt to taste

Heat the oil in the cooker. Sizzle the cumin, fennel, and black mustard seeds over medium-high heat just until they begin to pop, 5 to 10 seconds. Stir in the ginger, garlic, and onions and continue to cook, stirring frequently, for another minute. Add the carrots, boiling water (stand back to avoid sputtering oil), split peas, and curry powder. Stir well to be sure that no bits of onion or spices have gotten stuck to the bottom of the pot.

Lock the lid in place. Over high heat, bring to high pressure. Lower the heat just enough to maintain high pressure and cook for 6 minutes. For a hearty texture, quick-release the pressure by setting the pot under cold running water. For a smoother texture, allow the pressure to come down naturally. Remove the lid, tilting it away from you to allow any excess steam to escape.

Stir in salt. If the soup is too thick, thin it slightly with water or stock.

TIPS & TECHNIQUES

For best results, make sure that your curry powder is fresh and flavorful. Taste a bit: If it leaves a bitter aftertaste, replace it. Better yet, try my recipe for home-made curry powder on page 20.

If you are not partial to the licorice taste of fennel, reduce the amount to ½ teaspoon.

Owners of jiggle-top cookers: Please see Tips in preceding recipe, page 44.

VARIATIONS

Stir in ⅓ cup minced fresh coriander when you add the salt.

To bring out flavors and reduce the need for salt, experiment by stirring in freshly squeezed lemon juice, a tablespoon at a time, until you achieve a pleasant balance of flavors.

At the end of cooking, stir in 1 to 2 cups finely chopped Swiss chard or beet greens and simmer until tender, 2 to 3 minutes.

For a sweeter edge, cook the soup with ⅓ cup raisins or substitute parsnips for the carrots.

Tarragon-Scented White Bean Soup

8 minutes high pressure

This recipe is one I turn to regularly for a quick meal, and I never fail to be amazed at how tarragon adds elegance to anything it touches. ***Serves 4 to 6***

1½ cups dried navy (pea) beans, picked over and rinsed, soaked overnight in ample water to cover or speed-soaked (page 185)

5 cups boiling water

1 tablespoon safflower or canola oil (optional, except for owners of jiggle-top cookers)

1 cup thinly sliced leeks (white and light green parts) or coarsely chopped onions

2 large carrots, halved lengthwise and cut into ½-inch slices

2 large celery ribs, finely diced

2 large bay leaves

2 teaspoons dried tarragon leaves

. . . .

1 teaspoon salt, or to taste

Drain and rinse the beans. Place them in the cooker with the water, oil (if needed), leeks, carrots, celery, bay leaves, and tarragon.

Lock the lid in place. Over high heat, bring to high pressure. Lower the heat just enough to maintain high pressure and cook for 8 minutes. Allow the pressure to come down naturally or use a quick-release method. Remove the lid, tilting it away from you to allow any excess steam to escape. If the beans are not quite tender, either return to high pressure for another minute or two or replace (but do not lock) the lid and simmer until the beans are done.

Remove the bay leaves and add salt. If the soup is too thin, with a slotted spoon, transfer about 1 cup of the beans to a food processor or blender, and purée. Stir the purée back into the soup.

TIPS & TECHNIQUES

If using leeks, add a few of the greens for extra flavor. Remove them before serving.

VARIATIONS

For a more elegant soup, purée the entire batch.

Use Great Northern instead of navy beans. Cooking time remains the same.

WHITE BEAN GAZPACHO

8 minutes high pressure

This is a wonderful version of the traditional gazpacho, made by cooking white beans with garlic, onions, and sweet paprika, and then puréeing the mixture. The resultant creamy, salmon-colored bisque sets the stage for chopped tomatoes, cucumbers, red onion, and green pepper. A splash of vinegar is added at the end, giving the soup a refreshing lilt, much appreciated on a hot summer's day. ***Serves 6***

> **1½ cups dried navy (pea) beans, picked over and rinsed, soaked overnight in ample water to cover or speed-soaked (page 185)**
>
> **4 cups boiling water**
>
> **1 tablespoon olive oil (optional, except for owners of jiggle-top cookers)**
>
> **2 teaspoons minced garlic**
>
> **1 cup coarsely chopped onions**
>
> **2 large bay leaves**
>
> **2 teaspoons sweet paprika**
>
> **Generous pinch of crushed red pepper flakes**
>
> . . . .
>
> **Salt to taste**
>
> **1 cup seeded and finely chopped fresh plum tomatoes**
>
> **½ cup diced green bell pepper**
>
> **1 cup peeled, seeded, and diced cucumber (Kirbys are nice)**
>
> **¼ to ⅓ cup finely chopped red onion or scallion greens**
>
> **1 tablespoon full-flavored olive oil**
>
> **1 to 3 tablespoons red wine vinegar (sherry wine vinegar is especially good)**

Drain and rinse the beans. Place them in the cooker with the water, oil (if needed), garlic, onions, bay leaves, paprika, and red pepper flakes.

Lock the lid in place. Over high heat, bring to high pressure. Lower the heat just enough to maintain high pressure and cook for 8 minutes. Allow the pressure to come down naturally or use a quick-release method. Remove the lid, tilting

TIPS & TECHNIQUES

There are some interesting alternatives for finishing off this soup. Instead of stirring in the vegetable garnishes, you can serve them in small bowls, allowing each diner to choose among them. (If you do this, it would be a good idea to double the amounts as some people will take a bit more than I've allotted here.)

Another possibility is to combine all of the chopped vegetables and set a mound of the mixture in the center of each bowl of soup.

After chilling, the soup might have to be thinned slightly with vegetable stock (preferred) or water.

it away from you to allow any excess steam to escape. The beans should be quite soft. If they are not, return to high pressure for a few more minutes or replace (but do not lock) the lid and simmer until the beans are done.

Remove the bay leaves and purée the soup in two to three batches in a blender (preferred) or food processor. Add salt. Transfer to a large storage container, cover, and chill. Just before serving, stir in the tomatoes, green pepper, cucumber, red onion, olive oil, and vinegar to taste. (The soup should have a slight piquant edge.)

QUINOA VEGETABLE SOUP

7 minutes high pressure

The soup pot is an unusual place for quinoa to make its appearance, but my testers and I all agreed that it offers a delightful surprise. If quinoa isn't a staple in your kitchen, use white rice instead. Although this soup is quite pretty and full-flavored, it requires relatively little time spent doing prep work. It is hearty enough to serve as the focal point of a meal. *Serves 6*

2 teaspoons safflower or canola oil

2 teaspoons finely minced garlic

2 cups coarsely chopped onions

5 cups boiling vegetable stock

2 tablespoons tomato paste

Generous ½ cup (½ ounce) sliced dried mushrooms, soaked if necessary (page 22)

3 large carrots, halved lengthwise and cut into ¼-inch slices

3 large celery ribs, diced

½ cup dried split peas, picked over and rinsed

½ cup quinoa, thoroughly washed (page 172) and drained

2 large bay leaves

1 tablespoon dried dill

. . . .

Salt and freshly ground pepper to taste

TIPS & TECHNIQUES

The split peas are added primarily to thicken the soup and give it body. They will probably not hold their shape.

If using instant stock, it's most convenient to bring water to the boil in a tea kettle and pour it directly into the cooker. Then stir in the instant stock powder.

VARIATIONS

Substitute red lentils for split peas. Cooking time remains the same.

Add 1 to 2 cups of winter squash cut into 1-inch chunks (peeling optional) along with the other vegetables.

Instead of dried mushrooms, use ½ pound sliced fresh mushrooms.

Heat the oil in the cooker. Cook the garlic and onion over medium-high heat, stirring frequently, for 3 minutes. Stir in the stock (stand back to avoid sputtering oil), tomato paste, mushrooms, carrots, celery, split peas, quinoa, bay leaves, and dill.

Lock the lid in place. Over high heat, bring to high pressure. Lower the heat just enough to maintain high pressure and cook for 7 minutes. Reduce the pressure with a quick-release method. Remove the lid, tilting it away from you to allow any excess steam to escape.

Remove the bay leaves and add salt and pepper. Stir well when serving to distribute the quinoa, which tends to sink to the bottom.

SOUPE AU PISTOU

2 minutes high pressure

Here is a thick, stewlike soup redolent with the flavors of southern France. It is especially delicious when the subtle anise flavor of fresh fennel is added. Although the classic recipe calls for a pestolike paste made with raw garlic and basil and stirred in at the end, I prefer the mellower flavor of garlic that is browned and cooked with the soup.

I like to add pasta and perhaps navy beans (see Variation) if I'm planning to serve this soup as an entree. A nice alternative is to omit the pasta and serve the soup as the first course, followed by pasta and a salad.

I usually rely on the food processor when prepping the vegetables because this recipe requires a fair amount of chopping. *Serves 8*

TIPS & TECHNIQUES

If using canned tomatoes, substitute the drained juice for an equal amount of water.

VARIATION

After cooking, add 1 to 2 cups cooked navy or cannellini beans. Simmer until they are heated before adding the basil and additional seasonings.

2 tablespoons olive oil

2 to 3 teaspoons minced garlic

2 cups thinly sliced leeks (white and light green parts) or coarsely chopped onions

5 cups boiling water

1 large fennel bulb, coarsely chopped (1½ to 2 cups), or 1½ cups chopped celery plus ½ teaspoon whole fennel seeds

2 large carrots, halved lengthwise and cut into ¼-inch slices

½ pound fresh green beans, trimmed and cut into 2-inch pieces

3 cups coarsely chopped fresh or canned (drained) plum tomatoes

1 large zucchini, cut into 1-inch chunks

1 teaspoon dried oregano leaves

Pinch of crushed red pepper flakes

½ cup orzo, tubettini, or other small pasta (optional)

. . . .

2 cups loosely packed fresh basil leaves, coarsely chopped

2 to 4 tablespoons freshly squeezed lemon juice

Salt and freshly ground pepper to taste

Freshly grated Parmesan or Gruyère cheese (optional)

Heat 1 tablespoon of the oil in the cooker. Cook the garlic over medium-high heat, stirring constantly, until lightly browned. Immediately add the leeks and cook, stirring frequently, for 1 minute. Add the water (stand back to avoid sputtering oil), fennel, carrots, green beans, tomatoes, zucchini, oregano, red pepper flakes, and orzo (if using).

Lock the lid in place. Over high heat, bring to high pressure. Lower the heat just enough to maintain high pressure and cook for 2 minutes. Reduce the pressure with a quick-release method. Remove the lid, tilting it away from you to allow any excess steam to escape.

If the soup seems too thin, with a slotted spoon, transfer a cupful of the vegetables to a food processor or blender, purée them, and stir the purée back in. Stir in the remaining tablespoon of olive oil, the basil, and lemon juice and salt and pepper to taste. Stir well when serving to distribute the orzo, which tends to sink to the bottom. Garnish with grated cheese, if desired.

RATATOUILLE SOUP

3 minutes high pressure

This chunky soup is a meal in itself, accompanied by a green salad and a loaf of crusty bread. In hot weather, I like to serve it chilled. Leftovers are nice over cooked pasta.
Serves 6

1 to 2 tablespoons olive oil
2 teaspoons minced garlic
2 cups coarsely chopped onions
1 pound eggplant, peeled and cut into ½-inch dice
One 28-ounce can peeled plum tomatoes, coarsely chopped, including juice
1 pound large zucchini, cut into 1-inch slices
1 cup boiling vegetable stock
1 bay leaf
2 teaspoons dried basil leaves
1 teaspoon whole fennel seeds
Generous pinch of crushed red pepper flakes
1 teaspoon salt, or to taste
Freshly ground pepper to taste
. . . .
Freshly grated Parmesan cheese or balsamic vinegar to taste

Heat 1 tablespoon of the oil in the cooker. Cook the garlic and onions over medium-high heat, stirring frequently, for 1 minute. Add the eggplant, tomatoes and their juice, zucchini, stock (stand back to avoid sputtering oil), bay leaf, basil, fennel, red pepper flakes, salt, and pepper.

Lock the lid in place. Over high heat, bring to high pressure. Lower the heat just enough to maintain high pressure and cook for 3 minutes. Reduce the pressure with a quick-release method. Remove the lid, tilting it away from you to allow any excess steam to escape. If the vegetables are not quite tender, replace (but do not lock) the lid and simmer until they are done.

Remove the bay leaf and add the remaining tablespoon of olive oil, if desired. Serve in bowls with a sprinkling of Parmesan cheese on top. Alternatively, stir in 1 to 2 teaspoons of balsamic vinegar, if desired, to sharpen the flavors.

Only 1 cup of stock is added to this soup because the vegetables give off so much liquid during cooking.

DILLED CABBAGE SOUP WITH RICE

5 minutes high pressure

A very full-flavored and satisfying soup that belies the ease of preparation. For a rib-sticking cold weather meal, follow it up with the Winter Vegetable Ragout. **Serves 8**

2 teaspoons safflower or canola oil

2 cups coarsely chopped onions

6 cups boiling vegetable stock

½ cup extra-long-grain or basmati white rice

3 tablespoons tomato paste

2 large bay leaves

4 whole black peppercorns

1 teaspoon salt, or to taste

1 tablespoon dried dill

1 large cabbage (about 2½ pounds), quartered, cored, and thinly shredded

3 large carrots, halved lengthwise and thinly sliced

2 large celery ribs, thinly sliced

. . . .

2 to 3 teaspoons balsamic or other red wine vinegar

Heat the oil in the cooker. Cook the onions over medium-high heat, stirring frequently, for about 1 minute. (If time permits and you are so inclined, sweat the onions, covered, over low heat, stirring occasionally, for about 10 minutes, to bring out their sweetness.)

Add the stock (stand back to avoid sputtering oil), rice, tomato paste, bay leaves, peppercorns, salt, dill, cabbage, carrots, and celery.

Lock the lid in place. Over high heat, bring to high pressure. Lower the heat just enough to maintain high pressure and cook for 5 minutes. Reduce the pressure with a quick-release method. Remove the lid, tilting it away from you to allow any excess steam to escape.

Remove the bay leaves and peppercorns (if you happen to notice them). Add vinegar to taste. Stir well when serving to distribute the rice, which tends to sink to the bottom.

TIPS & TECHNIQUES

Don't be concerned if the cabbage reaches to the top of the cooker. It will shrink dramatically as it heats up, allowing sufficient space for the pressure to rise.

VARIATIONS

Use lemon juice instead of vinegar.

Cook the soup with ¼ cup dried currants. Substitute ⅓ cup quinoa, thoroughly washed (page 172) and drained, for the rice.

BEET BORSCHT

6 minutes high pressure

TIPS & TECHNIQUES

The beets are cut smaller than the potatoes because they are more dense and take longer to cook. It isn't necessary to peel either vegetable. Just scrub them well and pare away any rough spots.

If you are planning to make a puréed summer soup, you can save chopping time by cutting the potatoes and beets into slightly larger chunks. Increase cooking time to 8 minutes under pressure.

This recipe creates a soup that can have two different personalities, both of them delicious and visually stunning. In summer, purée the whole batch and serve it chilled. In winter, leave it partly chunky and serve it piping hot. Either way, you'll have a substantial main course. *Serves 8*

1 tablespoon safflower or canola oil

2 cups coarsely chopped onions or thinly sliced leeks
   (white and light green parts)

3½ to 4 cups boiling water (use the smaller amount if
   you like your soup very thick)

1 pound beets, trimmed, scrubbed, and cut into ½-inch
   chunks

½ pound thin-skinned potatoes, scrubbed and cut into 1-
   inch chunks

1 pound cabbage, cored and thinly shredded

2 tablespoons tomato paste

2 large bay leaves

2 teaspoons dried dill seeds or dill weed

. . . .

Salt and freshly ground pepper to taste

3 to 4 tablespoons freshly squeezed lemon juice

Optional garnishes:

   Sour cream, yogurt, or roasted shallot cream
      (page 24)

   1 cucumber, peeled, seeded, and diced

   ¼ cup minced fresh dill

Heat the oil in the cooker. Cook the onions over medium-high heat, stirring frequently, for 1 minute. Add the water (stand back to avoid sputtering oil), beets, potatoes, cabbage, tomato paste, bay leaves, and dill seeds.

Lock the lid in place. Over high heat, bring to high pressure. Lower the heat just enough to maintain high pressure and cook for 6 minutes. Reduce the pressure with a quick-release method. Remove the lid, tilting it away from you to allow any excess steam to escape. If the beets are not fork tender, replace (but do not lock) the lid and simmer until they are done. Remove the bay leaves.

For a winter soup: Purée about one third of the soup in a food processor or blender. Return the purée to the pot, reheat, and stir in salt and pepper. Add lemon juice to taste just before serving. Garnish with a dollop of sour cream, if desired.

For a summer soup: Purée the soup in several batches in a food processor or blender. Add salt and pepper. Transfer to a large storage container, cover, and chill. Just before serving, add lemon juice to taste. Serve with a dollop of sour cream, yogurt, or roasted shallot cream, topped with cucumber and dill.

HERBED CAULIFLOWER-TOMATO SOUP

4 minutes high pressure

An elegant puréed soup with lovely flavor and a pale rosy hue. It is nice served hot in winter and especially good chilled in late summer, when tomatoes and cauliflower are abundant in northern climes. A bean or grain salad makes a pleasant second course. ***Serves 4 to 6***

1 tablespoon olive oil
½ to 2 teaspoons minced garlic (see Tips)
2 cups coarsely chopped onions
4 cups coarsely chopped fresh or canned (drained) plum
    tomatoes
½ cup water
2 tablespoons tomato paste
1 large bay leaf
1 teaspoon dried oregano or marjoram leaves
1 teaspoon dried basil leaves
¼ teaspoon dried rosemary leaves
Generous pinch of crushed red pepper flakes
Generous pinch of ground cinnamon
1 large head cauliflower (about 2½ pounds), trimmed
    and cut into 2-inch florets
Salt and freshly ground pepper to taste
. . . .
¼ cup minced fresh dill or parsley

Heat the oil in the cooker. Cook the garlic and onions over medium-high heat, stirring frequently, for 1 minute. Add the tomatoes, water (stand back to avoid sputtering oil), tomato paste, bay leaf, oregano, basil, rosemary, red pepper flakes, cinnamon, cauliflower, and salt and pepper.

Lock the lid in place. Over high heat, bring to high pressure. Lower the heat just enough to maintain high pressure and cook for 4 minutes. Allow the pressure to come down naturally or use a quick-release method. Remove the lid, tilting it away from you to allow any excess steam to escape.

TIPS & TECHNIQUES

My testers and I are at odds about how much garlic to use in this recipe. I prefer 1 to 2 teaspoons, but some feel that a hint of garlic (about ½ teaspoon) creates a better balance of flavors. I thought I'd leave the decision to you.

If using canned tomatoes, substitute ½ cup of the drained juice for the water.

Before puréeing the soup, you may wish to hold aside about 1 cup of cooked cauliflower florets to use as garnish.

If tomato skins bother you, purée the soup through a food mill.

Remove the bay leaf. Purée the soup in two or three batches in a food processor or blender. Transfer to a large storage container, cover, and chill before serving, if desired. Garnish with dill.

CELERY, CORN, AND POTATO CHOWDER

4 minutes high pressure, 2 to 3 minutes simmering

I love corn for its flavor, color, and texture. In this recipe, I play with the last characteristic in a variety of ways. Some of the kernels are cooked with the soup, some are blended to release their milk and add creaminess, and a final batch is added at the end to contribute crunch. The result is a pretty, rich-tasting soup that is very low in fat. If you don't mind tipping the caloric balance in the other direction, follow it up with some Guacamole Rice Salad.

If you are using fresh corn (the best choice), cook the shucked cobs with the soup for added sweetness and flavor. Break them in half, if necessary, to fit into the cooker.
Serves 6

2 teaspoons safflower or canola oil

2 cups coarsely chopped onions, preferably red onions

4 cups boiling vegetable stock

1 pound thin-skinned potatoes, peeled and cut into ½-inch dice

1 large red bell pepper, seeded and diced

4 cups fresh or frozen (defrosted) corn kernels

4 large celery ribs, diced

½ teaspoon dried thyme leaves

. . . .

⅓ cup minced fresh dill

Salt and freshly ground pepper to taste

VARIATIONS

If using fresh corn, you can cut an additional cob into 1-inch chunks and cook them with the soup. Very pretty.

If fresh dill is not readily available, cook the soup with 1 tablespoon of dried dill.

For a richer chowder, reduce the stock to 3½ cups and stir in ½ cup of milk after cooking.

continued

Heat the oil in the cooker. Cook the onions over medium-high heat, stirring frequently, for 1 minute. Add the stock (stand back to avoid sputtering oil), potatoes, red bell pepper, 1 cup of corn, corn cobs (if using), celery, and thyme.

Lock the lid in place. Over high heat, bring to high pressure. Lower the heat just enough to maintain high pressure and cook for 4 minutes. Reduce the pressure with a quick-release method. Remove the lid, tilting it away from you to allow any excess steam to escape.

Remove the corn cobs (if used). With a slotted spoon, transfer about 2 cups of cooked vegetables to a food processor or blender, and purée them together with 2 cups of the uncooked corn kernels. (Do not overprocess or the potatoes will become gummy.) Stir the purée back into the soup together with the remaining 1 cup of uncooked corn. Add the dill and salt and pepper. Simmer until the just-added corn is tender, 2 to 3 minutes.

ORIENTAL EGGPLANT SOUP

4 minutes high pressure

Here is an elegant purée, redolent of eggplant and toasted sesame. It's good hot and also delicious as a cold summer soup. Complete the meal with a quick stir-fry or Thai-Style Vegetable Curry accompanied by rice. ***Serves 6***

4 cups vegetable stock

1 tablespoon tamari soy sauce

2 large eggplants (2½ to 3 pounds total), peeled and cut into 1-inch chunks

2 cups coarsely chopped onions

2 tablespoons finely minced fresh ginger

2 teaspoons finely minced garlic

1 small dried red chili pepper, or a generous pinch of crushed red pepper flakes

. . . .

1 to 2 tablespoons toasted (Oriental) sesame oil

1 tablespoon brown rice vinegar, approximately

Additional tamari soy sauce to taste

¼ cup thinly sliced scallion greens

¼ cup minced fresh coriander

Bring the stock and tamari to the boil in the cooker as you add the eggplant, onions, ginger, garlic, and chili pepper.

Lock the lid in place. Over high heat, bring to high pressure. Lower the heat just enough to maintain high pressure and cook for 4 minutes. Allow the pressure to come down naturally or use a quick-release method. Remove the lid, tilting it away from you to allow any excess steam to escape.

Pass the soup through a food mill (most convenient) or press it with the back of a spoon through a wide-meshed strainer (this will take a bit of time). Discard the eggplant seeds and other solid bits of vegetable. Unless you are planning to serve the soup chilled, return the purée to the pot to heat as you stir in the toasted sesame oil, vinegar, and additional soy sauce.

Ladle the soup into a tureen or individual bowls. Garnish with scallion greens and coriander.

TIPS & TECHNIQUES

Eggplants must be peeled because their skins don't soften sufficiently in the short time it takes for the pressure cooker to turn their flesh into a soft purée. If you're planning to pass the cooked soup through a food mill, however, you don't have to bother peeling the eggplant.

Double Mushroom Barley Soup

18 minutes high pressure

Here is an intensely flavored soup made with both fresh and dried mushrooms. It is ideal for an impromptu supper accompanied by whole-grain bread and a mixed green salad. *Serves 6*

2 teaspoons safflower or canola oil

1 teaspoon finely minced garlic

2 cups coarsely chopped onions or thinly sliced leeks (white and light green parts)

6 cups boiling vegetable stock, approximately

½ cup pearl barley

½ pound fresh mushrooms, sliced or quartered

Generous ½ cup (½ ounce) sliced dried mushrooms, soaked if necessary (page 22)

2 large carrots, halved lengthwise and thinly sliced

2 large celery ribs, diced

2 large bay leaves

1½ tablespoons dried dill, approximately

Salt and freshly ground pepper to taste

Heat the oil in the cooker. Cook the garlic and onions over medium-high heat, stirring constantly, for 1 minute. Add the stock (stand back to avoid sputtering oil), barley, fresh and dried mushrooms, carrots, celery, bay leaves, dill, and salt and pepper.

Lock the lid in place. Over high heat, bring to high pressure. Lower the heat just enough to maintain high pressure and cook for 18 minutes. Allow the pressure to come down naturally or use a quick-release method. (Set the cooker under cold running water if you experience any sputtering while quick-releasing the pressure.) Remove the lid, tilting it away from you to allow any excess steam to escape.

Discard the bay leaves and add a bit more dried dill, salt, and pepper if the flavors need a boost. The soup will thicken considerably upon standing. Thin it to the desired consistency with additional vegetable stock.

VARIATIONS

Substitute peeled parsnips for the carrots.

After the soup is cooked, add 1 cup frozen (defrosted) baby limas and simmer until tender, 1 to 2 minutes.

CREAMY APPLE-SQUASH SOUP

5 minutes high pressure

A lovely fall soup with a caramel-orange color and the smooth elegance of silk. The apples add a subtly tart edge, an intriguing counterpoint to the sweetness of the squash. Although it contains almost no fat, the soup tastes quite rich and is best served in modest portions as an appetizer rather than as a main dish. ***Serves 8 to 10***

- 1 tablespoon safflower or canola oil
- 1½ cups thinly sliced leeks (white and light green parts) or coarsely chopped onions
- 4 cups boiling water
- 3 pounds butternut squash, seeded and cut into 1½-inch chunks
- 3 Granny Smith apples, peeled, cored, and quartered
- ⅓ cup uncooked old-fashioned oatmeal
- 2 tablespoons finely minced fresh ginger
- 1½ tablespoons mild curry powder
- 1 teaspoon salt, or to taste

. . . .

- 1 to 2 tablespoons snipped chives, fennel fronds, or thinly sliced scallion greens (optional)

Heat the oil in the cooker. Cook the leeks over medium-high heat, stirring frequently, for 1 minute. Add the water (stand back to avoid sputtering oil), squash, apples, oatmeal, ginger, curry powder, and salt.

Lock the lid in place. Over high heat, bring to high pressure. Lower the heat just enough to maintain high pressure and cook for 5 minutes. Allow the pressure to come down naturally or use a quick-release method. Remove the lid, tilting it away from you to allow any excess steam to escape. If the squash is not fork-tender, replace (but do not lock) the lid and let cook for a few more minutes in the residual heat.

Purée the soup in two or three batches in a blender (preferred) or food processor and return to the cooker to reheat before serving. Garnish with chives, if desired.

TIPS & TECHNIQUES

It's not necessary to peel the squash (if it's unwaxed and organic) because the pressure cooker does a nice job of softening the skin.

The oatmeal adds body, creaminess, and sheen to the soup.

Potato Soup with Spinach

6 minutes high pressure, 2 to 3 minutes simmering

There is something so satisfying about a thick potato soup. And if leeks are available, you'll understand why they are traditionally paired with America's favorite tuber.

The green flecks of spinach are very pretty against the pale, creamy backdrop of potatoes. *Serves 4 to 6*

VARIATIONS

Season the soup with ¼ teaspoon saffron threads in addition to the oregano and rosemary.

Substitute ½ pound chopped kale, Swiss chard, beet greens, or escarole for the spinach.

2 teaspoons safflower or canola oil

2 teaspoons finely minced garlic

2 cups coarsely chopped leeks (white and light green parts) or onions

4 cups boiling vegetable stock

2 pounds thin-skinned potatoes, peeled and cut into ½-inch dice

2 large carrots, halved lengthwise and cut into ¼-inch slices

2 large celery ribs, halved lengthwise and cut into ¼-inch slices

1½ teaspoons dried oregano leaves

½ teaspoon dried rosemary leaves

2 large bay leaves

⅛ to ¼ teaspoon crushed red pepper flakes

. . . .

1 pound fresh spinach, trimmed and chopped, or 10 ounces frozen (defrosted) chopped spinach

1 large red bell pepper, roasted (page 17), seeded, and diced (optional, but highly recommended)

Salt and freshly ground pepper to taste

1 to 2 tablespoons freshly squeezed lemon juice (optional)

Heat the oil in the cooker. Cook the garlic and leeks over medium-high heat, stirring frequently, for 3 minutes. Add the stock (stand back to avoid sputtering oil), potatoes, carrots, celery, oregano, rosemary, bay leaves, and red pepper flakes.

Lock the lid in place. Over high heat, bring to high pressure. Lower the heat just enough to maintain high pressure and cook for 6 minutes. Allow the pressure to come down naturally or use a quick-release method. Remove the lid, tilting it away from you to allow any excess steam to escape.

Remove the bay leaves. With a slotted spoon, transfer about 2 cups of potatoes and other vegetables to a food processor, and pulse to create a purée. (Do not overprocess or the potatoes will become gummy.) Stir the purée back into the soup together with the spinach, roasted red bell pepper (if using), and salt and pepper. Simmer until the spinach is cooked, 2 to 3 minutes. If desired to intensify the flavors, stir in lemon juice to taste just before serving. This recipe creates a fairly thick soup. You might want to thin it a bit with stock after cooking.

INTENSELY TOMATO— ROASTED PEPPER SOUP

3 minutes high pressure

This flashy fire-engine red tomato soup welcomes you back to the days of old-fashioned, straightforward flavor. But the addition of roasted red bell peppers gives it a refreshing contemporary twist.

Try making this soup when slightly bruised or overripe beefsteak tomatoes are on sale or screaming for your attention in the garden. It freezes well and is also good chilled, particularly as the base for a summer gazpacho. ***Serves 8***

½ cup water

3 pounds beefsteak tomatoes, cored and cut into chunks

2 large red bell peppers, roasted (page 17), seeded, and cut into eighths

1 cup coarsely chopped onions

2 teaspoons minced garlic

2 large bay leaves

¼ teaspoon saffron threads (optional, but highly recommended)

Salt to taste

. . . .

⅓ cup minced fresh basil or dill

TIPS & TECHNIQUES

The food mill is ideal for puréeing this soup, as it separates out the tomato skins and seeds. However, the food processor and blender both create a reasonably smooth purée.

Only a modest amount of water is needed since the tomatoes release so much liquid.

VARIATIONS

Stir 2 tablespoons of olive oil into the puréed soup.

Garnish with croutons as well as basil.

continued

Bring the water and tomatoes to the boil in the cooker as you prepare and add the peppers, onions, garlic, bay leaves, saffron (if using), and salt.

Lock the lid in place. Set the cooker on a heated Flame Tamer. Over high heat, bring to high pressure. Lower the heat just enough to maintain high pressure and cook for 3 minutes. Allow the pressure to come down naturally or quick-release pressure by placing the cooker under cold running water. (Other quick-release methods are likely to cause spitting at the vent.) Remove the lid, tilting it away from you to allow any excess steam to escape.

Purée the soup in three or four batches in a food mill (preferred), food processor, or blender. Return to the cooker to reheat before serving. Garnish with basil.

Tomato-Rice Soup

Add 1 to 1½ cups cooked brown or white rice to the puréed soup and simmer until the rice is quite soft. (Cooked quinoa is also a nice addition.)

ZUCCHINI BISQUE WITH TOMATOES AND FRESH BASIL

4 minutes high pressure

This elegant purée—pale salmon with flecks of green—is smooth and creamy, although very low in fat. It's great to prepare in the summer, when zucchini, tomatoes, and basil are in abundance.

Good hot or chilled. Try Warm Bean Vinaigrette or an All-Purpose Bean Salad for the second course. *Serves 6*

2 teaspoons olive oil

1 teaspoon minced garlic

1 cup coarsely chopped onions

2 pounds zucchini, cut into 1-inch chunks

¾ pound thin-skinned potatoes, scrubbed and cut into
    1-inch chunks

1 pound fresh plum tomatoes, seeded (optional) and
    diced

1 small red bell pepper, seeded and diced

3 cups boiling water

2 large bay leaves

. . . .

½ cup minced fresh basil

2 to 3 tablespoons freshly squeezed lemon juice

Salt to taste

Heat the oil in the cooker. Cook the garlic over medium-high heat, stirring constantly, until lightly browned. Add the onions and continue to cook, stirring frequently, for 1 minute. Add the zucchini, potatoes, tomatoes, red bell pepper, water (stand back to avoid sputtering oil), and bay leaves.

Lock the lid in place. Over high heat, bring to high pressure. Lower the heat just enough to maintain high pressure and cook for 4 minutes. Allow the pressure to come down naturally or use a quick-release method. Remove the lid, tilting it away from you to allow any excess steam to escape.

Allow the soup to cool slightly. Remove the bay leaves. Purée the soup in three or four batches in a blender (for a smoother soup) or a food processor. If serving hot, return to the cooker to reheat. If serving cold, transfer to a large storage container, cover, and chill. Just before serving, stir in the basil, lemon juice to taste, and salt.

BASIC VEGETABLE STOCK

10 minutes high pressure, optional natural pressure release

Although there need be no strict recipe for vegetable stock, the following will give you some guidelines.

This stock has optimum flavor when used within 2 to 3 days. It may be frozen for up to 3 months, but there will be some loss of flavor. You may find it convenient to freeze stock in different quantities and defrost as needed. For a big batch like this I usually put half in a 1-quart container and the remainder in 2-cup portions that are suitable for cooking grains and beans. Some cooks find it convenient to freeze stock in ice cube trays. ***Makes 1½ quarts***

8 cups water

8 cups scrubbed and coarsely chopped miscellaneous vegetables (see Potential Candidates for the Stockpot, page 69)

2 medium onions, coarsely chopped (include skins for a darker stock)

1 to 2 garlic cloves, finely chopped (optional)

3 large carrots, cut into 3 to 4 chunks

4 large celery ribs, cut into 3 to 4 chunks

1 to 2 parsnips, cut into 3 to 4 chunks (optional; makes the stock sweeter)

2 bay leaves

Small bunch of fresh parsley stalks

A few sprigs of fresh thyme or oregano, or ½ teaspoon dried thyme or dried oregano (optional)

. . . .

Salt to taste

TIPS & TECHNIQUES

I prefer to make my stocks free of fat and extra labor, but there's no question that you'll attain a richer and more intensely flavored stock if you brown the vegetables for 10 to 15 minutes in 1 to 2 tablespoons of oil before adding the water. Because fat carries flavor, this process also enables you to freeze the stock with less loss of taste.

For maximum flexibility, cook the stock without salt, then add salt once the stock has been incorporated into the finished dish. If you intend to use the stock for making a bean soup, it would be detrimental to add salt, which toughens bean skins and lengthens cooking time.

Place the water in the cooker and begin bringing to the boil as you prepare and add the remaining ingredients, except the salt.

Lock the lid in place. Over high heat, bring to high pressure. Lower the heat just enough to maintain high pressure and cook for 10 minutes. If time permits, allow the pressure to come down naturally. Otherwise, reduce pressure with a quick-release method. Remove the lid, tilting it away from you to allow any excess steam to escape.

Allow the stock to cool slightly. Pour the stock through a strainer into one or more storage containers. Press the vegetables against the sides of the strainer with a large spoon to extract all of the liquid. Add salt, if desired. Cool and refrigerate for up to 3 days or freeze up to 3 months.

POTENTIAL CANDIDATES FOR THE STOCKPOT

Asparagus and broccoli stalks

Zucchini

Corn cobs and husks

Celery, parsnip, and carrot chunks, peelings, and trimmings

Onions (including skins)

Garlic (including skins)

Leek greens and roots

Scallions (including root ends)

Kale stalks (for a strong, distinctive flavor suggesting cabbage)

Wilted celery, lettuce, and watercress

Winter squash (avoid waxed peels)

Turnips (peel them to avoid bitterness)

Potatoes and potato skins (be sure to remove any green spots; skins will make the stock darker)

Sprigs of parsley or other fresh herbs

Bay leaves or a few pinches of dried herbs

Peeled sweet potatoes, apples, or pears (for a slightly sweet stock)

Tomatoes or lemon slices (for a slightly acid stock)

CANDIDATES TO AVOID

Beets and beet skins (unless you desire a magenta-colored stock)

Turnip skins (they are bitter)

Most members of the cabbage family, such as cabbage and brussels sprouts (they easily overpower the stock)

Green peppers, eggplant, and leafy greens such as collards and mustard (they may impart a bitter taste)

Asian Vegetable Stock

10 minutes high pressure, 10-minute natural pressure release

This stock is fun to use for cooking grains that will be served with a stir-fried Oriental-style vegetable dish. It's also very tasty as a soup on its own, with perhaps a few of the cooked mushrooms and some thinly sliced scallions floating on top.

An added bonus is that your kitchen will be filled with an exotic aroma, transporting you to faraway places.

Makes about 1¹/₂ quarts

6 cups water
1 bunch scallions, coarsely chopped
3 to 4 large garlic cloves, coarsely chopped
8 quarter-size slices fresh ginger
1 ounce dried shiitake or Chinese dried mushrooms, rinsed
2 cups shredded bok choy or other cabbage
1 large bunch coriander, including well-washed roots, coarsely chopped (about 2 cups loosely packed)
2 teaspoons dried, ground lemongrass or 1 stalk fresh, chopped lemongrass (optional)

. . . .

2 to 3 tablespoons tamari soy sauce
2 to 3 teaspoons toasted (Oriental) sesame oil

Place the water in the cooker and begin bringing to the boil as you prepare and add all of the remaining remaining ingredients, except the soy sauce and sesame oil.

Lock the lid in place. Over high heat, bring to high pressure. Lower the heat just enough to maintain high pressure and cook for 10 minutes. Allow the pressure to come down naturally for 10 minutes. Quick-release any remaining pressure. Remove the lid, tilting it away from you to allow any excess steam to escape.

Allow the stock to cool slightly. Pour the stock through a fine-meshed strainer into one or more storage containers, leaving in the pot any sandy dregs that have sunk to the bottom. Press the vegetables against the sides of the strainer with a

TIPS & TECHNIQUES

If you've used shiitake mushrooms, remove and discard the stems after cooking. Slice the mushrooms and toss them into cooked grains or add them to soups.

VARIATION

This stock makes a great base for miso soup. Omit the soy sauce and sesame oil, and stir in your choice of miso to taste. (I use about 1 teaspoon per small soup bowl.) Add a few cubes of tofu and garnish with sliced scallions.

large spoon to extract all of the liquid. Add soy sauce and sesame oil to taste. Cool and refrigerate for up to 3 days or freeze up to 3 months.

GARLIC-PARSLEY STOCK

10 minutes high pressure

A great boon for garlic lovers, made in a flash since the garlic does not have to be peeled. Garlic-parsley stock brings complexity to the final product when used as the base for soups, stews, and grains.

If you wish, when using this stock, eliminate any extra garlic called for in a particular recipe. As for me, a dish can never have too much garlic.

This recipe may be doubled. Leftovers may be frozen for up to 3 months, but there will be some slight loss of flavor.

Makes approximately 3 cups

4 cups water
2 medium heads garlic (about 5 ounces total)
1 medium bunch parsley, thoroughly rinsed

. . . .

Salt to taste

Place the water in the cooker and begin bringing to the boil as you remove the thin paperlike covering on the garlic bulbs. Break off the individual cloves and discard the root. Set the unpeeled cloves and parsley in the water.

Lock the lid in place. Over high heat bring to high pressure. Lower the heat just enough to maintain high pressure and cook for 10 minutes. Allow the pressure to come down naturally or use a quick-release method. Remove the lid, tilting it away from you to allow any excess steam to escape.

Allow the stock to cool slightly. Pour the stock through a strainer into one or more storage containers. Discard the parsley. If you wish, you may squeeze the garlic out of the skins and mash or purée it. Stir the mashed garlic into the stock to thicken it. Alternatively, use the garlic purée as a spread for bread. Add salt to taste, if desired. Cool and refrigerate for up to 3 days or freeze up to 3 months.

VEGETABLES

Vegetable stews cooked under pressure have the kind of long-simmered taste we all love. The pressure cooker is also a boon for pressure steaming the longer-cooking vegetables, such as beets, potatoes, and artichokes, making it possible to incorporate them into spontaneous daily fare.

Although many people have told me that they love pressure-cooked vegetables of all kinds, I generally shy away from exposing quick-cooking items like asparagus and green beans to the intense heat of the cooker. The danger of overcooking is so great that I much prefer to use a traditional steaming technique and stay out of harm's way. Nevertheless, for those among you who wish to live dangerously, I've provided some guidance.

The chart on pages 74 and 75 will give you the specific timing and particulars for pressure cooking a wide variety of vegetables. Basic instructions for pressure cooking vegetables are on page 76.

Vegetable Cooking Times at a Glance

For basic instructions on cooking vegetables, see page 76

Note: Timing is based on setting vegetables on a rack over water that is already boiling.

	Minutes High Pressure	Total Cooking Time°	Comments
Artichokes			Avoid large artichokes: The outer leaves become overcooked by the time the heart is tender. Trim bottoms and set on rack or stack pyramid-fashion, as needed.
Medium (6 to 8 ounces)	6–8		
Baby (1 ounce each)	3–4		
Asparagus			Snap off tough part of stalk and reserve for stock.
Average		1½–2	
Pencil		1–1½	
Beans, green (string)			Trim off ends.
Whole or cut into thirds		2–3	
Beets			Scrub well; peeling optional, but trim off "hair" and rough spots.
Medium to large, whole (5 – 6 ounces each)	20–22		
Small, whole (3 – 4 ounces each)	11–13		
¼-inch slices	3–5		
Broccoli			If cooking florets and stalks together, slice stalks as thinly as possible.
Large florets (3½ inches across top)		2–3	
Stalks, peeled, cut into ¼-inch slices		3–4	
Brussels sprouts			Avoid cooking whole sprouts except when they are very small. In general, the older and larger the sprouts, the longer they take to become tender.
Medium, cut into ¼-inch slices		2–3	
Cabbage (red and green)			Avoid cooking red cabbage on its own, since it requires contact with an acid (such as vinegar) to retain its color.
1 large (about 3 pounds), quartered and cored		3–4	
Carrots			Hold their shape beautifully, even when cooked longer, as in soups and stews.
Large, cut into 2-inch chunks	4–5		
¼-inch slices	1–2		
Cauliflower			
Large florets (about 2½ inches across the top)		2–3	
Celeriac (celery root)			Opt for small roots. After peeling, set pieces in acidulated water to prevent browning. Good in vegetable purées.
½-inch dice		3–4	
Celery			
1-inch slices		3–4	
Collard greens			See page 84.
Thinly sliced	3–4		

°Timing begins as soon as the lid is locked into place (rather than when the cooker reaches high pressure).

	Minutes High Pressure	Total Cooking Time*	Comments
Corn on the cob			Break the cobs in half, if necessary, to fit into the cooker. Layer pyramid-fashion if cooking in quantity.
Old, large		3–4	
Young, fresh		2–3	
Eggplant			Best to peel. Will not hold its shape.
1½-inch chunks	2–3		
Kale	1–2		See instructions for cooking collards, page 84.
Leeks			Wash thoroughly to remove sand, as directed in the Glossary.
Large, whole (over 1½-inch diameter)		3–4	
Small, whole (about 1-inch diameter)		2–3	
Okra			Trim on the line where the stem meets the pod.
Large, whole (3 to 4 inches long)	3		
Small, whole (2 inches and under)	1		
Onions			Peel before cooking.
Medium to small white (2 ounces each)	4–5		
Small, white (pearl)	2–3		
Parsnips			Opt for young, slender parsnips. If using large ones, cut the wider slices into 2 or 3 pieces.
1-inch chunks	2–4		
¼-inch slices	1		
Potatoes, thin-skinned (all varieties)			Best when braised in 1 to 2 inches of liquid rather than steamed on a rack. Large potatoes cook more evenly when quartered. Peel for aesthetic reasons only.
Medium to large, quartered	5–7		
Whole, small (1 ounce each)	5–6		
¼-inch slices	2–3		
Potatoes, sweet			Always peel before pressure cooking. They sometimes "collapse" under pressure and don't hold their shape.
Large, quartered	4–6		
Rutabaga (swede)			Always peel off skin.
½-inch dice	5–6		
Squash, winter			Peeling is optional if the squash is unwaxed and organically grown; the pressure cooker does a good job of tenderizing the skin.
Acorn, halved	6–7		
Butternut, ½-inch slices	2–3		
Pattypan (about 2 pounds), whole	10–12		
All peeled winter squash, 1½-inch chunks	3–4		
Turnips			Always peel off the skin.
Medium to large (4 ounces each), quartered	3–4		
Small, whole (1½ ounces each)	7		
¼-inch slices	1–2		
Zucchini			Tends to "collapse" under pressure.
1-inch slices	1		

*Timing begins as soon as the lid is locked into place (rather than when the cooker reaches high pressure).

Basic Instructions for
Pressure Cooking Vegetables

1. Wash, peel, and trim the vegetable. Cut as directed in the chart.
2. Place 1 cup of water and the steaming rack in the cooker. Bring to the boil.
3. Distribute the vegetables evenly on the rack. (If your cooker comes with a steaming basket, fill the basket with the vegetables and lower it in after the water begins to boil.)
4. Lock the lid in place. Over high heat, bring to high pressure. Lower the heat just enough to maintain high pressure and cook for the number of minutes indicated in the chart.

    NOTE: Some quick-cooking vegetables are done before the cooker actually reaches high pressure. See Total Cooking Time, page 7.
5. Always use the quick-release method immediately after cooking time is up. Otherwise you run the risk of overcooking the vegetables.
6. Remove the lid, tilting it away from you to allow any excess steam to escape.
7. If the vegetable is not quite tender, replace (but do not lock) the lid and simmer until done.

General Tips and Techniques

Unless specified, the peeling of vegetables is optional. For example, I usually peel carrots unless they are organic, in which case I scrub them well.

It's best to cut large, hard vegetables like beets and potatoes into quarters or dice. Otherwise, by the time the insides are cooked, the outsides can be a bit soggy.

Do not allow the vegetables to pile up beyond the three-quarter fill line, unless you are cooking leafy greens (which will shrink dramatically).

Vegetables with the same cooking times may be pressure-steamed together.

QUANTITY COOKING
....
Unlike with the microwave, cooking time under pressure is not generally altered if the quantity of vegetables is increased. However, if you are cooking an especially large batch and notice that it takes longer than 3 minutes for the cooker to come up to pressure, decrease time under pressure by 1 minute for every 2 additional minutes beyond the 3.

RED FLANNEL HASH

8 minutes high pressure

A vegetarian version of that New England classic. As you might guess, the beets cloak the potatoes and cabbage in glorious color. Serve this hash as part of a New England dinner menu with Celery, Corn, and Potato Chowder and Revisionist Boston Brown Bread. **Serves 6**

½ cup water

1 tablespoon tomato paste

1 cup coarsely chopped onions

1 pound thin-skinned potatoes, scrubbed or peeled and cut into ¾-inch dice

½ pound beets, trimmed, scrubbed, and cut into ½-inch dice

1 pound cabbage, cored and shredded

½ teaspoon salt, or to taste

. . . .

1 tablespoon maple syrup

1 to 2 tablespoons apple cider vinegar

Combine the water and tomato paste in the cooker and bring to the boil. Add the onions, potatoes, and beets. Set the cabbage on top and sprinkle with salt.

Lock the lid in place. Over high heat, bring to high pressure. Lower the heat just enough to maintain high pressure and cook for 8 minutes. Reduce the pressure with a quick-release method. Remove the lid, tilting it away from you to allow any excess steam to escape.

If there is more than a tablespoon or two of liquid in the bottom of the pot, drain off the excess. Mash the vegetables with a fork to create a coarse mixture. (The potatoes will mash easily while the beets are likely to remain in little chunks.) Drizzle on the maple syrup and 1 tablespoon of vinegar. Stir and taste, adding a bit more vinegar, if desired, to achieve a delicate sweet-sour balance. Reheat before serving, if necessary.

TIPS & TECHNIQUES

Since the cabbage and onion will release a good deal of liquid, ½ cup water should be sufficient to bring the vegetables up to pressure. If you are experiencing difficulty, add ½ cup more water.

VARIATION

Serve the vegetables as is rather than mashing them.

Tarragon Cabbage and Potatoes

3 minutes high pressure

If you think that a dish of cabbage and potatoes can't be elegant, try adding some tarragon and you'll be in for a nice surprise. The tomatoes give it a nice boost of color, which also helps elevate this dish from its humble roots.

Despite the presence of potatoes, this dish goes nicely with brown rice or quinoa. Serve some pickled beets on the side for color. A tossed green salad rounds out the meal. ***Serves 6***

1½ pounds cabbage

2 teaspoons olive oil

1 cup thinly sliced leeks (white and light green parts) or
    coarsely chopped onions

1 cup water

1 tablespoon tomato paste

1 pound potatoes, peeled and cut into ½-inch dice

2 cups chopped fresh or canned (drained) plum tomatoes

1½ teaspoons dried tarragon leaves

1 teaspoon salt, or to taste

Remove any tough or bruised outer leaves from the cabbage. Quarter it, and cut away the dense white core. Shred by cutting very thin slices along the length as if you were preparing coleslaw. Set aside.

Heat the oil in the cooker. Cook the leeks over medium-high heat, stirring frequently, for 1 minute. Add the water (stand back to avoid sputtering oil) and blend in the tomato paste. Layer the reserved cabbage, potatoes, and tomatoes. Then sprinkle the tarragon and salt on top. (See Tips.)

Lock the lid in place. Set the cooker on a heated Flame Tamer. Over high heat, bring to high pressure. Lower the heat just enough to maintain high pressure and cook for 3 minutes. Reduce the pressure with a quick-release method. Remove the lid, tilting it away from you to allow any excess steam to escape.

Stir well. If time permits, let the dish stand at room temperature for 20 minutes—the potatoes will release starch and thicken the mixture. Then reheat before serving. Serve as a side dish in small bowls or ladle out the vegetables and cooking liquid and serve over grains in large soup plates.

TIPS & TECHNIQUES

To avoid scorching, set the cabbage on the bottom of the cooker. Place the potatoes on the cabbage and the tomatoes on top. Do not stir until cooking is done.

I like this dish best when prepared with fresh plum tomatoes, but canned are preferred when only the tasteless "Styrofoam" variety of fresh is available. If using canned tomatoes, substitute the drained juice for an equivalent amount of water. Eliminate the tomato paste.

SWEET AND SOUR RED CABBAGE

4 minutes high pressure

If you enjoy the play of sweet against sour, this colorful preparation will become a favorite vegetable side dish. It goes well with bulgur, rice, and millet pilafs. ***Serves 4 to 6***

1 medium red cabbage (about 2¼ pounds)

1 tablespoon safflower or canola oil

2 cups coarsely chopped onions, preferably red onions

1 large carrot, halved lengthwise and thinly sliced

½ cup apple cider or juice

2 to 3 tablespoons apple cider vinegar (use 3 for a more pronounced sour edge)

⅔ cup tightly packed chopped or snipped dried apricots

⅛ teaspoon ground allspice

½ teaspoon salt, or to taste

. . . .

2 tablespoons freshly squeezed lemon juice, approximately

Remove any tough or bruised outer leaves from the cabbage. Quarter it, and cut away the dense white core. Shred by cutting very thin slices along the length as if you were preparing coleslaw. Set aside.

Heat the oil in the cooker. Cook the onions over medium-high heat, stirring frequently, for 1 minute. Add the cabbage, carrot, apple cider (stand back to avoid sputtering oil), vinegar, apricots, allspice, and salt.

Lock the lid in place. Over high heat, bring to high pressure. Lower the heat just enough to maintain high pressure and cook for 4 minutes. Reduce the pressure with a quick-release method. Remove the lid, tilting it away from you to allow any excess steam to escape.

Stir in enough lemon juice to achieve the sweet-sour balance that suits you. To serve the cabbage on a plate, lift it out with a slotted spoon. Otherwise, serve the cabbage in small bowls.

TIPS & TECHNIQUES

The acid in the cider vinegar preserves the color of the red cabbage.

Do not be concerned if the cabbage goes beyond the maximum fill line. It will quickly shrink, providing enough room for the steam pressure to gather.

Paprika Carrots

2 minutes high pressure

Cooking carrots with cumin and paprika is characteristic of the kitchens of Uzbekistan in Central Asia. I first learned of this approach from the superb Russian cookbook *Please to the Table* by Anya von Bremzen and John Welchman (Workman, 1990). The traditional dish uses both sweet and hot paprika and is slowly braised. I have reduced the fat, added the red bell pepper (for a jolt of color), altered the proportions and seasonings—and cut down the cooking time by about 25 minutes!

Serve Paprika Carrots with Armenian Vegetable Stew and some kasha. ***Serves 4***

2 teaspoons olive oil

1 teaspoon whole cumin seeds

2 teaspoons minced garlic

1½ cups coarsely chopped onions

1 small red bell pepper, seeded and diced

½ to 1 cup water (use manufacturer's recommended liquid minimum)

1 tablespoon tomato paste

1 teaspoon sweet Hungarian paprika, or ¾ teaspoon sweet and ¼ teaspoon hot paprika

1 pound carrots, cut on the diagonal into ½-inch slices

½ teaspoon salt, or to taste

Heat the oil in the cooker. Sizzle the cumin seeds over medium-high heat just until they begin to pop, 5 to 10 seconds. Add the garlic, onions, and red bell pepper, and cook, stirring frequently, for 1 minute. Add the water (stand back to avoid sputtering oil) and blend in the tomato paste and paprika. Add the carrots and salt.

Lock the lid in place. Over high heat, bring to high pressure. Lower the heat just enough to maintain high pressure and cook for 2 minutes. Reduce the pressure with a quick-release method. Remove the lid, tilting it away from you to allow any excess steam to escape. If the carrots aren't sufficiently tender, replace (but do not lock) the lid and let them continue to cook for another minute or two in the residual heat.

To create a thick sauce, mash some of the carrots by hand or purée about a cupful in a food processor or blender and stir the purée back in. Adjust seasonings before serving.

CORIANDER CARROTS

2 minutes high pressure

A festive preparation, nice to serve with Black Bean Chili that has been mounded on top of rice or polenta.
Serves 4 to 6

1 tablespoon safflower or canola oil

½ cup finely sliced leeks (white and light green parts) or coarsely chopped onions

¾ to 1 cup water (use manufacturer's recommended liquid minimum)

¼ cup dried currants or raisins

1 tablespoon ground coriander seeds

1 bay leaf

½ teaspoon salt, or to taste

1½ pounds carrots, cut on the diagonal into ½-inch slices

. . . .

1 to 2 tablespoons freshly squeezed lemon juice (optional)

1 tablespoon minced fresh parsley

Heat the oil in the cooker. Cook the leeks over medium-high heat, stirring frequently, for 1 minute. Add the water (stand back to avoid sputtering oil), currants, coriander, bay leaf, salt, and carrots.

Lock the lid in place. Over high heat, bring to high pressure. Lower the heat just enough to maintain high pressure and cook for 2 minutes. Reduce the pressure with a quick-release method. Remove the lid, tilting it away from you to allow any excess steam to escape. If the carrots are not quite tender, replace (but do not lock) the lid and let them continue to cook for another minute or two in the residual heat.

Just before serving, stir in the lemon juice (if using) and parsley.

Currants are not quite as sweet as raisins, so I prefer using them in dishes such as this one. Golden raisins make a nice change if you prefer the added sweetness.

For vibrant flavor, grind the coriander seeds just before using.

Carrot Tsimmes

4 minutes high pressure

This sweet mixed vegetable dish from the Jewish kitchen is a festive and tasty way to enjoy your daily quota of beta carotene. The sweet potatoes become quite soft and melt into a purée that envelops the other vegetables. Have an extra lemon on hand to perk up the flavors, if desired.

I like to serve the tsimmes as part of an eastern European meal that includes Double Mushroom Barley Soup, kasha or steamed potatoes, and a green vegetable. *Serves 6*

1 pound carrots, cut on the diagonal into ½-inch slices

½ pound butternut squash, seeded and cut into 1-inch chunks (peeling optional)

1 pound (2 large) sweet potatoes or garnet yams, peeled, halved lengthwise, and cut into ½-inch slices

½ teaspoon salt, or to taste

½ teaspoon ground cinnamon

¼ teaspoon ground allspice

1 lemon, scrubbed, quartered, and pitted

1 cup pitted prunes, halved

1 cup boiling water

Freshly squeezed lemon juice (optional)

Place all the ingredients except the optional lemon juice in the cooker.

Lock the lid in place. Over high heat, bring to high pressure. Lower the heat just enough to maintain high pressure and cook for 4 minutes. Reduce the pressure with a quick-release method. Remove the lid, tilting it away from you to allow any excess steam to escape.

Remove the lemon quarters and stir well. Season with lemon juice, if desired.

VARIATIONS

Substitute ½ cup apricots for half of the pitted prunes.

For a sweeter version, use ½ cup apple or orange juice instead of an equivalent amount of water.

Try parsnips, peeled and cut into ½-inch slices, instead of butternut squash.

CREOLE OKRA STEW

1 to 3 minutes high pressure

I had this recipe in mind for many months before any okra appeared in the markets, and when it became available I could find only very large pods. I normally opt for tiny specimens (under 2 inches long) as they are the most tender, but keeping in mind the pressure cooker's capacity to tenderize in short order, I tested this recipe using pods that were a tough-looking 4 inches long. The result—in only 3 minutes—was amazing.

Many people avoid okra because of its slippery texture, but I find that by cooking the vegetable with a bit of apple cider vinegar, the whole concoction develops a pleasing silken quality, with a thickness that is ideal for a stew.

Serve Creole Okra Stew as a side dish in a small bowl. Alternatively, use the stew as a delicious topping for rice or pasta. And don't forget to pass the Tabasco. *Serves 4*

2 teaspoons olive oil

2 teaspoons minced garlic

2 cups coarsely chopped onions or thinly sliced leeks
    (white and light green parts)

1 pound okra, trimmed and cut into ½-inch slices

2 cups coarsely chopped fresh or canned (drained) plum
    tomatoes

1 cup water (or substitute juice from drained canned
    tomatoes, plus water to equal 1 cup)

1 tablespoon apple cider vinegar, approximately

2 celery ribs, cut into ½-inch slices

1 large red bell pepper, seeded and diced

1 teaspoon dried oregano leaves

½ teaspoon dried thyme leaves

1 large bay leaf

Pinch of crushed red pepper flakes

1 teaspoon salt, or to taste

Heat the oil in the cooker. Cook the garlic over medium-high heat, stirring constantly, until browned. Immediately add the onions and continue cooking, stirring frequently, for 1 min-

If you'd like to replicate the flavor of bacon or smoked ham so often used in Creole recipes, after cooking, stir in some liquid smoke flavoring, readily available in supermarkets.

ute. Add the okra, tomatoes, water (stand back to avoid sputtering oil), vinegar, celery, red bell pepper, oregano, thyme, bay leaf, red pepper flakes, and salt.

Lock the lid in place. Set the cooker on a heated Flame Tamer. Over high heat, bring to high pressure. Lower the heat just enough to maintain high pressure and cook for 1 minute (young, small okra) to 3 minutes (older, large pods). Reduce the pressure with a quick-release method. Remove the lid, tilting it away from you to allow any excess steam to escape.

Stir well and add a bit more cider vinegar, if desired, to sharpen the flavors.

COLLARD SPAGHETTI

1 to 3 minutes high pressure

Collards are a good candidate for pressure cooking as they can be quite tough and are one of the longer-cooking greens. To assure that they maintain a sprightly color, finish off the greens by standard cooking so that you can keep peeking and tasting until they are just right.

Use the 3-minute timing for mature collard greens, those that have a 7-inch or wider leaf span. For younger collards, reduce cooking time under pressure to 1 to 2 minutes.

Collards are a natural companion for a Southern supper of Black-eyed Pea Gumbo, baked sweet potatoes, and corn bread. *Serves 2 (collard lovers) to 4 (dainty portions)*

**1 pound collards (pretrimmed weight), washed and
    drained**
1 cup water
**1 large garlic clove, minced (optional, but highly
    recommended for garlic lovers)**
Pinch of salt (optional)

Cut off the stems and stack the collards on top of each other. Roll them up tightly into a long tube with the stem end at one side and the leaf tips at the other. Starting at the stem end, slice the collards as thin as possible to create spaghettilike strands. (It's fine to slice some of the stems if they aren't too thick and fibrous. Otherwise, save them for stock.)

Like most greens, collards shrink dramatically. A pound will yield a little more than 2 cups of cooked greens. If you wish to double or triple the amount of greens, you need not increase the amount of water. You can also fill the cooker almost up to the top with raw greens, as they will shrink quickly, leaving the necessary space for the pressure to rise.

Select collards that are perky; avoid those that are limp or have yellowed edges.

If you wish to serve the collards at room temperature, run them under cold water as soon as they are done. This will set their color and prevent any further cooking.

Bring the water, garlic (if using), and salt (if using) to the boil in the cooker. Add the collards.

Lock the lid in place. Over high heat, bring to high pressure. Lower the heat just enough to maintain high pressure and cook for 1 minute (young collards) to 3 minutes (mature collards). Reduce the pressure with a quick-release method. Remove the lid, tilting it away from you to allow any excess steam to escape.

Taste the collards. If they are still a little tough, replace (but do not lock) the lid and cook over medium-high heat until tender. Taste frequently to avoid overcooking.

When the collards are done, drain well and serve hot.

Collard Hash

When cooking mature collards, you can add ½ pound of thin-skinned potatoes that have been scrubbed and cut into ½-inch dice. Set these in the water and place the collards on top. Cook under high pressure for 3 minutes. Drain off most of the cooking liquid. Mash the potatoes against the side of the cooker and stir the mixture well before serving. Add salt to taste.

VARIATIONS

Chopped kale and mustard greens can be cooked using the same technique. Allow 1 minute under high pressure for young greens and 2 minutes for mature ones.

Toss the cooked collard spaghetti in a bit of tomato sauce. Consider mixing the collards with cooked pasta.

Season the collards with olive oil and freshly squeezed lemon juice or umeboshi plum vinegar (available in health food stores).

Coat the collards with a bit of toasted (Oriental) sesame oil and tamari soy sauce. Sprinkle with toasted sesame seeds.

PARSNIPS WITH INDIAN SPICES

2 minutes high pressure

F riends claim I'm on a one-woman mission to introduce new-comers to the pleasures of parsnips. In this country we are just not in the habit of using them, which is a great shame since they are delicious, readily available, and easy to cook.

Because of their mellow flavor, parsnips make a great back-drop for the assertive Indian seasonings used in this recipe. For a flavor-packed menu, try serving them with Cauliflower-Potato Curry, Curried Quinoa Pilaf, Sun-Dried Tomato Chutney, and a mixed green salad. *Serves 5 to 6*

2 pounds parsnips
1 tablespoon safflower or canola oil
1 teaspoon whole black mustard seeds
1 teaspoon whole cumin seeds
¼ teaspoon whole fenugreek seeds (optional)
1 small red chili pepper, stemmed and partially seeded
    (wear rubber gloves when handling chili peppers), or
    a generous pinch of crushed red pepper flakes
1½ cups coarsely chopped onions
1 teaspoon minced garlic
1½ tablespoons minced fresh ginger
½ to 1 cup boiling water (use manufacturer's
    recommended liquid minimum)
½ teaspoon ground turmeric
⅛ teaspoon ground cardamom
1 teaspoon salt, or to taste

. . . .

2 to 3 tablespoons minced fresh coriander

Scrub the parsnips if they are organic and have thin skins. Otherwise, peel them. Cut them on the diagonal into ½-inch slices and slice the thick upper pieces in half. Set aside.

Heat the oil in the cooker. Sizzle the mustard, cumin, and fenugreek seeds plus the chili pepper over medium-high heat just until the seeds begin to pop, 5 to 10 seconds. Add the onions, garlic, and ginger and cook, stirring frequently, for 1

TIPS & TECHNIQUES

When selecting parsnips, choose slender to medium specimens; older, thick ones tend to be woody, with a hard central core.

VARIATION

Use carrots instead of parsnips.

minute. Add the water (stand back to avoid sputtering oil), turmeric, cardamom, and salt. Stir to blend. As soon as the water returns to the boil, add the reserved parsnips.

Lock the lid in place. Over high heat, bring to high pressure. Lower the heat just enough to maintain high pressure and cook for 2 minutes. Reduce the pressure with a quick-release method. Remove the lid, tilting it away from you to allow any excess steam to escape. If the parsnips are not quite tender, replace (but do not lock) the lid and continue to cook for a minute or two in the residual heat.

Stir in the coriander just before serving. To serve, lift out the parsnips with a slotted spoon.

GARLIC POTATOES

3 minutes high pressure

These chunky mashed potatoes are infused with the sublime flavor that garlic offers when the cloves are cooked whole rather than minced. Portion size is especially subjective here: If serious garlic and potato lovers are in town, double the quantities (but use only 1 cup of stock) to assure that there's enough to go around. ***Serves 3 to 4***

½ to 1 cup vegetable stock (use manufacturer's
     recommended liquid minimum)
1 bay leaf
¾ teaspoon salt, or to taste (less if using salted stock)
1 large head garlic (about 2 ounces), broken into cloves
     and peeled
1½ pounds thin-skinned potatoes, scrubbed and cut into
     ½-inch dice

. . . .

1 to 2 tablespoons olive oil
Freshly ground pepper to taste (optional)
1 to 2 tablespoons minced fresh parsley

Bring the stock, bay leaf, and salt to the boil in the cooker. Add the garlic and potatoes.

Lock the lid in place. Over high heat, bring to high pressure. Lower the heat just enough to maintain high pressure and cook for 3 minutes. Reduce the pressure with a quick-release method. Remove the lid, tilting it away from you to allow any excess steam to escape.

Remove the bay leaf. Drain off all but about ½ cup of the liquid (reserve for stock or for cooking grains). Mash the potatoes and garlic coarsely with a fork or ricer and stir in the olive oil, pepper (if using), and parsley, plus additional salt, if desired.

POTATOES PAPRIKASH

3 minutes high pressure

This is a simple dish with excellent flavor and a lovely pale-salmon color. It received rave reviews from my testers, who considered it comfort food at its best.

These potatoes seem at home on an eastern European menu, accompanied by kasha and steamed brussels sprouts. You can start off the meal with Dilled Cabbage Soup.

Serves 4 to 6

1 tablespoon safflower or canola oil

1 cup finely chopped shallots, leeks (white and light
    green parts), or onions

½ cup water or vegetable stock

1 tablespoon sweet Hungarian paprika

1 cup puréed fresh or canned (drained) plum tomatoes

2 pounds thin-skinned potatoes, scrubbed, halved, and
    cut into ¼-inch slices

1 teaspoon salt, or to taste

Freshly ground pepper

. . . .

3 to 4 tablespoons plain low-fat yogurt (soy or dairy),
    sour cream, or roasted shallot cream (page 24)

Heat the oil in the cooker. Cook the shallots over medium-high heat, stirring frequently, for 1 minute. Add the water (stand back to avoid sputtering oil) and scrape up any bits of shallot that might be sticking to the bottom of the pot. Stir in the paprika and puréed tomatoes and bring to the boil. Add the potatoes, salt, and pepper.

Lock the lid in place. Set the cooker on a heated Flame Tamer. Over high heat, bring to high pressure. Lower the heat just enough to maintain high pressure and cook for 3 minutes. Reduce the pressure with a quick-release method. Remove the lid, tilting it away from you to allow any excess steam to escape. If the potatoes are not quite tender, replace (but do not lock) the lid and let them steam for a few minutes in the residual heat.

Stir in the yogurt and adjust the seasonings before serving.

To create an instant sauce, finely mince 1 of the raw potatoes. These small bits will virtually dissolve under pressure and thicken the water when you stir the cooked dish.

POTATOES AND ONIONS THAI-STYLE

5 minutes high pressure

This recipe was inspired by a similar preparation in *Thai Vegetarian Cooking* by Vatcharin Bhumichitr (Clarkson Potter, 1991). I like the texture best as a coarse mash, but you can also leave the potatoes in chunks and create a thick sauce by puréeing a small amount of them. For a punch of color, I've added the chopped red bell pepper.

Since this dish is rich, steamed broccoli or string beans and a green salad would be ideal accompaniments. Try Oriental Eggplant if you're in the mood for a soup. **Serves 4–6**

1 cup coconut milk (page 19)

2 teaspoons minced garlic

2 teaspoons ground coriander seeds

1 stalk fresh lemongrass, outer layer removed, cut into 1-inch pieces, or ½ teaspoon finely ground dried lemongrass

1 tablespoon tamari soy sauce, approximately

1 teaspoon sugar (optional)

1½ pounds thin-skinned potatoes, peeled and cut into 1-inch chunks

½ pound (about 8) small white onions, trimmed, peeled, and halved from root to top, or 1 pound medium onions, trimmed, peeled, and cut into eighths

½ cup diced red bell pepper

. . . .

½ cup minced fresh basil or coriander

Place all the ingredients except the basil in the cooker.

Lock the lid in place. Over high heat, bring to high pressure. Lower the heat just enough to maintain high pressure and cook for 5 minutes. Reduce the pressure with a quick-release method. Remove the lid, tilting it away from you to allow any excess steam to escape. If the potatoes are not quite tender, replace (but do not lock) the lid and let steam for a few more minutes in the residual heat.

Coarsely mash some or all of the potatoes with a fork. If you've used fresh lemongrass, remove the pieces. Stir in the basil, and additional soy sauce, if desired.

MAPLE-GLAZED TURNIPS WITH PRUNES

3 minutes high pressure

A crowd-pleasing recipe that brings out the subtle sweetness of turnips. Rich taste belies the fact that this is a fat-free recipe.

I like to serve this dish on Thanksgiving with Fall Harvest Rice Casserole and steamed broccoli. Creamy Apple-Squash would be my first choice for soup. *Serves 6*

¾ to 1 cup water (use manufacturer's recommended liquid minimum)

3 tablespoons maple syrup

½ teaspoon ground cinnamon

½ teaspoon salt, or to taste

2 pounds medium turnips, peeled and quartered

1 cup pitted prunes, halved

. . . .

1 to 2 tablespoons freshly squeezed lemon juice (optional)

Combine the water, maple syrup, cinnamon, and salt in the cooker. Bring to the boil. Add the turnips and prunes.

Lock the lid in place. Over high heat, bring to high pressure. Lower the heat just enough to maintain high pressure and cook for 3 minutes. Reduce the pressure with a quick-release method. Remove the lid, tilting it away from you to allow any excess steam to escape. If the turnips are not tender (they should be firm but easily pierced with a fork), replace (but do not lock) the lid and simmer until they are done.

With a slotted spoon, transfer about a cup of the turnips to a food processor or blender, and purée. Stir the purée back into the liquid to create a sauce. Stir in lemon juice to taste, if desired.

TIPS & TECHNIQUES

It's essential to peel turnips because their skins can be quite bitter.

SOUTHWEST SUCCOTASH

2 minutes high pressure, 2 to 3 minutes simmering

This alluring dish will become a favorite of anyone devoted to the sacred three sisters: beans, corn, and squash. It's great with Black Bean Chili. **Serves 6**

1 tablespoon safflower or canola oil

¾ teaspoon whole cumin seeds

2 teaspoons finely minced garlic

1 cup coarsely chopped onions

1 medium red bell pepper, seeded and diced

1 to 2 jalapeño peppers, seeded and diced, or 1 dried
    chipotle pepper, stemmed, seeded, and snipped into
    bits (wear rubber gloves when handling chili peppers),
    or a generous pinch of crushed red pepper flakes

1 cup water

2 tablespoons tomato paste

1½ pounds butternut or kabocha squash, peeled, seeded,
    and cut into 1-inch chunks

2 cups fresh or frozen corn kernels

¾ teaspoon salt, or to taste

. . . .

2 cups frozen (defrosted) baby limas

¼ to ⅓ cup minced fresh coriander or parsley

Heat the oil in the cooker. Sizzle the cumin seeds over medium-high heat just until they begin to pop, 5 to 10 seconds. Add the garlic and cook, stirring frequently, until it turns light brown. Add the onions, red bell pepper, and jalapeño pepper, and continue cooking, stirring frequently, for 1 minute. Add the water (stand back to avoid sputtering oil), tomato paste, squash, corn, and salt.

Lock the lid in place. Over high heat, bring to high pressure. Lower the heat just enough to maintain high pressure and cook for 2 minutes. Reduce the pressure with a quick-release method. Remove the lid, tilting it away from you to allow any excess steam to escape. If the squash is not almost tender, replace (but do not lock) the lid and allow the vegetables to cook for a few more minutes in the residual heat.

Stir in the limas and simmer, covered, until cooked, 2 to 3 minutes. Stir in the coriander just before serving.

If you enjoy a smoky resonance in food, go out of your way to obtain a dried chipotle chili pepper. It really makes a difference.

Some of the squash will remain chunky. The rest will soften and contribute toward making a thick sauce.

One ear of corn yields about 1 cup of kernels.

VARIATION

Cook the succotash with an extra ear of corn, sliced into 1-inch chunks.

SWEET AND SOUR ZUCCHINI

1 minute high pressure

This classic Sicilian recipe cooks in a flash and makes a nice summer side dish. It also can double as an interesting topping for pasta when the zucchini are cut into smaller pieces (after cooking). The flavors are intensified if the dish is allowed to sit for 15 minutes or so before eating. Serve it hot or at room temperature. *Serves 4 to 6*

1 tablespoon olive oil

2 teaspoons minced garlic

½ to 1 cup water (use manufacturer's recommended liquid minimum)

2 tablespoons red wine vinegar, preferably balsamic

2 pounds large zucchini, halved lengthwise and cut into 1-inch slices

¼ cup raisins or dried currants

⅛ teaspoon ground cinnamon

½ teaspoon salt, or to taste

Freshly ground pepper to taste

. . . .

3 tablespoons minced fresh parsley

Heat the oil in the cooker. Cook the garlic over medium-high heat, stirring constantly, until it begins to brown. Immediately add the water (stand back to avoid sputtering oil), vinegar, zucchini, raisins, cinnamon, salt, and pepper.

Lock the lid in place. Over high heat, bring to high pressure. Lower the heat just enough to maintain high pressure and cook for 1 minute. Reduce the pressure with a quick-release method. Remove the lid, tilting it away from you to allow any excess steam to escape. If the zucchini is not done (it should be firm but easily pierced with a fork), replace (but do not lock) the lid and let it cook for a minute or two in the residual heat.

Stir in the parsley while the zucchini is still hot. Serve in small bowls with a bit of the cooking liquid or lift the zucchini with a slotted spoon and serve on plates.

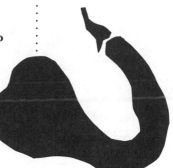

VARIATION

. . . .

Use 1½ pounds zucchini and ½ pound small mushrooms, cut in half.

VEGETABLE STEWS

The following recipes use a variety of vegetables and are substantial enough to make memorable entrees.

ARMENIAN VEGETABLE STEW

3 minutes high pressure

I first ran across this unusual stew made sweet with apricots and apples in *The Food and Cooking of Russia* (Penguin, 1982) by British food writer Lesley Chamberlain.

The dish goes nicely with bulgur or rice, a salad of spicy greens (such as arugula or watercress), and a hearty peasant loaf or some Armenian flat bread or pita.

Good straight from the pot and even better the next day.

Serves 4

1 tablespoon safflower or canola oil

1 cup coarsely chopped onions

2 cups coarsely chopped fresh or canned (drained) plum tomatoes

1 pound small (about 2 ounces each) thin-skinned potatoes, scrubbed or peeled and halved, or larger thin-skinned potatoes, scrubbed or peeled and cut into 1-inch chunks

¾ pound fresh green beans, trimmed and cut into thirds

1 red bell pepper, seeded and cut into 1-inch pieces

1 Granny Smith apple, peeled, cored, and cut into eighths

⅓ cup coarsely chopped or snipped dried apricots

Salt and freshly ground pepper to taste

. . . .

Roasted shallot cream (page 24) or yogurt and fresh mint leaves (optional)

TIPS & TECHNIQUES

The liquid in this recipe is provided by the tomatoes, onions, and apple. If you have any problem bringing up the pressure, push the ingredients aside and pour ½ cup water into the bottom of the cooker.

VARIATION

Add 1 cup cooked chickpeas after cooking.

Heat the oil in the cooker. Cook the onions over medium-high heat, stirring frequently, for 1 minute. Add the tomatoes, potatoes, green beans, red bell pepper, apple, apricots, and salt and pepper.

Lock the lid in place. If using a jiggle-top cooker, or if your cooker has a thin bottom, set it on a heated Flame Tamer. Over high heat, bring to high pressure. Lower the heat just enough to maintain high pressure and cook for 3 minutes. Reduce the pressure with a quick-release method. Remove the lid, tilting it away from you to allow any excess steam to escape. If the potatoes are not quite tender, replace (but do not lock) the lid and let the vegetables cook for a few more minutes in the residual heat.

Adjust the seasonings and garnish with a dollop of roasted shallot cream and fresh mint leaves, if desired.

SANCOCHO

A CARIBBEAN STEW

5 minutes high pressure

This most delicious Caribbean stew includes the starchy vegetables that are central to the diet in that part of the world. In recent years, yuca (cassava), taro, and boniato (white sweet potato) have become more readily available all over the United States.

With the help of colleague and friend Elizabeth Schneider, author of the authoritative *Uncommon Fruits & Vegetables: A Commonsense Guide* (Harper & Row, 1986), I learned how to select and prepare them for cooking.

Elizabeth was delighted to discover that pressure cooking starchy tubers not only made fast work of preparing them, but actually enhanced their flavor and texture. In the process, she became committed to using the pressure cooker and I became committed to eating more yuca.

In making this dish, you can use one type of vegetable or a variety. The calabaza (West Indian pumpkin) dissolves to thicken and sweeten the delicious sauce, while the other vegetables retain their shape.

Serve the stew in large bowls over rice. It's filling, so you won't need much more than a green salad to complete the main course. **Serves 6**

1 tablespoon annatto oil (page 16) or canola oil

1 tablespoon minced garlic

2 cups coarsely chopped onions

1 large green bell pepper, seeded and cut into strips about ½ inch wide by 3 inches long

1 large red bell pepper, seeded and cut into strips about ½ inch wide by 3 inches long

1 jalapeño pepper, seeded and diced, or a generous pinch of crushed red pepper flakes

1 cup boiling water

1 teaspoon salt, or to taste

1½ to 2 pounds starchy vegetables such as yuca, taro, and boniato, peeled and cut into ¾-inch dice

1 pound calabaza (West Indian pumpkin) or butternut squash, peeled and finely chopped

2 ears corn, shucked and cut into 1-inch slices (or substitute 2 cups fresh or frozen [defrosted] corn kernels)

. . . .

1½ cups tomato sauce
1 tablespoon red wine vinegar (optional)

Heat the oil in the cooker. Cook the garlic over medium-high heat, stirring constantly, until light brown. Immediately add the onions and continue to cook, stirring frequently, for 1 minute. Add the bell peppers and jalapeño pepper, water (stand back to avoid sputtering oil), salt, starchy vegetables, calabaza, and corn. Stir well.

Lock the lid in place. Over high heat, bring to high pressure. Lower the heat just enough to maintain high pressure and cook for 5 minutes. Reduce the pressure with a quick-release method. Remove the lid, tilting it away from you to allow any excess steam to escape. If the vegetables are not sufficiently tender, replace (but do not lock) the lid and simmer until done.

Add the tomato sauce as you stir well to distribute the squash and create a thick sauce. Add a bit of vinegar to perk up the flavors, if desired.

Tropical Vegetables in Coconut Milk

5 minutes high pressure

Here is a very simple one-pot dish that is outrageously good. The starchy vegetables (see page 96) form a perfect union with their tropical companion, the coconut. Thanks to the curry powder, the stew takes on a fetching saffron color with flecks of vibrant squash orange and tomato red. Serve it over white or brown rice, accompanied by a steamed green vegetable, and perhaps some fried plantains. Try some fresh mango or papaya for dessert. ***Serves 4 to 6***

1 tablespoon annatto oil (page 16) or canola oil

1 teaspoon minced garlic

1 red or green chili pepper, seeded and thinly sliced
   (wear rubber gloves when handling chili peppers)

2 cups coconut milk (page 19)

2½ pounds starchy vegetables such as yuca, taro, and
   boniato, peeled and cut into ¾-inch dice

1 pound calabaza (West Indian pumpkin) or butternut
   squash, peeled and finely chopped

1 cup finely chopped fresh or canned (drained) plum
   tomatoes

1 tablespoon mild curry powder

1 teaspoon salt, or to taste

Heat the oil in the cooker. Cook the garlic over medium-high heat, stirring constantly, until lightly browned. Immediately add the chili pepper, coconut milk (stand back to avoid sputtering oil), starchy vegetables, calabaza, tomatoes, curry powder, and salt.

Lock the lid in place. Set the cooker on a heated Flame Tamer. Over high heat, bring to high pressure. Lower the heat just enough to maintain high pressure and cook for 5 minutes. Reduce the pressure with a quick-release method. Remove the lid, tilting it away from you to allow any excess steam to escape. If the vegetables are not sufficiently tender, replace (but do not lock) the lid and simmer until done.

Stir well to distribute the calabaza and create a thick sauce.

CAULIFLOWER-POTATO CURRY

3 minutes high pressure

The vegetables in this recipe are cooked in coconut milk, giving the final dish a smooth finish and a tantalizing balance of flavors. For those of you who prefer a lower-fat version, I offer a variation made with water that also produces very satisfying results (see directions following the recipe).

I like to serve this curry with white basmati rice and Sun-Dried Tomato Chutney. It's nice to begin the meal with Split Pea Dal with Apple and Coconut or serve the dal in small bowls on the side with the main course. ***Serves 4 to 6***

1 large head cauliflower (about 2½ pounds)

2 teaspoons safflower or canola oil

2 teaspoons whole cumin seeds

1½ cups coconut milk (page 19)

2 tablespoons tomato paste

2 tablespoons mild curry powder

1 teaspoon ground coriander seeds

¼ teaspoon ground cinnamon

1 teaspoon salt, or to taste

Pinch of cayenne

1½ pounds thin-skinned potatoes, scrubbed and cut into ½-inch dice

½ cup diced red bell pepper

. . . .

¼ cup minced fresh coriander (optional)

Cut the cauliflower into florets about 2 inches wide across the top. Set aside.

Heat the oil in the cooker. Sizzle the cumin seeds over medium-high heat just until they begin to pop, 5 to 10 seconds. Turn off the heat and add the coconut milk (stand back to avoid sputtering oil) and tomato paste. While stirring with a fork, sprinkle in the curry powder, coriander, cinnamon, salt, and cayenne. Bring to the boil. Set the potatoes and red bell pepper in the liquid and place the cauliflower florets on top.

Lock the lid in place. Over high heat, bring to high pressure. Lower the heat just enough to maintain high pressure and cook for 3 minutes. Reduce the pressure with a quick-release method. Remove the lid, tilting it away from you to allow any excess steam to escape. If the potatoes are not quite done, replace (but do not lock) the lid and let them cook for a few more minutes in the residual heat.

Stir well to combine the cauliflower and the potatoes. While stirring, the cauliflower will break up into small pieces and amalgamate with the cooking liquid to create a thick sauce. Mix in the coriander (if using) before serving.

Low-Fat Cauliflower-Potato Curry

In order to create a full-flavored dish, I have decreased the amount of liquid and intensified some of the flavorings. Use 1 cup of water instead of the coconut milk and increase the seasonings as follows: 1 tablespoon whole cumin seeds, 3 tablespoons tomato paste, and 1½ teaspoons ground coriander seeds. In all other respects, proceed with the recipe as directed.

THAI-STYLE VEGETABLE CURRY

2 minutes high pressure, 3 to 4 minutes additional cooking

For its range of exotic and complex tastes, I find Thai cuisine quite captivating. I've built a variety of textures into this flavor-packed stew by cooking the sweet potatoes, broccoli stalks, and mushrooms under pressure and then steaming the quick-cooking broccoli florets and green beans at the end.

Serve it with brown basmati rice and a crisp green salad. For a heartier meal, add Thai Chickpeas. *Serves 4 to 6*

TIPS & TECHNIQUES
. . . .
If your dried lemongrass isn't finely ground, place the "bits" into a tea ball or a cheesecloth bundle.

1 large bunch broccoli

1 tablespoon safflower or canola oil

2 teaspoons minced garlic

2 cups coconut milk (page 19)

2 tablespoons tamari soy sauce

1 stalk fresh lemongrass, outer layer removed, cut into
1½-inch pieces, or 1½ teaspoons finely ground dried
lemongrass

1 teaspoon dried basil leaves (omit if using fresh basil at
the end)

½ teaspoon ground coriander seeds

⅛ teaspoon ground cinnamon

⅛ teaspoon ground cardamom

Generous pinch of crushed red pepper flakes

1 pound sweet potatoes, peeled and coarsely chopped

½ pound fresh mushrooms, halved or quartered

¼ pound fresh green beans, trimmed and cut into thirds
(optional)

10 large fresh basil leaves, snipped (optional)

Cut the florets from the broccoli stalks and cut each floret
so that the top measures about 1 inch across. Peel off the thick
outer skin of the stalks and cut the stalks into ½-inch dice. Set
aside.

Heat the oil in the cooker. Cook the garlic over medium-
high heat, stirring constantly, just until it begins to brown. Add
the coconut milk (stand back to avoid sputtering oil), soy
sauce, lemongrass, dried basil (if using), spices, red pepper
flakes, reserved broccoli stalks, sweet potatoes, and mushrooms.

Lock the lid in place. Over high heat, bring to high pressure. Lower the heat just enough to maintain high pressure
and cook for 2 minutes. Reduce the pressure with a quick-
release method. Remove the lid, tilting it away from you to
allow any excess steam to escape.

If you've used fresh lemongrass, remove the pieces. Stir in
the broccoli florets and green beans (if using). Replace (but
do not lock) the lid and cook over medium heat until they are
tender-crisp, 3 to 4 minutes. Stir in the fresh basil (if using)
just before serving.

POTATO RAGOUT WITH ROASTED BELL PEPPERS

4 minutes high pressure, 1 minute simmering

It's nice to marry the faintly charred flavor of roasted bell peppers with the slightly sweet blandness of potatoes. Once you get into the habit of roasting bell peppers, they are likely to become a regular part of your repertoire.

This dish is substantial enough to be the focal point on a plate, surrounded by one or two steamed vegetables and accompanied by a green salad. *Serves 4 to 6*

1 tablespoon olive oil

2 teaspoons minced garlic

2 cups coarsely chopped onions

1 cup boiling water

1 tablespoon tomato paste

1 teaspoon dried marjoram or oregano leaves

1 teaspoon salt, or to taste

2 pounds medium thin-skinned potatoes, scrubbed and cut into eighths

. . . .

2 large red bell peppers, roasted (page 17), seeded, and cut into ½-inch strips

2 large green bell peppers, roasted (page 17), seeded, and cut into ½-inch strips

¼ to ⅓ cup minced fresh parsley or basil

Heat the oil in the cooker. Cook the garlic over medium-high heat, stirring constantly, until it turns golden brown. Immediately add the onions and cook, stirring frequently, for an additional minute. Add the water (stand back to avoid sputtering oil), tomato paste, marjoram, salt, and potatoes.

Lock the lid in place. Over high heat, bring to high pressure. Lower the heat just enough to maintain high pressure and cook for 4 minutes. Reduce the pressure with a quick-release method. Remove the lid, tilting it away from you to allow any excess steam to escape.

If you'd like to create a sauce of the cooking liquid, with a slotted spoon, transfer about a cupful of the potatoes to a food processor or blender, and purée. Stir the purée back into the vegetables. Alternatively, you can drain off the liquid. Stir in the roasted bell peppers and simmer just until the peppers get warm, about 1 minute. Stir in the parsley just before serving.

WINTER VEGETABLE RAGOUT

5 minutes high pressure

Here is a wonderfully satisfying dish, with a hint of smokiness, thanks to the flavor of dried chestnuts. Serve with white rice or millet to absorb some of the flavorful sauce. For optimum appearance, eat this dish right after it's made.
Serves 4 to 6

½ cup dried chestnuts, soaked overnight in 1½ cups
    water or speed-soaked (page 16)

Water

1 tablespoon olive oil

2 cups coarsely chopped leeks (white and light green
    parts) or onions

¾ pound small thin-skinned potatoes, scrubbed and
    quartered

¾ pound rutabaga or white turnip, peeled and cut into
    ¾-inch dice

½ pound butternut, kabocha, or delicata squash, peeled,
    seeded, and cut into 1½-inch chunks

½ pound cabbage, preferably red, cored and thinly
    shredded

1 large bay leaf

½ teaspoon salt, or to taste

1 teaspoon dried thyme leaves, marjoram leaves, or
    winter savory

. . . .

¾ pound fresh or 10 ounces frozen (defrosted) brussels
    sprouts, trimmed, sliced, and cooked until tender-
    crisp

2 tablespoons minced fresh parsley

continued

Strain the chestnuts, reserving the soaking water in a liquid measuring cup. Discard any bits of brown skin sticking to the chestnuts and coarsely chop them. Add enough water to the soaking liquid to make a total of 1½ cups and return the chopped chestnuts to the liquid. Set aside.

Heat the oil in the cooker. Sauté the leeks, stirring frequently, for 1 minute. (If you are so inclined, you can sweat the leeks over low heat, covered, for about 10 minutes to bring out their sweetness.) Add the reserved chestnut soaking water (stand back to avoid sputtering oil), chestnuts, potatoes, rutabaga, squash, cabbage, bay leaf, salt, and thyme.

Lock the lid in place. Over high heat, bring to high pressure. Lower the heat just enough to maintain high pressure and cook for 5 minutes. Reduce the pressure with a quick-release method. Remove the lid, tilting it away from you to allow any excess steam to escape.

Remove the bay leaf and mash about a cup of the potatoes against the side of the cooker with a fork to thicken the cooking liquid. Stir in the brussels sprouts. Serve the ragout in bowls, sprinkled with the parsley.

VEGETABLE PURÉES

The pressure cooker provides a handy way to turn out vegetable purées in a flash. Since there is no worry about overcooking (you want the vegetables to be very soft anyway), it's a great way to relax and invent interesting combinations. Here are a few that I came up with. By checking the chart (pages 74 and 75) for vegetables with approximately the same cooking times, you can come up with some of your own.

Serve these purées as vegetable side dishes.

CHESTNUT-SQUASH PURÉE

5 minutes high pressure

The smokiness of the dried chestnuts and the bright orange of the squash remind me in an appealing way of the look and smell of fall. *Serves 4*

½ cup dried chestnuts, soaked overnight in 1 cup water
    or speed-soaked (page 16)
1½ pounds butternut, kabocha, or delicata squash,
    peeled, seeded, and cut into 1-inch chunks
Water
½ teaspoon dried sage leaves
½ teaspoon salt, or to taste

Strain the chestnuts, reserving the soaking water in a liquid measuring cup. Discard any bits of brown skin sticking to the chestnuts and chop them fine.

Place the chestnuts and squash in the cooker. Add enough water to the soaking liquid to make a total of 1 cup and pour over the chestnuts and squash. Add the sage and salt.

Lock the lid in place. Over high heat, bring to high pressure. Lower the heat just enough to maintain high pressure and cook for 5 minutes. Allow the pressure to come down naturally or use a quick-release method. Remove the lid, tilting it away from you to allow any excess steam to escape.

With a slotted spoon, transfer the squash and chestnuts to a food processor, and pulse to create a coarse purée, adding a bit of the cooking liquid if needed to achieve the right texture. Reheat before serving.

TIPS & TECHNIQUES

Use leftover cooking liquid for cooking grains.

POTATO-BROCCOLI PURÉE

6 minutes high pressure

VARIATION
. . . .
Thin any leftovers with
vegetable stock to make a
creamy broccoli-potato
soup.

Ône of my favorite purées, this is comfort food at its very best. It's also a great use for broccoli stalks, which are always a challenge to cook in appealing ways.

If you use red-skinned potatoes, tiny red flecks peek through the purée—a nice little bonus. But for a lighter, greener purée, you may opt to peel whatever type of potato you use. *Serves 4*

½ to ¾ **pound broccoli stalks (from 1 large bunch)**
1 **cup water**
1 **pound thin-skinned potatoes, scrubbed or peeled and**
    cut into 1-inch chunks
1 **cup coarsely chopped onions**
1 **to 2 garlic cloves, minced**
2 **teaspoons dried dill**
1 **teaspoon salt, or to taste**
Freshly ground pepper to taste
. . . .
1 **tablespoon olive oil (optional, but delicious)**
2 **tablespoons minced fresh parsley**

Cut off the tough bottoms of the broccoli stalks and discard. Peel the stalks and cut them into 1-inch chunks. (You should have about 2 cups.) Begin bringing the water to the boil in the cooker as you add the broccoli, potatoes, onions, garlic, dill, salt, and pepper.

Lock the lid in place. Over high heat, bring to high pressure. Lower the heat just enough to maintain high pressure and cook for 6 minutes. Allow the pressure to come down naturally or use a quick-release method. Remove the lid, tilting it away from you to allow any excess steam to escape.

With a slotted spoon, transfer the vegetables to a food processor and pulse, adding as much of the cooking liquid as needed to create a coarse, fairly thick purée. (Take care not to overprocess as the potatoes will get gummy.) Stir in the olive oil, if desired. Reheat and garnish with parsley before serving.

SWEET POTATO–BEET PURÉE

5 minutes high pressure

As you might have guessed, the beets color this purée a brilliant magenta, making it a real highlight on any plate. A dollop of yogurt or roasted shallot cream (page 24) on top makes a nice addition. ***Serves 5 to 6***

1 pound sweet potatoes, peeled and cut into 1-inch
    chunks

1 pound beets, scrubbed, trimmed, and cut into ½-inch
    dice

1 juice orange

Water

1 tablespoon minced fresh ginger

½ teaspoon salt

Place the sweet potatoes and beets in the cooker. Remove the peel from the orange (see lemon peel, page 22) and mince it. Add ½ tablespoon of the minced peel to the vegetables. If you have any leftover peel, reserve it for possible use after the purée is done. Squeeze the juice from the orange into a liquid measuring cup; add enough water to equal 1 cup. Add this liquid and the ginger and salt to the cooker.

Lock the lid in place. Over high heat, bring to high pressure. Lower the heat just enough to maintain high pressure and cook for 5 minutes. Allow the pressure to come down naturally or use a quick-release method. Remove the lid, tilting it away from you to allow any excess steam to escape.

With a slotted spoon, transfer the mixture to a food processor, and pulse to create a coarse purée. If needed, add a bit of the cooking liquid to create the texture you desire. Stir in additional orange peel, if you like. Reheat before serving.

TIPS & TECHNIQUES

The beets don't have to be peeled because the pressure cooker does such a fine job of softening their skins.

Because the sweet potatoes purée more readily than the beets, you might find that small bits of beet remain intact. I actually like this variation in texture, but if you want an absolutely smooth purée, pass the mixture through a food mill.

Rutabaga–Sweet Potato Purée

6 minutes high pressure

A sweet and festive combination made of sweet potato purée flecked with bits of rutabaga. *Serves 6*

1½ pounds rutabaga, peeled and cut into 1-inch chunks

1 pound sweet potatoes, peeled and cut into 1½-inch chunks

1 cup water or apple juice (for a sweeter version)

¾ teaspoon ground cinnamon

½ teaspoon salt, or to taste

. . . .

Freshly ground nutmeg to taste

⅓ cup coarsely chopped walnuts (optional)

Place the rutabaga, sweet potatoes, water, cinnamon, and salt in the cooker.

Lock the lid in place. Over high heat, bring to high pressure. Lower the heat just enough to maintain high pressure and cook for 6 minutes. Allow the pressure to come down naturally or use a quick-release method. Remove the lid, tilting it away from you to allow any excess steam to escape.

With a slotted spoon, transfer the vegetables in two batches to a food processor. Pulse to create a purée, adding just enough cooking liquid to achieve a medium-thick consistency. (Take care not to overprocess or the potatoes may become gummy.) Add nutmeg to taste. Reheat before serving. Garnish with walnuts, if desired.

TIPS & TECHNIQUES

The sweet potato is cut into larger chunks because it cooks more quickly than the rutabaga.

SEA VEGETABLES

Exotic vegetables from the sea are finally taking their proud place on fine restaurant menus around the country. Since they contain ten to twenty times more minerals than land plants, it's a good idea for you to incorporate some sea vegetables in your home cooking, too. They are excellent sources of iodine, chlorophyll, calcium, vitamins, and protein.

I took to them right away, but, despite your best intentions, you may find them an acquired taste. In the following recipes, I've put them in familiar surroundings so you won't feel too far at sea.

HIJIKI WITH PASTA AND OLIVES

4 minutes high pressure

VARIATION
. . . .
Instead of spaghetti, use an equivalent amount of brightly colored beet, carrot, or spinach fettuccine.

Since cooked hijiki looks like long strands of black spaghetti, it's fun to pair the two. The combination also works well because hijiki's intense flavor is modulated by the easy going taste of pasta.

This recipe produces something akin to a warm pasta salad rather than a sauced pasta. It's also nice to serve at room temperature. Either way, add a green salad or steamed green vegetable and you'll have the makings of a memorable meal.

Serves 4

1 package (approximately 2.1 ounces) hijiki, rinsed, then soaked in ample water to cover for 15 minutes

1 tablespoon olive oil

1½ tablespoons coarsely chopped garlic

3 cups coarsely chopped onions

2 teaspoons dried basil leaves

¼ teaspoon crushed red pepper flakes

1 cup boiling water

1 tablespoon tamari soy sauce (preferred), or ½ teaspoon salt, approximately

. . . .

8 ounces dried spaghetti, cooked al dente

1 large red bell pepper, roasted (page 17), seeded, and cut into thin strips

½ to ¾ cup coarsely chopped pitted green olives (pimiento-stuffed add more color)

¼ cup minced fresh coriander or parsley

Pour the soaked hijiki into a colander and run cold water over it. Drain the hijiki and set aside.

Heat the oil in the cooker. Cook the garlic and onions over medium-high heat, stirring frequently, for 2 minutes. Stir in the basil, red pepper flakes, reserved hijiki, water (stand back to avoid sputtering oil), and soy sauce.

Lock the lid in place. Over high heat, bring to high pressure. Lower the heat just enough to maintain high pressure and cook for 4 minutes. Reduce the pressure with a quick-release method. Remove the lid, tilting it away from you to allow any excess steam to escape.

Stir the cooked pasta, roasted red bell pepper, olives, and coriander into the hijiki. Adjust the seasonings, adding more tamari or salt to taste.

GARLICKY WAKAME WITH POTATOES

2 minutes high pressure

Here is a homey approach to wakame, a sea vegetable that resembles okra in its slightly slippery quality. This is a dish for all who love the briny flavor of sea vegetables, but probably not a good choice for the uninitiated.

What really brings this dish to life is a dollop of fine-quality mustard on the side. Serve it as you would any potato side dish. *Serves 3 to 4*

1 ounce wakame, rinsed, then soaked in ample water to
   cover for 15 minutes
1 tablespoon olive oil
2 cups coarsely chopped onions
4 large garlic cloves, finely minced
1¼ pounds thin-skinned potatoes, peeled, halved, and
   cut into ½-inch dice
1 large carrot, cut on the diagonal into ¼-inch slices
1 small red bell pepper, seeded and diced
1 teaspoon dried basil leaves
½ to 1 cup water (use manufacturer's recommended
   liquid minimum)

. . . .

Salt and freshly ground pepper to taste
1 to 2 teaspoons balsamic vinegar (optional)

Pour the wakame into a colander and run cold water over it. Drain, then coarsely chop the wakame and set aside.

Heat the oil in the cooker. Cook the onions and garlic over medium-high heat, stirring frequently, for 2 minutes. (If time permits, cook them until the onions are browned around the edges, about 2 minutes longer.) Add the reserved wakame, potatoes, carrot, red bell pepper, basil, and water.

Lock the lid in place. Over high heat, bring to high pressure. Lower the heat just enough to maintain high pressure and cook for 2 minutes. Reduce the pressure with a quick-release method. Remove the lid, tilting it away from you to allow any excess steam to escape. If the potatoes are not quite

---

TIPS & TECHNIQUES
. . . .
Sometimes wakame has a thick central rib that requires longer cooking than the rest of the leaf. With the timing of this recipe, it becomes pleasantly chewy; however, if you find it unpleasant, you can always cut the thick rib away after you've soaked the wakame.

tender, replace (but do not lock) the lid and let them cook for a few more minutes in the residual heat.

If there is any liquid remaining in the bottom of the cooker, you may either lift the mixture out with a slotted spoon, or purée about ½ cup of the potatoes in a food processor or blender and stir the purée into the liquid to create a sauce. Stir in the salt and pepper, and vinegar, if desired.

SHIITAKE SEA PALM

3 minutes high pressure

TIPS & TECHNIQUES

Use any leftover cooking liquid for stirring into cooked grains.

Sea palm is my favorite sea vegetable. It is milder than many others, and a good one to try for newcomers to the category. In combination with shiitake, sea palm makes an elegant vegetable side dish and a wonderful topping for pasta or brown rice. If not available locally, you can order it from Gold Mine Natural Food Co. (see Mail-Order Sources). *Serves 3 to 4*

2 ounces (about 2½ cups loosely packed) dried shiitake
    mushrooms

2 cups boiling water

2 ounces (about 2 cups loosely packed) sea palm, soaked
    in ample water to cover for 5 minutes

1 teaspoon minced garlic

1 to 2 teaspoons tamari soy sauce

1 to 2 teaspoons toasted (Oriental) sesame oil

Set the shiitake in a 4-cup liquid measure or bowl and pour the boiling water on top. Soak, covered, for 10 minutes. Occasionally push the shiitake that are on top to the bottom, making sure that all the mushrooms get submerged. Drain the shiitake, reserving the soaking liquid. Slice off the tough stems and discard or save for stock. Slice the caps into ¼-inch slivers.

Drain and rinse the sea palm. Snip or chop the vegetable into 2-inch strips (approximately), discarding any tough "roots" to which the strands are attached. Place the sea palm, shiitake, mushroom soaking water, garlic, and 1 teaspoon of soy sauce in the cooker.

Lock the lid in place. Over high heat, bring to high pressure. Lower the heat just enough to maintain high pressure and cook for 3 minutes. Reduce the pressure with a quick-release method. Remove the lid, tilting it away from you to allow any excess steam to escape.

Add additional soy sauce, if desired, and toasted sesame oil to taste. Serve over pasta or grains with a bit of the cooking liquid or lift with a slotted spoon and serve on plates.

GRAINS

Grains — whether in the form of bread, pasta, or rice — offer a level of satiety and nourishment unequaled by other foods. Indeed, if I go a day or two without a bowl of rice or a serving of polenta, I feel as though I haven't quite been eating.

Once again, the pressure cooker comes to the rescue, putting the multifaceted world of grains at our doorstep, planting wheat berries and brown rice firmly in the category of daily fare.

General Tips and Techniques

Shopping for Grains: With their oil-rich germ intact, whole grains are more prone to rancidity than refined products (such as white rice). Markets that do not store grains under refrigeration should sell only those that come sealed in airtight packages.

If your only option is to shop from unrefrigerated bulk bins, be sure to do so at a store that has high turnover. Before making your purchase, sniff the grains and make sure they smell sweet and not musty. If you are not satisfied with your local source of grains, I can highly recommend that you order by mail from Gold Mine Natural Food Co. (see Mail-Order Sources). This source offers high-quality, fresh, organic grains.

Storing: Place grains in the freezer (best) or refrigerator either in their own packaging or in heavy-duty zippered plastic bags. Label each with date of purchase and make an effort to use them within 4 to 5 months.

The only exception to this storage rule is white rice, a refined grain that may be stored at room temperature. (I keep mine in the refrigerator anyway.)

Rinsing: Clean only the amount of grain that you are planning to cook.

Pour the measured amount into a strainer and plunge the strainer up and down about ten times in a large bowl filled with cold water. When the grain is under water, stir it gently with your fingers. If the grain seems quite dirty, repeat this process once or twice more, or until the water remains almost clear.

Give the grains a final brief rinse under cold running water while stirring.

Allow the grains to drain while you proceed with the recipe. Do not let them sit indefinitely, however, as they will begin to absorb liquid and soften, which will throw off the cooking time.

Optional Toasting: Before cooking grains, you have the option of dry-toasting them in a heavy skillet or in the bottom of the cooker (if it is heavy-bottomed enough to do so without scorching). Toasting brings out the nuttiness in grains and opens their pores, allowing them to absorb liquid more readily.

Toasting can take as long as 15 minutes—with considerable stirring—and I rarely find it's worth the effort, except for millet, which cooks more thoroughly and develops a much fluffier texture when pretoasted. If you wish to experiment with toasting other grains, follow the instructions in the recipe for Basic Millet.

Soaking: Soaking long-cooking grains overnight reduces their cooking time by about 40 percent. Some experts maintain that it makes grains more digestible. A practical reason for soaking is to enable you to cook a particular whole grain with ingredients that require a shorter cooking time.

Preparing to Cook: Measure the grains in a dry-cup measure (the type of cup that nestles into others). Measure the liquid using a glass measuring cup.

Pressure Cooking Grains

I have come up with grain-cooking formulas that work quite well, but because the moisture content of grains may vary from one batch to the next, you may occasionally need to make minor adjustments as follows:

If cooking time is up and the grains are not sufficiently tender, replace (but do not lock) the lid and continue to cook in the residual heat until the grains are done.

If the grain is not thoroughly cooked and the mixture seems dry, stir in 2 to 6 tablespoons of boiling water or vegetable stock. Replace (but do not lock) the lid and simmer until the grains are done.

If there is excess water left after the grains are tender, simply tip it off or lift the grains from the cooker with a slotted spoon. (A small amount of excess liquid will be absorbed if the grains are allowed to sit for 5 to 10 minutes with the lid slightly ajar.)

Use a Flame Tamer (page 6) if you experience scorching or sticking on the bottom of the pot.

Attention Users of Jiggle-Top Cookers

To accommodate for loss of steam, add ¼ cup extra liquid as indicated in the ingredients lists. If you experience excessively dry grains or scorching, increase liquid by ¼ cup until you achieve the right formula. Better yet, get in the habit of using the Basic Casserole Brown Rice technique (page 121) for cooking rice and other grains; this approach will leave you casualty-free.

The addition of 1 tablespoon of oil will help to control foaming in some jiggle-top cookers. However, others operate perfectly well without oil. If you're not sure about the requirements of your cooker and prefer to leave your grains oil-free, experiment by leaving the oil out. Do not fill the cooker more than halfway. Stay close at hand to intercede if you hear any loud hissing noises.

FLAVORING OPTIONS

When preparing plain brown or white rice (or other grains) to serve with Italian, French, Spanish, or American Southern food, *before cooking* add one or more of the following flavorings to the pot per 1 cup of dry grain:

1 large garlic clove, crushed or thinly sliced
1 bay leaf
½ to 1 teaspoon dried oregano, basil, or thyme leaves
Dash of cayenne
½ teaspoon sweet Hungarian paprika

Or stir in any of the following *after cooking:*

1 tablespoon finely minced or grated orange or lemon peel (colored part only, organic if possible)

¼ cup toasted pine nuts or coarsely chopped walnuts, hazelnuts, or pecans
1 to 2 teaspoons poppy seeds
¼ cup finely chopped fresh herbs such as basil, parsley, dill, or coriander

When serving grains with Indian, Moroccan, or Middle Eastern food, consider substituting orange or apple juice for half of the water and *before cooking* add one or more of the following to the pot per 1 cup of dry grain:

One 3-inch cinnamon stick, broken in two, or ½ teaspoon ground cinnamon
2 to 3 crushed cardamom pods or ¼ teaspoon ground cardamom
1 to 2 teaspoons ground coriander seeds

2 to 3 teaspoons mild curry powder
2 to 3 whole cloves or ⅛ teaspoon ground cloves
⅛ teaspoon ground allspice
2 to 3 quarter-size slices fresh ginger or ¼ teaspoon ground ginger
¼ cup toasted pine nuts
⅓ cup raisins, dried currants, chopped dried apricots, or prunes

When serving grains with Oriental food, *before cooking* try adding one or more of the following to the pot per 1 cup of dry grain:

1 tablespoon finely minced fresh ginger
1 tablespoon tamari soy sauce
1 tablespoon toasted sesame seeds

What About Salt?

Cooking grains with salt is a matter of personal taste. In some recipes I have suggested a moderate amount as an optional addition. In my own case, I rarely add salt to unseasoned brown rice since I enjoy its natural sweetness. However, I am inclined to add salt to other grains.

A good way to cut down on the need for salt is to add one or more of the seasonings suggested in the Flavoring Options.

Certain grains—such as wheat berries, triticale, and Wehani brown rice—do not absorb liquid properly if they are cooked with salt. These grains are indicated with an asterisk on the grain cooking chart (page 159). You may add salt after cooking, if desired.

Doubling Recipes

It is tricky to double grain recipes, since the liquid is not automatically doubled. When increasing the amount of rice, use the proportions suggested in the rice cooking charts (pages 120 and 140) as a guideline. When doubling other grain recipes, use one and a half times the liquid called for in the grain cooking chart (page 159).

Rehydrating and Reheating Cooked Grains

On cool days, cooked grains may be left at room temperature for up to 24 hours, covered. During hot weather or if you need to keep them longer than a day, store them in a tightly sealed container in the refrigerator. Unfortunately, grains dry out and harden under refrigeration. To rehydrate and reheat them, place the grains in a heatproof bowl and set the uncovered bowl on a rack in the cooker (or another pot) over a few inches of boiling water. Cover the pot and steam over medium-high heat, stirring once or twice, until the grains are rehydrated and heated throughout, 2 to 5 minutes depending upon the quantity and type of grain.

Basic Casserole Brown Rice Cooking Chart

For basic cooking instructions, see page 121.

This chart can be used for all varieties of brown rice.
Remember that short-grain brown rice cooks an additional
5 minutes under high pressure (see the note on Cooking Times).

Cups Brown Rice	Cups Liquid	Teaspoons Optional Salt	Approximate Yield in Cups	Minimum Casserole Size in Quarts
1	1½	½	2½	1
1½	1¾	¾	3½	1½
2	2¼	1	5	2

COOKING TIMES: Cook long-grain brown, Wehani, or brown basmati rice for 20 minutes under high pressure plus a 20-minute natural pressure release.
Cook short-grain brown rice for 25 minutes under high pressure plus a 20-minute natural pressure release.

Brown Rice Cooking Chart

For basic cooking instructions, see page 122.

For a dry rice, use the smaller amount of liquid.
For a moist rice and in jiggle-top cookers, use the maximum.

Cups Brown Rice	Cups Boiling Liquid	Teaspoons Optional Salt	Tablespoons Optional Oil	Approximate Yield in Cups
1	1¾–2	½	1	2¼
1½	2½–2¾	¾	1	3½
2	3½–4	1	1½	5
3	5–5½	1½	2	7

NOTE: Do not fill the cooker more than halfway.

BASIC CASSEROLE BROWN RICE

20 to 25 minutes high pressure, 20-minute natural pressure release

Everyone who tries it loves this foolproof method. The grains are steamed to perfection in a 1½- or 2-quart heat-proof casserole that is placed on a rack over water in the pressure cooker. There should be at least ½ inch of space between the casserole and the sides of the cooker.

With this method, the rice is initially mixed with less water than normal and the grains absorb just the amount of moisture they need from the steam inside the cooker.

After it has cooked, you can serve the rice right in the casserole: No fuss to cook and no pot to clean.

Here's a recipe for cooking 1½ cups of any variety of brown rice. In the basic casserole brown rice cooking chart (page 120), you'll find the formulas for cooking other quantities. *Makes 3½ cups*

1½ **cups brown rice, rinsed and drained**

1¾ **cups water**

Flavoring options (page 118)

¾ **teaspoon salt (optional)**

In a 1½- or 2-quart casserole, combine all the ingredients. Place the rack and 2 cups of water in the cooker. Lower the uncovered casserole onto the rack with the aid of a foil strip (page 9).

Lock the lid in place. Over high heat, bring to high pressure. Lower the heat just enough to maintain high pressure and cook for 20 minutes (for long-grain brown, Wehani, brown basmati, etc.) or 25 minutes (for short-grain brown). Allow the pressure to come down naturally for 20 minutes. Remove the lid, tilting it away from you to allow any excess steam to escape. If the rice is not quite tender, replace (but do not lock) the lid and allow it to steam for a few more minutes in the residual heat.

Lift the casserole from the cooker with the aid of the foil strip. Fluff up the rice before serving.

BASIC BROWN RICE

15 to 50 minutes high pressure, 10-minute natural pressure release

TIPS & TECHNIQUES

If you prefer eating rice whose grains fall away from each other, try a ceramic rice pot (page 117) or opt for the Basic Casserole Brown Rice recipe (page 121). This "no-risk" approach is also excellent if you experience scorching or sticking on the bottom of the cooker, and is the preferred method if you are using a jiggle-top cooker.

VARIATIONS

Blend different types of brown rice to vary texture. It's nice to use about 25 percent Wehani rice to add specks of dark amber.

See the recipes that follow for blends of rice and other grains.

This is the basic recipe that I use for all types of brown rice, including brown basmati and Wehani.

Fifteen minutes under pressure will result in a very chewy rice; by increasing the cooking time, you will increase the softness and digestibility of the rice. Experiment to find your own preference. I find 25 minutes under high pressure plus a 10-minute natural pressure release a good compromise.

In general, the pressure cooker produces rice that is slightly stickier than you may be accustomed to. I have gotten quite used to the texture and actually prefer it.

For details on preparing different quantities, check the brown rice cooking chart on page 120. ***Makes about 3½ cups***

2½ to 2¾ cups water (use higher amount in jiggle-top cookers)

1½ cups brown rice, rinsed and drained

Flavoring options (page 118)

¾ teaspoon salt, or to taste (optional)

Bring the water to the boil in the cooker. Add the rice, flavorings as desired, and salt (if using).

Lock the lid in place. Set the cooker on a heated Flame Tamer. Over high heat, bring to high pressure. Lower the heat just enough to maintain high pressure and cook for 15 to 50 minutes, as desired. Allow the pressure to come down naturally for 10 minutes. Quick-release any remaining pressure. Remove the lid, tilting it away from you to allow any excess steam to escape. Fluff up the rice before serving.

Sushi Brown Rice

Increase water to 3 cups (3½ cups for jiggle-top cookers) and proceed as directed, cooking under pressure for 40 minutes. The extra water will create a stickier rice. Set the cooker on a Flame Tamer if your cooker has a thin bottom. For instructions on making sushi rolls, see page 180.

QUINOA RICE

25 minutes high pressure, 10-minute natural pressure release

Quinoa and rice make a delightful combination, with the quinoa contributing lightness and interesting texture to the final product. *Makes about 4 cups*

2½ to 2¾ cups water (use higher amount in jiggle-top cookers)

1 cup short-grain brown rice, rinsed and drained

½ cup quinoa, thoroughly washed (page 172) and drained

Flavoring options (page 118)

½ teaspoon salt, or to taste

Bring the water to the boil in the cooker. Add the rice, quinoa, flavorings as desired, and salt.

Lock the lid in place. Over high heat, bring to high pressure. Lower the heat just enough to maintain high pressure and cook for 25 minutes. Allow the pressure to come down naturally for 10 minutes. Quick-release any remaining pressure. Remove the lid, tilting it away from you to allow any excess steam to escape. Fluff up the mixture before serving.

Add ¾ teaspoon caraway seeds to the pot before cooking.

Stir 1 tablespoon tomato paste into the cooking water.

Use stock instead of water.

BULGUR AND BROWN RICE

25 minutes high pressure, 10-minute natural pressure release

This combination has an appealing rustic look and a pleasantly nutty flavor. Don't expect a fluffy product: The texture is hearty and moist. *Makes about 4 cups*

2½ to 2¾ cups water (use higher amount in jiggle-top cookers)
½ cup coarse bulgur, rinsed and drained
1 cup long- or short-grain brown rice, rinsed and drained
Flavoring options (page 118)
¾ teaspoon salt, or to taste

Bring the water and bulgur to the boil in the cooker. Add the rice, flavorings as desired, and salt.

Lock the lid in place. If your cooker has a thin bottom, set it on a heated Flame Tamer. Over high heat, bring to high pressure. Lower the heat just enough to maintain high pressure and cook for 25 minutes. Allow the pressure to come down naturally for 10 minutes. Quick-release any remaining pressure. Remove the lid, tilting it away from you to allow any excess steam to escape. Stir well before serving.

RICE 'N' RYE

35 minutes high pressure, 10-minute natural pressure release

Mixing rice with a whole grain such as rye berries produces a cooked grain with nice color variation and a pleasing chewiness. *Makes 3½ cups*

2¼ to 2½ cups water (use higher amount in jiggle-top cookers)

1 cup short-grain brown rice, rinsed and drained

⅓ cup rye berries (whole-grain rye), rinsed and drained

Flavoring options (page 118)

½ teaspoon salt, or to taste

Bring the water to the boil in the cooker. Add the rice, rye berries, flavorings as desired, and salt.

Lock the lid in place. If using a jiggle-top cooker, set it on a heated Flame Tamer. Over high heat, bring to high pressure. Lower the heat just enough to maintain high pressure and cook for 35 minutes. Allow the pressure to come down naturally for 10 minutes. Quick-release any remaining pressure. Remove the lid, tilting it away from you to allow any excess steam to escape. Fluff up the mixture before serving.

VARIATION

Substitute wheat berries (whole-grain wheat), triticale, or kamut for the rye berries.

MILLET RICE OREGANATO

25 minutes high pressure, 10-minute natural pressure release

VARIATIONS

Stir in ¼ cup finely chopped olives or oil-packed sun-dried tomatoes after cooking.

Stir in 3 to 4 tablespoons minced fresh basil or parsley after cooking.

This flavorful combination has a polentalike consistency and is particularly nice served with Italian food. Try it with a topping of Tofu Spaghetti Sauce. (Warning: This mixture sticks to the bottom of some jiggle-top cookers.)

Serves 4 to 6

1 tablespoon olive oil
1 tablespoon minced garlic
2½ to 2¾ cups boiling water (use higher amount in jiggle-top cookers)
1 cup short-grain brown rice, rinsed and drained
½ cup millet, rinsed and drained (toasting optional, page 167)
1 to 1½ teaspoons dried oregano leaves
1 large bay leaf
Generous pinch of crushed red pepper flakes (optional)
¾ teaspoon salt, or to taste

Heat the oil in the cooker. Cook the garlic over medium-high heat, stirring frequently, until golden brown. Immediately add the water (stand back to avoid sputtering oil). When the water returns to the boil, add the rice, millet, oregano, bay leaf, red pepper flakes (if using), and salt.

Lock the lid in place. If using a jiggle-top cooker, set it on a heated Flame Tamer. Over high heat, bring to high pressure. Lower the heat just enough to maintain high pressure and cook for 25 minutes. Allow the pressure to come down naturally for 10 minutes. Quick-release any remaining pressure. Remove the lid, tilting it away from you to allow any excess steam to escape.

Remove the bay leaf. Stir well to distribute and fluff up the grains before serving.

TAMARI BROWN RICE WITH BARLEY

35 minutes high pressure, 10-minute natural pressure release

This is a great approach for grains that you plan to serve with Oriental foods. The soy sauce turns the grains an appealing golden brown and gives them a complex taste. The addition of barley results in a stickier rice than usual, so you'll need to stir vigorously with a fork to fluff it up.

For a wonderful Double Sesame Grain Salad based on this recipe, see page 179. ***Makes about 5½ cups***

> 3 to 3¼ cups water (use higher amount in jiggle-top cookers)
>
> 1 to 2 tablespoons tamari soy sauce
>
> 1 cup hulled or pearl barley, rinsed and drained
>
> 1 cup short-grain brown rice, rinsed and drained

Bring the water to the boil in the cooker. Stir in 1 tablespoon of the soy sauce, the barley, and rice.

Lock the lid in place. If using a jiggle-top cooker, set it on a heated Flame Tamer. Over high heat, bring to high pressure. Lower the heat just enough to maintain high pressure and cook for 35 minutes. Allow the pressure to come down naturally for 10 minutes. Quick-release any remaining pressure. Remove the lid, tilting it away from you to allow any excess steam to escape.

Fluff up the mixture before serving. Stir in a bit more soy sauce, if desired.

TIPS & TECHNIQUES

Barley foams while cooking. If you experience loud hissing noises, turn off the heat, release the pressure under cold running water, and thoroughly clean the lid and vent. Add 1 tablespoon of oil to the mixture, return to high pressure, and continue cooking.

If using pearl barley, try the type found in the health food store, which is less refined than the barley found in the supermarket.

Since the barley gives this combination a slight stickiness, you can mold the mixture into attractive single servings by pressing it into lightly oiled ½-cup measures. Unmold and sprinkle with some chopped chives or minced fresh herbs.

For a yield of about 2½ cups, use 2 to 2¼ cups water, ½ tablespoon tamari soy sauce, ⅔ cup brown rice, and ⅓ cup barley.

VARIATIONS

Cook the grains with 1 to 2 tablespoons finely minced ginger.

Toss in ¼ cup minced scallion greens and a few teaspoons of toasted (Oriental) sesame oil after the mixture is cooked.

Mushrooms and Leeks with Saffron Rice

25 minutes high pressure, 10-minute natural pressure release

The estimable combination of mushrooms and leeks goes at least as far back as the Middle Ages.

For an appealing menu, serve this dish with Parsnips with Indian Spices and Cauliflower-Potato Curry. *Serves 4*

2 teaspoons safflower or canola oil

1 teaspoon minced garlic

2 cups thinly sliced leeks (white and green parts)

1½ cups long-grain brown rice, rinsed and drained

2 to 2¼ cups boiling water (use higher amount in jiggle-top cookers)

½ pound small fresh button or wild mushrooms, cut into ½-inch slices

1 large carrot, diced

1 teaspoon whole fennel seeds

¾ teaspoon salt, or to taste

¼ teaspoon saffron threads

⅛ teaspoon freshly ground pepper

. . . .

1 to 2 tablespoons minced fresh parsley

Heat the oil in the cooker. Cook the garlic and leeks over medium-high heat, stirring frequently, for 2 minutes. Stir in the rice. Add the water (stand back to avoid sputtering oil), mushrooms, carrot, fennel, salt, saffron, and pepper.

Lock the lid in place. If using a jiggle-top cooker, set it on a heated Flame Tamer. Over high heat, bring to high pressure. Lower the heat just enough to maintain high pressure and cook for 25 minutes. Allow the pressure to come down naturally for 10 minutes. Quick-release any remaining pressure. Remove the lid, tilting it away from you to allow any excess steam to escape.

Stir well to distribute the mushrooms. If any liquid remains, stir while simmering until it is absorbed. Garnish with parsley before serving.

TIPS & TECHNIQUES

A less-than-normal amount of water is used because the leeks and mushrooms give up considerable liquid when cooking. Indeed, the mixture usually comes out quite moist, with a risotto-like texture.

BROWN RICE WITH SPINACH, RAISINS, AND PINE NUTS

25 minutes high pressure, 10-minute natural pressure release, 2 to 3 minutes simmering

A very colorful and festive rice dish inspired by the age-old southern Italian tradition of combining greens, raisins, and pine nuts. I like to cook the rice with half of the pine nuts, which adds a delicious richness to the dish. The remaining half is stirred in at the end to add a bit of crunch.

This dish is interesting enough to serve as the focal point of a meal that might also include a large green salad and a bean soup to start. ***Serves 3 to 4***

2 to 2¼ cups water (use higher amount in jiggle-top cookers)

1 cup long-grain brown rice, rinsed and drained

1 tablespoon finely minced fresh ginger

⅓ cup raisins or dried currants

⅓ cup toasted pine nuts

¾ teaspoon salt, or to taste

. . . .

5 ounces frozen (defrosted) chopped spinach

Freshly grated nutmeg to taste (optional)

Bring the water to the boil in the cooker. Add the rice, ginger, raisins, 2 tablespoons of the pine nuts, and the salt.

Lock the lid in place. Over high heat, bring to high pressure. Lower the heat just enough to maintain high pressure and cook for 25 minutes. Allow the pressure to come down naturally for 10 minutes. Quick-release any remaining pressure. Remove the lid, tilting it away from you to allow any excess steam to escape.

Stir in the spinach, remaining pine nuts, and nutmeg (if using). Simmer, covered, until the spinach is heated, 2 to 3 minutes.

TIPS & TECHNIQUES

Although I usually squeeze excess water out of defrosted spinach before adding it, in this case I find that the additional liquid is needed for those few extra minutes of simmering. Use your judgment.

VARIATIONS

Instead of using nutmeg, drizzle on freshly squeezed lemon juice to taste.

Substitute 1 to 1½ cups finely chopped cooked kale for the spinach.

Replace the pine nuts with coarsely chopped toasted walnuts or blanched almonds.

BROWN RICE WITH BASIL AND SUN-DRIED TOMATOES

25 minutes high pressure, 10-minute natural pressure release

An ideal choice during the late summer and early fall when fresh basil is abundant. Delicious hot and at room temperature, with perhaps a drizzle of olive oil and lemon juice. Steamed broccoli and a green salad rounds out the meal nicely. *Serves 3 to 4*

1 tablespoon olive oil (or use the oil from the sun-dried tomatoes)
½ cup thinly sliced leeks (white part only) or finely chopped onion
½ teaspoon minced garlic
1 cup long-grain brown rice, rinsed and drained
1¾ to 2 cups boiling water (use higher amount in jiggle-top cookers)
1 tablespoon tomato paste
¾ teaspoon salt, or to taste
. . . .
¼ cup finely chopped oil-packed sun-dried tomatoes
⅓ cup minced fresh basil

Heat the oil in the cooker. Cook the leeks and garlic over medium-high heat, stirring frequently, for 1 minute. Stir in the rice, boiling water (stand back to avoid sputtering oil), tomato paste, and salt.

Lock the lid in place. If using a jiggle-top cooker, set it on a heated Flame Tamer. Over high heat, bring to high pressure. Lower the heat just enough to maintain high pressure and cook for 25 minutes. Allow the pressure to come down naturally for 10 minutes. Quick-release any remaining pressure. Remove the lid, tilting it away from you to allow any excess steam to escape.

Stir in the sun-dried tomatoes and basil before serving.

VARIATIONS

Stir in ½ to 1 cup shredded smoked mozzarella while the rice is still warm.

Use ½ cup pitted, chopped oil-cured olives instead of the sun-dried tomatoes.

Add 1 cup cooked black beans when you stir in the basil and sun-dried tomatoes. Add more salt or 1 to 2 teaspoons of balsamic vinegar to perk up the flavors, if desired.

CARIBBEAN RICE AND BEANS

25 minutes high pressure, 10-minute natural pressure release

As far as I'm concerned, coconut rice is one of the great contributions tropical kitchens have given the world. In this recipe, I've parted from tradition in a number of ways. First, I've used brown rice. (See also the simple recipe for Coconut White Rice.) Second, I've called for grated coconut rather than coconut milk.

Aside from eliminating the extra step of buying or preparing coconut milk, this technique results in a deliciously flavored rice dish with crunch.

For a magnificent finish, fry up some ripe plantains and set them decoratively on top. A steamed green vegetable and a green salad will complete the meal. *Serves 4 to 6*

1 tablespoon olive oil (or try annatto oil, page 16, if you
    like)

2 teaspoons minced garlic

1 cup coarsely chopped onions

1 hot red chili pepper, seeded and chopped (wear
    rubber gloves when handling chili peppers), or a
    generous pinch of crushed red pepper flakes

1 cup diced red bell pepper

1 cup coarsely chopped fresh or canned (drained) plum
    tomatoes

2 to 2¼ cups boiling water (use higher amount in jiggle-
    top cookers)

1½ cups long-grain brown rice, rinsed and drained

½ cup dried, grated, unsweetened coconut

½ teaspoon dried thyme or oregano leaves

1 teaspoon salt, or to taste

. . . .

1 cup firm-cooked pigeon or black-eyed peas

¼ cup finely minced fresh coriander (optional)

2 very ripe plantains, peeled, cut on the diagonal into
    thin slices, and fried in a heavy skillet lightly
    brushed with oil

continued

TIPS & TECHNIQUES

Plantains look like large green bananas until they are fully ripened, at which time they turn completely black and are at their sweetest. To peel plantains, cut shallow incisions down the length at about 1½-inch intervals and remove the skin. (Plantains resist peeling more than bananas do.)

Heat the oil in the cooker. Cook the garlic, onions, and chili pepper over medium-high heat, stirring frequently, for 1 minute. Add the red bell pepper, tomatoes, water (stand back to avoid sputtering oil), rice, coconut, thyme, and salt.

Lock the lid in place. If using a jiggle-top cooker, set it on a heated Flame Tamer. Over high heat, bring to high pressure. Lower the heat just enough to maintain high pressure and cook for 25 minutes. Allow the pressure to come down naturally for 10 minutes. Quick-release any remaining pressure. Remove the lid, tilting it away from you to allow any excess steam to escape.

As you add the peas and coriander (if using), stir well to distribute the coconut. Serve in mounds, topped with fried plantains.

MEXICAN GREEN RICE WITH CORN

25 minutes high pressure, 10-minute natural pressure release

Traditionally used with white rice, this technique of "greening" the grain with fresh parsley and coriander turns out a delicious brown rice. I like adding corn to the standard recipe—it provides a bit of bright color and crunch. If poblano peppers are available, they give the dish a nice kick.

This rice pairs up beautifully with Creole Okra Stew. Leftovers are delicious served at room temperature, revived with a splash of fresh lime juice. *Serves 4*

1 cup water
20 parsley sprigs, thick stems removed, cut into 3 pieces
20 coriander sprigs, thick stems removed, cut into 3 pieces
2 large poblano or green bell peppers, roasted (page 17), seeded, and coarsely chopped
1 tablespoon safflower or canola oil
2 teaspoons minced garlic
½ cup coarsely chopped onion

VARIATIONS

For a hotter dish, add a jalapeño pepper, seeded and diced, to the green purée.

To create a more substantial dish, stir in a cup of cooked black beans when you add the olives, red bell pepper, and coriander.

1½ cups long-grain brown rice, rinsed and drained

½ to ¾ cup boiling water (use higher amount in jiggle-top cookers)

2 teaspoons mild chili powder

1 teaspoon salt, or to taste

2 cups fresh or frozen (defrosted) corn kernels

. . . .

⅓ cup chopped pitted green olives

½ cup diced roasted red bell pepper (page 17)

⅓ cup minced fresh coriander

In a blender, combine the water, parsley, coriander, and poblano peppers to create a thin purée. Set aside.

Heat the oil in the cooker. Cook the garlic over medium-high heat, stirring frequently, until brown. Immediately add the onion and continue to cook, stirring frequently, for 1 minute. Stir in the rice, reserved green purée (stand back to avoid sputtering oil), boiling water, chili powder, salt, and corn.

Lock the lid in place. Set the cooker on a heated Flame Tamer. Over high heat, bring to high pressure. Lower the heat just enough to maintain high pressure and cook for 25 minutes. Allow the pressure to come down naturally for 10 minutes. Quick-release any remaining pressure. Remove the lid, tilting it away from you to allow any excess steam to escape.

Fluff up the rice and stir in the olives, red bell pepper, and minced coriander before serving.

HERBED HIJIKI RICE

25 minutes high pressure, 10-minute natural pressure release

Here's a recipe for lovers of sea vegetables. The jet-black flecks of hijiki lend a briny flavor and rich rust color to the rice, while the herbs provide a welcome echo of familiarity. Paprika Carrots and steamed brussels sprouts make good accompaniments.

Toss leftovers with a bit of olive oil and lemon juice for a tasty room-temperature salad. *Serves 3 to 4*

> 1 ounce dried hijiki, rinsed, then soaked in ample water
>   to cover for 15 minutes
> 1 tablespoon olive oil
> 1½ cups finely chopped onions
> 2 teaspoons finely minced garlic
> 1 celery rib, halved lengthwise and thinly sliced
> 1 large carrot, halved lengthwise and thinly sliced
> 1½ teaspoons dried basil leaves
> 1 teaspoon dried oregano leaves
> ½ teaspoon whole fennel seeds
> 1 bay leaf
> Generous pinch of crushed red pepper flakes
> 1 cup long-grain brown rice, rinsed and drained
> 1½ to 1¾ cups boiling water (use higher amount in
>   jiggle-top cookers)
> ¾ teaspoon salt, or to taste
> . . . .
> ⅓ cup finely chopped oil-packed sun-dried tomatoes
> ¼ cup minced fresh parsley

Pour the hijiki into a colander and run cold water over it. Drain the hijiki, coarsely chop it, and set aside.

Heat the oil in the cooker. Sauté the onions and garlic, stirring frequently, for 2 minutes. Add the reserved hijiki, the celery, carrot, basil, oregano, fennel, bay leaf, red pepper flakes, and rice. Stir well. Pour in the boiling water (stand back to avoid sputtering oil) and salt.

Lock the lid in place. If using a jiggle-top cooker, set it on a heated Flame Tamer. Over high heat, bring to high pressure. Lower the heat just enough to maintain high pressure and cook for 25 minutes. Allow the pressure to come down naturally for 10 minutes. Quick-release any remaining pressure. Remove the lid, tilting it away from you to allow any excess steam to escape.

Remove the bay leaf. Fluff up the rice and stir in the sun-dried tomatoes and parsley before serving.

BASIC WILD RICE

22 to 28 minutes high pressure

Because the time and amount of water needed to prepare wild rice varies, I pressure cook it in ample liquid, then drain off any excess and dry out the rice by letting it steam in the covered pot for a minute or two. I think you'll find most batches are properly butterflied (split open) in 22 minutes. If not, just bring the pressure back up for another few minutes.

It's festive to use wild rice as the stuffing for baked squash or to include it in a grain salad. I find it dense on its own and like it most when mixed with other grains—a practical approach because it is so expensive. *Makes 2½ to 3 cups*

1 cup wild rice, rinsed and drained
2 teaspoons safflower or canola oil (optional, except for
     owners of jiggle-top cookers)
3 cups water or vegetable stock
¼ teaspoon salt, or to taste

Combine the rice, oil (if needed), stock, and salt in the cooker.

Lock the lid in place. Over high heat, bring to high pressure. Lower the heat just enough to maintain high pressure and cook for 22 minutes. Allow the pressure to come down naturally or use a quick-release method. Remove the lid, tilting it away from you to allow any excess steam to escape.

If more than half of the rice is not butterflied, return to high pressure for a few more minutes or replace (but do not lock) the lid and simmer until the rice is done.

Drain (reserve the liquid for stock, if desired) and return to the pot. Cover and let steam over low heat until dry. Fluff up the rice before serving.

TOASTED SESAME WILD RICE

*25 minutes high pressure, 10-minute natural
pressure release*

This recipe was developed by my friend Paul Hess, an inventive cook who is in love with the pressure cooker. Leftovers taste good at room temperature and make a tasty base for a grain salad. *Serves 4*

3 tablespoons unhulled sesame seeds

½ cup wild rice, rinsed and drained

1 cup long-grain brown rice, rinsed and drained

2¾ to 3 cups boiling water (use higher amount in jiggle-
   top cookers)

1 teaspoon salt, or to taste

. . . .

1 to 2 teaspoons toasted (Oriental) sesame oil (optional)

Toast the sesame seeds and wild rice in the bottom of the cooker over medium-high heat (no oil is needed), stirring constantly, until the sesame seeds begin to darken slightly and pop, 2 to 3 minutes. Stir in the brown rice, water (stand back to avoid sputtering), and salt.

Lock the lid in place. Set the cooker on a heated Flame Tamer. Over high heat, bring to high pressure. Lower the heat just enough to maintain high pressure and cook for 25 minutes. Allow the pressure to come down naturally for 10 minutes. Quick-release any remaining pressure. Remove the lid, tilting it away from you to allow any excess steam to escape.

Drizzle in the toasted sesame oil (if using) as you fluff up the rice before serving.

TIPS & TECHNIQUES

If the bottom of your cooker is thin, it's best to toast the sesame seeds and wild rice in a heavy cast-iron skillet.

VARIATION

For an elegant twist, toast black instead of the standard buff-colored sesame seeds. (The black seeds will not darken but will pop.)

Fall Harvest Rice Casserole

*25 minutes high pressure, 20-minute natural
pressure release*

Here's a mellow combination of brown and wild rices,
dried chestnuts, and celery. Scented with sage, the mixture is an ideal starch accompaniment in a holiday meal and
also works beautifully as a stuffing for baked squash. The pilaf
is steamed in a heatproof casserole lowered into the cooker.

I love cooking with dried chestnuts for the mild sweet-
smokiness they impart. They are available in most health food
stores and by mail order. *Serves 4*

½ cup dried chestnuts, soaked overnight in 2 cups water
    or speed-soaked (see page 16)

1 cup long-grain or basmati brown rice, rinsed and
    drained

½ cup wild rice, rinsed and drained

1 cup diced celery

2 tablespoons chopped celery leaves (optional)

1 large bay leaf

Generous teaspoon dried sage leaves

¾ teaspoon salt, or to taste

. . . .

¼ to ⅓ cup thinly sliced scallion greens

2 tablespoons minced fresh parsley

Strain the chestnuts, reserving the soaking water in a 2-
cup liquid measuring cup. Add enough water to the soaking
liquid to make a total of 2 cups. Discard any brown bits of
skin sticking to the chestnuts and coarsely chop them.

Place the chestnut soaking liquid, brown and wild rices,
chopped chestnuts, celery, celery leaves (if using), bay leaf,
sage, and salt in a 1½- or 2-quart casserole.

Place the rack and 2 cups of water in the cooker. Lower
the uncovered casserole onto the rack with the aid of a foil
strip (page 9).

Lock the lid in place. Over high heat, bring to high pressure. Lower the heat just enough to maintain high pressure
and cook for 25 minutes. Allow the pressure to come down
naturally for 20 minutes. Remove the lid, tilting it away from
you to allow any excess steam to escape.

Remove the casserole from the cooker with the aid of the foil strip. Remove the bay leaf and stir in the scallion greens and parsley as you fluff up the rice before serving.

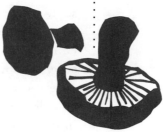

TRIPLE RICE BLEND WITH SHIITAKE MUSHROOMS

25 minutes high pressure, 10-minute natural pressure release

This recipe—using an appealing blend of Wehani, wild, and brown basmati rices—gets rave reviews in my household. It is prepared in a heatproof casserole rather than directly in the cooker.

This rice medley goes well with the Thai-Style Vegetable Curry as well as with an informal stir-fry. ***Serves 4***

Generous ½ cup (¾ ounce) dried shiitake mushrooms
2 cups boiling water
1 tablespoon tamari soy sauce, approximately
1 tablespoon finely minced fresh ginger
½ teaspoon finely minced garlic
¾ cup brown basmati rice, rinsed and drained
⅓ cup Wehani rice, rinsed and drained
⅓ cup wild rice, rinsed and drained

Place the mushrooms in a 4-cup measure or bowl and pour the boiling water on top. Cover with a plate or pot lid and let sit until the mushrooms are soft, 15 to 20 minutes.

Lift out the mushrooms with a slotted spoon. Slice off the stems and reserve them for stock. Cut the caps into slivers. Strain the mushroom soaking water directly into a 2-cup measure. Add water, if needed, to total 1¾ cups liquid. Stir in 1 tablespoon of the soy sauce.

continued

VARIATION

Use all brown rice instead of the blend.

Combine the soy sauce–mushroom stock plus the sliced mushrooms, ginger, garlic, and three types of rice in a 1½- or 2-quart casserole. Place the rack and 2 cups of boiling water in the cooker. Lower the uncovered casserole onto the rack with the aid of a foil strip (page 9).

Lock the lid in place. Over high heat, bring to high pressure. Lower the heat just enough to maintain high pressure and cook for 25 minutes. Allow the pressure to come down naturally for 10 minutes. Quick-release any remaining pressure. Remove the lid, tilting it away from you to allow any excess steam to escape. If the rice is not quite tender, replace (but do not lock) the lid and let it steam for a few more minutes in the residual heat.

When the rice is done, remove the casserole from the cooker with the aid of the foil strip. Fluff up the rice and evenly distribute the mushrooms before serving. Stir in extra soy sauce to taste, if desired.

White Rice Cooking Chart

For basic cooking instructions, see page 141.

Cups White Basmati or Extra-Long-Grain White Rice	Cups Liquid	Teaspoons Optional Salt	Yield in Cups
1	1½	½	3
1½	2¼	¾	4–4½
2	3	1	5½–6
3	4¼	1½	7½–8

NOTE: Do not cook more than 3 cups of dry white rice in a 6-quart cooker.

Basic White Basmati or Extra-Long-Grain Rice

3 minutes high pressure, 7-minute natural pressure release

I always have white basmati rice in the house, at the ready for a quick fix. Its delicate fragrance provides the ideal counterpart to the complex spicing of an Indian curry. For preparing larger quantities, check the white rice cooking chart (page 140). *Makes 2½ to 3 cups*

1½ cups water or vegetable stock

Flavoring options (page 118)

½ to ¾ teaspoon salt (less if using salted stock)

1 cup extra-long-grain or basmati white rice

Bring the water, flavorings as desired, and salt to the boil in the cooker. Stir in the rice.

Lock the lid in place. Over high heat, bring to high pressure. Lower the heat just enough to maintain high pressure and cook 3 for minutes. Allow the pressure to come down naturally for 7 minutes. Quick-release any remaining pressure. Remove the lid, tilting it away from you to allow any excess steam to escape. If the rice is not quite tender, replace (but do not lock) the lid and let it stream for another minute or two in the residual heat.

Fluff with a fork and adjust the seasonings before serving.

VARIATION

One of my favorite ways to dress up white rice is to cook it with 1 teaspoon of aniseed.

BASIC CASSEROLE-STEAMED WHITE RICE

5 minutes high pressure, 7- to 10-minute natural pressure release

Here is a handy way to pressure steam white rice in a heatproof casserole that you can bring right to the table. *Makes 2½ to 3 cups*

1 cup extra-long-grain or basmati white rice

1½ cups water

Flavoring options (page 118)

½ teaspoon salt, or to taste

Combine all the ingredients in a 1½- or 2-quart casserole. Place the rack and 2 cups of water in the cooker. Lower the uncovered casserole onto the rack with the aid of a foil strip (page 9).

Lock the lid in place. Over high heat, bring to high pressure. Lower the heat just enough to maintain high pressure and cook for 5 minutes. Allow the pressure to come down naturally, 7 to 10 minutes. Remove the lid, tilting it away from you to allow any excess steam to escape. If the rice is not quite tender, replace (but do not lock) the lid and let it steam for a few more minutes in the residual heat.

Remove the casserole from the cooker with the aid of the foil strip. Fluff up the rice before serving.

COCONUT RICE

3 minutes high pressure, 7-minute natural pressure release

Cooking plain white rice with dried coconut is a great way to dress it up quickly and easily. The coconut also provides some enjoyable crunch. I find that coconut rice goes especially well with Indian food, and I recommend preparing it with basmati white rice on such occasions. Don't forget to pass the chutney. *Serves 3 to 4*

> 2¼ cups water
>
> ½ cup dried, grated, unsweetened coconut
>
> 1 cup extra-long-grain or basmati white rice
>
> ¾ teaspoon salt, or to taste

Bring the water to the boil in the cooker. Add the coconut, rice, and salt.

Lock the lid in place. If using a jiggle-top cooker, set it on a heated Flame Tamer. Over high heat, bring to high pressure. Lower the heat just enough to maintain high pressure and cook for 3 minutes. Allow the pressure to come down naturally for 7 minutes. Quick-release any remaining pressure. Remove the lid, tilting it away from you to allow any excess steam to escape.

Stir well to distribute the coconut as you fluff up the rice before serving.

Cook the rice with any one of the following:

> 2 to 3 tablespoons dried currants
>
> 1 tablespoon finely chopped fresh ginger
>
> ¾ teaspoon ground turmeric (colors the rice yellow)

TRIPLE FENNEL RICE

3 minutes high pressure, 7-minute natural pressure release

A sophisticated preparation guaranteed to surprise and delight. In this dish, the subtle anise flavor of chopped fennel is enhanced by the addition of fennel seeds. Snipped fennel fronds add bright flecks of green to the finished dish.

Also very good when served as a room-temperature rice salad, with an extra drizzle of lemon on top. Fennel rice goes well with Mediterranean as well as Indian menus. *Serves 4*

1 large fennel bulb (about 1¼ pounds pretrimmed weight), including feathery fronds

1 tablespoon safflower or canola oil

¼ cup finely minced shallots, leeks (white and light green parts), or onions

1 cup extra-long-grain or basmati white rice

1½ cups boiling water

1 tablespoon tomato paste

¾ teaspoon salt, or to taste

1 small carrot, cut into matchsticks or halved lengthwise and thinly sliced

¾ to 1 teaspoon whole fennel seeds

. . . .

1 tablespoon freshly squeezed lemon juice (optional)

Slice off the root end and stalks from the fennel bulb. Remove any blemished outer layers. Cut the bulb in half from top to root. Cut out the hard core. Place each half cut side down and cut into ½-inch slices. Cut larger slices in half. (You should have 3 generous cups, loosely packed.) Set aside. Cut the fronds from the stalks; rinse and chop the fronds and set them aside. (Reserve the stalks for stock, if desired.)

Heat the oil in the cooker. Cook the shallots over medium-high heat, stirring frequently, for 1 minute. Add the rice, water (stand back to avoid sputtering oil), tomato paste, salt, about two thirds of the chopped fennel bulb, the carrot, and fennel seeds.

Lock the lid in place. Over high heat, bring to high pressure. Lower the heat just enough to maintain high pressure and cook for 3 minutes. Allow the pressure to come down naturally for 7 minutes. Quick-release any remaining pressure.

Because fennel has a very delicate flavor (even more so once cooked), I like to hold 1 cup aside and stir it in raw. In addition to intensifying the taste, it contributes a nice textural variation.

Remove the lid, tilting it away from you to allow any excess steam to escape. If the rice is not quite tender, replace (but do not lock) the lid and let it steam for a few more minutes in the residual heat.

Fluff up the rice as you evenly distribute the cooked fennel and stir in the remaining (raw) chopped fennel bulb and the fennel fronds before serving. Add lemon juice to taste, if desired.

CHUTNEY RICE

3 minutes high pressure, 7-minute natural pressure release

H ere's an interesting and festive way to prepare white rice. You can use Fruity Coconut Chutney or a favorite storebought mango chutney. Needless to say, this dish goes well with Indian food. *Serves 3 to 4*

TIPS & TECHNIQUES

If using storebought chutney, make sure it is a mild one.

1 tablespoon canola or safflower oil
1 teaspoon minced garlic
½ cup finely chopped red onion
1¾ cups water
½ cup finely chopped Fruity Coconut Chutney
    (page 235) or storebought chutney
½ teaspoon salt, or to taste
Pinch of cayenne or crushed red pepper flakes
    (optional)
1 cup extra-long-grain or basmati white rice

Heat the oil in the cooker. Cook the garlic and onion over medium-high heat, stirring frequently, for 1 minute. Add the water (stand back to avoid sputtering oil), chutney, salt, and cayenne (if using). Stir well to blend. Bring the mixture to the boil, then stir in the rice.

Lock the lid in place. Over high heat, bring to high pressure. Lower the heat just enough to maintain high pressure and cook for 3 minutes. Allow the pressure to come down naturally for 7 minutes. Quick-release any remaining pressure. Remove the lid, tilting it away from you to allow any excess steam to escape. If the rice is not quite tender, replace (but do not lock) the lid and allow it to steam for a few more minutes in the residual heat.

Stir well before serving.

Greek Cabbage and Rice Pilaf

3 minutes high pressure, 7-minute natural pressure release

TIPS & TECHNIQUES

I've used less than the usual amount of water because the cabbage and tomatoes give off so much liquid during cooking.

VARIATION

Diane Kochilas's recipe calls for cooking the rice with ½ cup of finely chopped blanched almonds. This would add a nice richness and crunch. If adding the nuts, you might want to eliminate the lemon juice and parsley.

This dish comes from Thrace in the northeastern corner of Greece and—with its raisins and cinnamon—reminds me of recipes from the Middle Ages, when the Arab influence on the culinary arts was very strong.

I adapted this recipe from Diane Kochilas's fine cookbook, *The Food and Wine of Greece* (St. Martin's, 1990). Serve it either as an entree or as a side dish. Baby Limas with Spinach and Dill or Crimson Bean Salad would make a good accompaniment. *Serves 4 to 6*

1 tablespoon olive oil
1 cup finely chopped onions
1½ cups extra-long-grain or basmati white rice
½ pound green cabbage, thinly shredded (3 cups)
2 cups boiling water
1 cup finely chopped fresh or canned (drained) plum
    tomatoes
⅓ cup dried currants or raisins
1 teaspoon salt, or to taste
1 teaspoon dried oregano leaves
¼ teaspoon ground cinnamon

1 to 2 tablespoons freshly squeezed lemon juice
2 tablespoons minced fresh parsley

Heat the oil in the cooker. Cook the onions over medium-high heat, stirring frequently, for 1 minute. Stir in the rice and then the cabbage. Add the water (stand back to avoid sputtering oil), tomatoes, currants, salt, oregano, and cinnamon.

Lock the lid in place. Over high heat, bring to high pressure. Lower the heat just enough to maintain high pressure and cook for 3 minutes. Allow the pressure to come down naturally for 7 minutes. Quick-release any remaining pressure. Remove the lid, tilting it away from you to allow any excess steam to escape. If the rice is not quite tender, replace (but do not lock) the lid and let it steam for a few more minutes in the residual heat.

Stir in lemon juice to taste and the parsley as you fluff up the rice and thoroughly distribute all the ingredients before serving.

CITRUS RICE WITH CURRANTS

3 minutes high pressure, 7-minute natural pressure release

The pale burnished color of this aromatic rice dish gives a hint of the orange juice and peel used to flavor it. Citrus rice goes particularly well with Mediterranean dishes and creates a nice trio with Ratatouille Soup and Warm White Bean Vinaigrette. This pilaf is good both hot and at room temperature. *Serves 4*

1 tablespoon olive oil

½ cup finely chopped leeks (white part only) or onions

1½ cups extra-long-grain or basmati white rice

1¾ cups boiling water

½ cup orange juice

¾ teaspoon salt, or to taste

¼ cup dried currants or raisins

. . . .

2 teaspoons freshly grated orange peel (page 23)

2 tablespoons minced fresh parsley

Heat the oil in the cooker. Cook the leeks over medium-high heat, stirring frequently, for 1 minute. Stir in the rice, water (stand back to avoid sputtering oil), orange juice, salt, and currants.

Lock the lid in place. Over high heat, bring to high pressure. Lower the heat just enough to maintain high pressure and cook for 3 minutes. Allow the pressure to come down naturally for 7 minutes. Quick-release any remaining pressure. Remove the lid, tilting it away from you to allow any excess steam to escape.

As you fluff up the rice, stir in the orange peel. Garnish with parsley just before serving.

TIPS & TECHNIQUES
. . . .
Remove the peel from the orange (page 22) before you squeeze out the juice. Two juice oranges will yield approximately ½ cup of juice.

VARIATION
. . . .
Substitute finely chopped dried apricots or pitted prunes for the currants.

PAELLA VEGETARIANA

3 minutes high pressure, 7-minute natural pressure release, 1 to 2 minutes standing

TIPS & TECHNIQUES

This recipe calls for less than the usual amount of water for cooking 2 cups of rice since the tomatoes and other vegetables give up liquid during cooking.

If using canned tomatoes, you can use the drained juice to replace an equivalent amount of water.

According to Penelope Casas, author of *The Foods and Wines of Spain* (Knopf, 1982), vegetable paella is associated with Murcia, a region in southeast Spain famous for its fine produce.

Using some of the vegetables she suggests, I have created this pressure-cooker version, which offers a very elegant and colorful main dish that is ideal for entertaining.

Although these quantities make six average portions, you may find—as one friend did—that there were no leftovers when she had four to dinner. It's that good!

Serve the paella preceded by a small serving of soup and accompanied by a large tossed salad. Leftovers are great at room temperature, freshened up with a sprinkling of fresh lemon juice or sherry wine vinegar. ***Serves 6***

1 tablespoon olive oil

1 tablespoon minced garlic

1 cup coarsely chopped onions

2 cups extra-long-grain or basmati white rice

2¼ cups boiling water

1½ cups coarsely chopped fresh or canned (drained) plum tomatoes

1 large carrot, halved lengthwise and cut into ¼-inch slices

One 10-ounce package frozen artichoke hearts (do not defrost)

1¼ teaspoons salt, or to taste

Generous ¼ teaspoon saffron threads

. . . .

1 large red bell pepper, roasted (page 17), seeded, and diced

1 cup cooked chickpeas

1½ cups fresh cooked or frozen (defrosted) peas

¼ cup minced fresh parsley

½ cup blanched, slivered almonds (toasted are nice)

Heat the oil in the cooker. Cook the garlic and onion over medium-high heat, stirring continuously, for 1 minute. Stir in the rice, water (stand back to avoid sputtering oil), tomatoes, carrot, artichoke hearts (they may remain in a frozen block), salt, and saffron.

Lock the lid in place. If using a jiggle-top cooker, set on a heated Flame Tamer. Over high heat, bring to high pressure. Lower the heat just enough to maintain high pressure and cook for 3 minutes. Allow the pressure to come down naturally for 7 minutes. Quick-release any remaining pressure. Remove the lid, tilting it away from you to allow any excess steam to escape.

Stir in the red bell pepper, chickpeas, and peas, taking care to evenly distribute all of the ingredients. Replace (but do not lock) the lid for a minute or two until the paella is heated through, or set the cooker over a very low flame if there is not enough residual steam to reheat. Stir in the parsley and almonds just before serving.

RISOTTO

More than any other dish, it's the creation of a 5-minute risotto that catapults the pressure cooker into the 1990s kitchen. Who can resist loving a pot that makes it possible to enjoy such an elegant, sophisticated, healthy dish at a moment's notice?

It is perhaps a little-known fact that many Italians use a pressure cooker for preparing risotto. They are aware that there is no compromise of taste or texture. See for yourself if you don't agree.

Unless otherwise noted, these risottos are substantial enough to serve as entrees. A large green or tri-colored salad makes a good accompaniment.

General Tips and Techniques

Risotto is traditionally made with a plump, medium-grained white rice. The most commonly available is called arborio, and it is sold in gourmet shops and by mail order. When arborio is cooked in a generous quantity of stock, a starch is released, creating a luscious creamy sauce. As with pasta, it's best to prepare risotto just before it is served.

When making risotto, do not rinse the rice. In this way, there is no loss of starch.

The pressure is always quick-released to avoid overcooking the rice.

Use the basic formula of 3½ to 4 cups of stock to 1½ cups of arborio to translate your favorite recipes to pressure-cooked versions, or to come up with your own renditions.

I don't hesitate to use instant stock if I have no homemade stock on hand. (Vogue Vege Base is a good brand. If your local health food store doesn't carry it, check Mail-Order Sources at the back of the book.)

Risotto is traditionally finished off by stirring in grated Parmesan cheese, which adds saltiness and sharpens all of the other flavors. For a non-dairy version, both balsamic vinegar and freshly squeezed lemon juice make excellent substitutes. Taste and gradually add one or the other until you achieve a good balance of flavors.

Leftover risotto can be shaped into patties and pan-fried or reheated on an oiled baking sheet in a moderate oven.

SAFFRON RISOTTO WITH VEGETABLES DU JOUR

5 minutes high pressure

Here is a good basic risotto that provides considerable versatility. The saffron adds a beautiful golden color, which acts as a backdrop for any cooked vegetable in season. Nice choices are peas, asparagus, and broccoli. ***Serves 6 as an appetizer, 4 as a main dish***

1 tablespoon olive oil

½ cup finely chopped leeks (white and light green
    parts), shallots, or onions

1½ cups arborio rice

3½ to 4 cups vegetable stock

Generous ¼ teaspoon saffron threads

1 teaspoon salt, or to taste

. . . .

1½ to 2 cups chopped cooked vegetables

2 to 3 tablespoons minced fresh parsley

½ cup freshly grated Parmesan cheese or 1 to 3
    tablespoons freshly squeezed lemon juice or 1 to 3
    teaspoons balsamic vinegar

Freshly ground pepper to taste

Heat the oil in the cooker. Cook the leeks over medium-high heat, stirring frequently, for 1 minute. Add in the rice, stirring to coat with the oil. Add 3½ cups of the stock (stand back to avoid sputtering oil), the saffron, and salt.

Lock the lid in place. Over high heat, bring to high pressure. Lower the heat just enough to maintain high pressure and cook for 5 minutes. Reduce the pressure with a quick-release method. Remove the lid, tilting it away from you to allow any excess steam to escape.

Stir in the vegetables, parsley, and Parmesan (if using). If the risotto isn't creamy, stir in a bit more stock. Cook over medium heat, stirring constantly, until the rice achieves the desired consistency (it should be tender but chewy) and the vegetables are thoroughly heated. Stir in lemon juice or vinegar (if using) and pepper. Serve immediately in shallow soup bowls.

VARIATIONS

It's fun to combine vegetables. I've done ¾ cup each cooked limas and corn and 1 cup each peas and carrots.

   Another nice addition for color and flavor is ½ cup chopped roasted red bell pepper.

Risotto with Broccoli Rabe and White Beans

5 minutes high pressure

VARIATION

Substitute steamed broccoli for the broccoli rabe.

Broccoli rabe is a most delicious green whose small buds resemble broccoli florets. It is much loved here and in Italy for its slightly bitter edge—a fine contrast to the mild taste of rice. In this recipe, the broccoli rabe is first steamed and then stirred into the cooked risotto. ***Serves 6 as an appetizer, 4 as a main dish***

1 to 1¼ pounds broccoli rabe

1 tablespoon olive oil

2½ teaspoons finely minced garlic

1 cup finely chopped leeks (white and light green parts) or onions

1 small red bell pepper, seeded and coarsely chopped

1½ cups arborio rice

3½ to 4 cups vegetable stock

1 teaspoon salt (less if using salted stock)

1½ cups firm-cooked white beans, such as cannellini or navy (pea) beans

Freshly ground pepper to taste

Freshly squeezed lemon juice or balsamic vinegar or freshly grated Parmesan cheese to taste

Trim off the browned, thick stem ends of the broccoli rabe. Cut the stems into 1-inch pieces and coarsely chop the leaves and florets. Bring about 1 inch of water to the boil in the cooker. Place the chopped stems in the water, cover (but do not lock the lid), and steam for 1 minute. Add the leaves and florets and steam, covered, until the broccoli rabe is tender, about 2 more minutes. Drain and refresh under cold running water. Set aside. (You may reserve the cooking liquid to use as part of the vegetable stock.) Rinse and dry the cooker.

Heat the oil in the cooker. Cook the garlic over medium-high heat, stirring constantly, just until it begins to brown. Immediately add the leeks and red bell pepper and continue to cook, stirring frequently, for another 2 minutes. Add in the rice, stirring to coat thoroughly with the oil. Stir in 3½ cups of the stock (stand back to avoid sputtering oil) and the salt.

Lock the lid in place. Over high heat, bring to high pressure. Lower the heat just enough to maintain high pressure and cook for 5 minutes. Reduce the pressure with a quick-release method. Remove the lid, tilting it away from you to allow any excess steam to escape.

Stir in the reserved broccoli rabe, the beans, and pepper. If the risotto isn't creamy, stir in a bit more stock. Cook over medium heat, stirring constantly, until the rice achieves the desired consistency (it should be tender but chewy) and the ingredients are thoroughly heated. Season to taste with lemon juice, vinegar, or grated Parmesan. (Alternatively, pass the grated Parmesan on the side.) Serve immediately in shallow soup bowls.

Risotto with Porcini

5 minutes high pressure

Porcini are expensive mushrooms, but they add an intense flavor uniquely their own. Here is a simple risotto worthy of a fine feast. ***Serves 6 as an appetizer, 4 as a main dish***

¾ ounce dried porcini mushrooms, quickly rinsed

1½ cups boiling water

2 to 2½ cups vegetable stock

1 tablespoon olive oil

1½ cups thinly sliced leeks (white and light green parts)

1 teaspoon finely minced garlic

½ teaspoon dried oregano leaves

1½ cups arborio rice

1 teaspoon salt, or to taste (less if using salted stock)

. . . .

2 tablespoons minced fresh parsley

⅓ to ½ cup freshly grated Parmesan cheese, or freshly squeezed lemon juice or balsamic vinegar to taste

Place the porcini in a 2-cup liquid measuring cup. Pour the boiling water on top, cover with a small plate, and set aside for 10 minutes.

Lift the porcini out with a slotted spoon. Carefully leaving behind any dirt that has settled to the bottom, pour the water through a fine-meshed strainer into a 4-cup liquid measuring cup. Add enough vegetable stock to the mushroom stock to measure 3½ cups. Rinse the mushrooms carefully to remove any grit. Cut off and discard any tough bits. Coarsely chop the mushrooms and set aside.

Heat the oil in the cooker. Cook the leeks and garlic over medium-high heat, stirring frequently, for 1 minute. Add the oregano and rice, stirring to coat the rice with the oil. Stir in the reserved porcini and porcini–vegetable stock mixture (stand back to avoid sputtering oil) and the salt.

Lock the lid in place. Over high heat, bring to high pressure. Lower the heat just enough to maintain high pressure and cook for 5 minutes. Reduce the pressure with a quick-release method. Remove the lid, tilting it away from you to allow any excess steam to escape.

Stir in the parsley and Parmesan cheese (if using). If the risotto isn't creamy, stir in a bit more stock. Cook over medium heat, stirring constantly, until the rice achieves the desired consistency (it should be tender but chewy) and the ingredients are thoroughly heated. Stir in lemon juice or vinegar to taste (if using) just before serving. Serve immediately in shallow soup bowls.

RISOTTO WITH KALE AND GREMOLATA

4 minutes high pressure, 4 to 5 minutes additional cooking

The talented Connecticut caterer Carole Peck suggested this great combination of tastes and textures during an animated conversation about risotto. Gremolata—a mixture of minced parsley, garlic, and lemon peel—is traditionally added at the end. My use of cooked garlic is a departure from the classic approach. *Serves 6 as an appetizer, 4 as a main dish*

1 tablespoon olive oil
1 to 2 tablespoons coarsely chopped garlic
1 cup finely chopped onions
1½ cups arborio rice
3½ to 4½ cups vegetable stock
¾ teaspoon salt, or to taste

. . . .

3 cups tightly packed finely chopped uncooked kale
    leaves (about ¼ pound)
2 tablespoons grated lemon peel (page 22)
¼ cup minced fresh parsley
Freshly ground pepper to taste
Freshly grated Parmesan cheese or freshly squeezed
    lemon juice to taste

continued

When chopping the kale leaves, cut away and discard any ribs thicker than ¼ inch in diameter.

Heat the oil in the cooker. Cook the garlic over medium-high heat, stirring constantly, until golden brown, then immediately add the onions and continue cooking, stirring frequently, for 1 minute. Add the rice, stirring to coat with the oil, then add 3½ cups of the vegetable stock (stand back to avoid sputtering oil) and the salt.

Lock the lid in place. Over high heat, bring to high pressure. Lower the heat just enough to maintain high pressure and cook for 4 minutes. Reduce the pressure with a quick-release method. Remove the lid, tilting it away from you to allow any excess steam to escape.

Stir in the kale and continue to cook uncovered, over medium heat, stirring constantly, until the kale is done and the rice is tender but still chewy, 4 to 5 minutes. If the risotto isn't creamy, stir in a bit more stock as the kale cooks.

Just before serving, stir in the lemon peel, parsley, and pepper. If using Parmesan cheese, pass it in a bowl on the side. If using lemon juice, stir in just enough to punch up the flavors. Serve immediately in shallow soup bowls.

Risotto with Winter Squash

5 minutes high pressure

In this luscious risotto, the squash cooks down into a sweet purée that gives the rice a light amber color. The sage provides a tantalizing herbal backdrop.

If you're not using Parmesan cheese, you'll probably want a bit more salt or a dash of balsamic vinegar to sharpen the flavors. *Serves 6 as an appetizer, 4 as a main dish*

1 tablespoon olive oil

1 cup finely chopped shallots or onions

Generous teaspoon dried sage leaves

1½ cups arborio rice

3½ to 4 cups vegetable stock

1 pound butternut squash, peeled, seeded, and cut into
   1-inch chunks (about 3 cups)

1 teaspoon salt, or to taste

. . . .

¼ cup freshly grated Parmesan cheese (optional) or
   balsamic vinegar to taste

Freshly grated pepper to taste

2 tablespoons minced fresh parsley

Heat the oil in the cooker. Cook the shallots over medium-high heat, stirring frequently, for 1 minute. Add the sage and rice, stirring to coat the rice with the oil. Stir in 3½ cups of the stock (stand back to avoid sputtering oil) and bring to the boil. Add the squash and salt.

Lock the lid in place. Over high heat, bring to high pressure. Lower the heat just enough to maintain high pressure and cook for 5 minutes. Reduce the pressure with a quick-release method. Remove the lid, tilting it away from you to allow any excess steam to escape.

If the risotto isn't creamy, stir in a bit more stock. Cook over medium heat, stirring constantly, until the rice achieves the desired consistency (it should be tender but chewy) and the squash is partially puréed. Stir in the Parmesan (if using) or vinegar, pepper, and parsley. Serve immediately in shallow soup bowls.

VARIATION

I have tried this recipe with unpeeled organic kabocha and delicata squashes with fine results. The skin becomes fork-tender and adds delightful flecks of color.

GREEN RISOTTO

5 minutes high pressure, 1 to 2 minutes cooking

It's nice to make this simple risotto when basil is in season. Otherwise, cook the rice with 2 teaspoons of dried dill for a quick and economical grain dish. This risotto isn't quite substantial enough to serve as an entree. *Serves 6 as an appetizer or side dish*

1 tablespoon olive oil
1 teaspoon finely minced garlic
½ cup finely chopped onion
1½ cups arborio rice
3½ to 4 cups vegetable stock

. . . .

10 ounces frozen (defrosted) chopped spinach
½ cup loosely packed chopped fresh basil leaves
Salt and freshly ground pepper to taste
Freshly grated Parmesan cheese or freshly squeezed
    lemon juice to taste

Heat the oil in the cooker. Cook the garlic over medium-high heat, stirring constantly, until golden brown, then immediately add the onion and continue cooking, stirring frequently, for 1 minute. Add the rice, stirring to coat with the oil, then add 3½ cups of the vegetable stock (stand back to avoid sputtering oil).

Lock the lid in place. Over high heat, bring to high pressure. Lower the heat just enough to maintain high pressure and cook for 5 minutes. Reduce the pressure with a quick-release method. Remove the lid, tilting it away from you to allow any excess steam to escape.

Stir in the spinach and continue to cook uncovered, over medium heat, stirring constantly, until the spinach is heated and the rice is tender but still chewy, 1 to 2 minutes. If the risotto isn't creamy, stir in a bit more stock as you add the basil, salt to taste, and lots of freshly ground pepper.

If using Parmesan cheese, pass it in a bowl on the side. If using lemon juice, stir in just enough to punch up the flavors. Serve immediately in shallow soup bowls.

VARIATIONS

Add ¼ cup chopped oil-packed sun-dried tomatoes or pitted black olives when you add the spinach.

Stir in ¼ cup toasted pine nuts or ⅓ cup coarsely chopped walnuts at the end.

OTHER GRAINS

In this section, you'll find recipes for a variety of grains beyond the rice family. For General Tips and Techniques on selecting, storing, and cooking grains, see pages 115-119.

Grain Cooking Times at a Glance

For basic cooking instructions, see pages 115 – 119 and check Index under individual listings.

Grain (1 Cup)	Cups Liquid	Teaspoons Optional Salt	Minutes Under High Pressure	Yield in Cups
Amaranth	1½–1¾**	½–1*	4 plus 10-minute npr§	2
Barley (hulled)	3†	½–1	35–45	3½–4
Barley (pearl)	3†	½–1	18–20	3½
Buckwheat	1¾†	½–1	3 plus 7-minute npr§	2
Bulgur	1½	½–1	5 plus 10-minute npr§	3
Job's Tears‡	2½	½–1	16 plus 10-minute npr§	3
Kamut	3†	½–1*	35–45	2¾
Millet‡	1¾–2**	½–1	10 plus 10-minute npr§	3½–4
Oats (whole groats)	3†	½–1	25–30	2–2½
Quinoa	1½	½–1	1 plus 10-minute npr§	3–3½
Rye berries	3	½–1	25–30	2½
Spelt	3	½–1*	35–45	2¼
Triticale	3	½–1*	35–45	2–2½
Wheat berries	3	½–1*	35–45	2¼
Wild rice	3	¼	22–28	2½–3

*To ensure proper absorption of water, add salt after cooking.
†Add 1 tablespoon oil to control foaming action.
‡Toast before boiling (page 167).
§npr = natural pressure release
**Use higher amount in jiggle-top cookers.

BASIC GRAINS

25 to 45 minutes high pressure

TIPS & TECHNIQUES
. . . .

I find the most efficient way to cook whole grains is to use an abundance of water and then drain off the excess, which can be reserved for stock.

Some grains do not cook properly if salt is added to the water. Please refer to the chart (page 159) for specifics.

To save time and energy, soak the grains overnight. You may cook them right in the soaking water. Reduce cooking time by 40 percent.

If using a jiggle-top cooker, always use 1 tablespoon of oil per cup of dry grain to control foaming action. If using a second-generation cooker, you may consider this optional.

The following recipe may be used for cooking whole-grain wheat (wheat berries), rye, triticale, spelt, kamut, hulled and pearl barley, and oat groats. Check the grain cooking chart (page 159) for precise timing on these and other grains.

When testing for doneness, keep in mind that most whole grains remain a bit chewy even when thoroughly cooked.

Yield: see Grain Cooking Times at a Glance, page 159

1 cup whole grains, rinsed and drained

3 cups water

Flavoring options (page 118)

1 tablespoon safflower or canola oil (to control foaming)

Place the grains, water, flavorings as desired, and oil in the cooker.

Lock the lid in place. Over high heat, bring to high pressure. Lower the heat just enough to maintain high pressure and cook for the number of minutes indicated on the chart (page 159). Quick-release the pressure by placing the cooker under cold running water. Remove the lid, tilting it away from you to allow any excess steam to escape. If the grains are not quite tender, replace (but do not lock) the lid and simmer until they are done.

Drain, reserving the cooking liquid for stock, if desired. Fluff up the grains before serving.

BASIC BULGUR

5 minutes high pressure, 10-minute natural pressure release

Bulgur is a refined form of the wheat berry that works nicely as a rice substitute. Although it comes in numerous grades, I prefer the medium or coarse bulgur for its hearty texture.

The best way I've found to pressure cook bulgur is in a 1½- or 2-quart heatproof casserole. ***Makes about 4 cups***

1½ **cups coarse bulgur, rinsed and drained**

2 **cups boiling water or vegetable stock**

½ **teaspoon salt, or to taste**

Flavoring options (page 118)

Place the bulgur in a 1½- or 2-quart casserole. Add the boiling water and stir in the salt and flavorings as desired.

Place the rack and 2 cups of water in the cooker. Lower the uncovered casserole onto the rack with the aid of a foil strip (page 9).

Lock the lid in place. Over high heat, bring to high pressure. Lower the heat just enough to maintain high pressure and cook for 5 minutes. Allow the pressure to come down naturally for 10 minutes. Quick-release any remaining pressure. Remove the lid, tilting it away from you to allow any excess steam to escape.

Taste the bulgur, and if it is not sufficiently tender, quickly stir the grain, adding a few tablespoons of boiling water if the mixture seems dry. Replace (but do not lock) the lid and continue to steam for a few more minutes in the residual heat.

Remove the casserole from the cooker with the aid of the foil strip. If the bulgur has not absorbed all of the water, drain it. Fluff up the grains with a fork before serving.

TIPS & TECHNIQUES

You can quickly dress up plain bulgur by tossing it with a few tablespoons of finely chopped fresh herbs, toasted pine nuts, or minced dried fruit.

Middle Eastern Potato Salad with Bulgur

5 minutes high pressure

This hearty salad can be a main dish (accompanied by a steamed green vegetable and a green salad), or you can serve it as a substitute for plain potatoes. I like it best when it is served just slightly warm or at room temperature. Finger-lings are my potato of choice for this dish. ***Serves 3 as a main dish, 4 to 5 as a side dish***

1¼ to 1½ cups water (use higher amount in jiggle-top cookers)

½ cup medium or coarse bulgur, rinsed and drained

2 teaspoons minced garlic

1½ teaspoons dried oregano or marjoram leaves

2 teaspoons dried mint leaves

1 pound thin-skinned potatoes, scrubbed and cut into 1-inch chunks

. . . .

¼ to ⅓ cup finely chopped red onion

1 to 2 tablespoons full-flavored olive oil

2 to 3 tablespoons freshly squeezed lemon juice

Salt to taste

½ cup minced fresh parsley

Place the water and bulgur in the cooker and bring to the boil. Stir in the garlic, oregano, mint, and potatoes.

Lock the lid in place. Set the cooker on a heated Flame Tamer. Over high heat, bring to high pressure. Lower the heat just enough to maintain high pressure and cook for 5 minutes. Reduce the pressure with a quick-release method. Remove the lid, tilting it away from you to allow any excess steam to es-cape. If the bulgur is not tender, replace (but do not lock) the lid and continue to steam for a few more minutes in the residual heat. (Stir in a few tablespoons of boiling water if the mixture seems dry.)

Stir in the onion, olive oil, and enough lemon juice to pro-vide a sharp edge. Add salt to taste. Stir in the parsley just before serving.

If you want the parsley to retain its bright green color, let the mixture cool slightly before adding it.

If there is any excess liquid after the bulgur is cooked, either drain it off or allow the mixture to stand, partially covered, until it is absorbed.

VARIATION

Add ⅓ cup chopped pimiento-stuffed green olives with the red onion.

BULGUR CASSEROLE WITH WINTER VEGETABLES

10 minutes high pressure, 10-minute natural pressure release

Here is a delicious one-pot meal—hearty, nutritious, colorful, and ideal for cold-weather appetites. Mound leftovers into the cavity of baked acorn squash.

For a bit of crunch and color, I hold aside a cupful of red cabbage and stir it into the cooked bulgur. ***Serves 6***

2 cups boiling water

2 tablespoons tomato paste

1½ cups coarse bulgur, rinsed and drained

2 teaspoons minced garlic

1 cup coarsely chopped onions

2 teaspoons dried winter savory or oregano leaves

½ teaspoon celery seeds

1 large bay leaf

1 teaspoon salt, or to taste

1½ pounds (2 medium) white turnips, peeled, halved, and cut into ½-inch slices

½ pound winter squash, peeled, seeded, and cut into 1-inch chunks

2 medium carrots, halved lengthwise and cut into ¾-inch dice

½ pound red cabbage, cored and finely shredded

. . . .

⅓ cup minced fresh parsley

Freshly ground pepper to taste

1 to 2 tablespoons freshly squeezed lemon juice (optional)

In a 2-quart heatproof casserole, blend the water and tomato paste. Stir in the bulgur, garlic, onions, winter savory, celery seeds, bay leaf, and salt. On top place the turnips, squash, carrots, and all but 1 cup of the cabbage.

Place the rack and 2 cups of water in the cooker. Lower the uncovered casserole onto the rack with the aid of a foil strip (page 9).

continued

Stir in 1 to 2 tablespoons of walnut, hazelnut, or olive oil at the end.

Lock the lid in place. Over high heat, bring to high pressure. Lower the heat just enough to maintain high pressure and cook for 10 minutes. Allow the pressure to come down naturally for 10 minutes. Quick-release any remaining pressure. Remove the lid, tilting it away from you to allow any excess steam to escape.

Taste the bulgur and vegetables, and if anything is not sufficiently tender, replace (but do not lock) the lid and continue to steam for a few more minutes in the residual heat.

Remove the casserole from the cooker with the aid of the foil strip. Transfer the mixture to a large serving bowl. Remove the bay leaf and stir in the reserved raw cabbage, parsley, pepper, and lemon juice, if desired, to sharpen the flavors.

MEDITERRANEAN VEGETABLE COUSCOUS

1 minute high pressure, 5 minutes standing

In this recipe, the vegetables are quickly pressure-cooked; then the couscous is added and left to steam for 5 minutes. There's a fair amount of chopping involved (so sharpen your chef's knife or get out the food processor), but after that it's a breeze. Any combination of vegetables can be used, so please consider this recipe a rule of thumb (see Tips).

This is a substantial dish that requires little more than a salad to make a complete meal. Leftovers are terrific at room temperature when drizzled with a bit of olive oil and lemon juice and garnished with cornichons. *Serves 6*

1 to 2 tablespoons olive oil

2 teaspoons minced garlic

1 cup coarsely chopped onions

1½ cups boiling vegetable stock or water

1 small fennel bulb, trimmed and cut into ½-inch strips
    (about 2½ cups; chop and reserve the fronds), or
      2 large celery ribs, halved lengthwise and cut into
      ½-inch slices, plus ½ teaspoon whole fennel seeds

1 large red bell pepper, seeded and cut into thin strips

When experimenting with different ingredients, be conscious of their water content. For example: onions, mushrooms, zucchini, and tomatoes all release considerable liquid, so I use 1½ cups of water for 1½ cups of couscous, although the ratio normally would be 2 to 1.

Dense vegetables like winter squash or parsnips release hardly any liquid, so you would need to add about 2¼ cups of water.

If I were adding dried ingredients, such as dried mushrooms or raisins, I'd have to take into account that they would absorb some liquid.

1 large carrot, halved lengthwise and cut into ½-inch
    slices

¼ pound medium fresh mushrooms, quartered or sliced

2 medium zucchini, cut into 1-inch slices

1½ cups coarsely chopped fresh or canned (drained)
    plum tomatoes

⅓ cup pitted oil-cured black olives

1½ teaspoons dried basil leaves

1½ teaspoons dried oregano leaves

1 teaspoon salt, or to taste

¼ teaspoon ground cinnamon

⅛ teaspoon freshly ground pepper

. . . .

1 to 3 tablespoons balsamic vinegar

1½ cups whole-wheat couscous

¼ cup minced fresh basil or parsley

Heat 1 tablespoon of the oil in the cooker. Cook the garlic over medium-high heat, stirring constantly, just until browned. Immediately add the onions and cook, stirring frequently, for 1 minute. Add the stock (stand back to avoid sputtering oil), fennel bulb, red bell pepper, carrot, mushrooms, zucchini, tomatoes, olives, basil, oregano, salt, cinnamon, and pepper.

Lock the lid in place. Over high heat, bring to high pressure. Lower the heat just enough to maintain high pressure and cook for 1 minute. Reduce the pressure with a quick-release method. Remove the lid, tilting it away from you to allow any excess steam to escape.

Stir in 1 tablespoon of balsamic vinegar and the couscous. Immediately replace (but do not lock) the lid and allow the mixture to steam in the residual heat until the couscous is tender, about 5 minutes.

Stir well to distribute the ingredients as you add the fennel fronds, basil, additional tablespoon of olive oil (if using), and just enough additional balsamic vinegar to make the flavors pop. If desired, you may also add a bit more salt.

Use freshly squeezed lemon juice instead of balsamic vinegar.

Stir in 2 tablespoons capers when you add the couscous.

TIPS & TECHNIQUES
. . . .
Harissa is available in
international groceries and
gourmet specialty shops.
Take a tiny taste of it
before adding, to
determine just how "hot"
it is.

SQUASH COUSCOUS WITH DATES

3 minutes high pressure, 5 minutes standing

This delicious and very simple recipe was inspired by a recent trip to Tunisia, where couscous and dates are staple foods. *Tabil*, a combination of ground coriander and caraway seeds, is a typical seasoning in that part of the world. I love the sweet, nutty taste of coriander seeds and use them in abundance in this recipe. What a discovery!

Serve this dish with a cooling cucumber salad and a steamed green vegetable. ***Serves 4 to 6***

1 tablespoon olive or canola oil

1 cup coarsely chopped onions

1 teaspoon minced garlic

2½ cups water

2 tablespoons tomato paste

1 to 3 teaspoons *harissa* (hot chili paste) or a generous
   pinch of crushed red pepper flakes

1½ tablespoons ground coriander seeds

1 teaspoon ground caraway seeds

1 teaspoon salt, or to taste

2½ pounds butternut squash, peeled, seeded, and cut
   into 1-inch chunks

. . . .

1½ cups couscous (whole-wheat or regular)

¾ cup diced pitted dates

Heat the oil in the cooker. Cook the onions and garlic over medium-high heat, stirring frequently, for 1 minute. Add the water (stand back to avoid sputtering oil) and blend in the tomato paste, *harissa*, coriander, caraway, and salt. Add the squash.

Lock the lid in place. Over high heat bring to high pressure. Lower the heat just enough to maintain high pressure and cook for 3 minutes. Reduce the pressure with a quick-release method. Remove the lid, tilting it away from you to allow any excess steam to escape.

Gently stir in the couscous and dates. Immediately replace (but do not lock) the lid and let steam in the residual heat until the couscous is tender, about 5 minutes.

BASIC MILLET

10 minutes high pressure, 10-minute natural pressure release

Millet is the grain most people love to hate. Usually it's cooked with too much water and turned into bland mush. In addition, millet gets rancid faster than any other grain I know — an explanation for the slight bitter edge that is an all too common characteristic.

It's worth incorporating millet into your "grain plan" because it's such a nutritional giant and so easy to digest. This recipe creates a pleasantly fluffy grain, akin to couscous. To ensure proper cooking and enhance flavor, pre-toasting the millet (as directed at right) is a necessary step.

Makes 3½ to 4 cups

1 cup millet, rinsed and drained

1¾ to 2 cups boiling water or vegetable stock (use
   higher amount in jiggle-top cookers)

½ teaspoon salt, or to taste

Place the millet in the cooker and toast as instructed. Turn off the heat and add the boiling water and salt (stand back to avoid sputtering).

Lock the lid in place. Over high heat, bring to high pressure. Lower the heat just enough to maintain high pressure and cook for 10 minutes. Allow the pressure to come down naturally for 10 minutes. Quick-release any remaining pressure. Remove the lid, tilting it away from you to allow any excess steam to escape.

Immediately fluff up the millet with a fork and serve.

TO TOAST MILLET

Put the rinsed and drained millet in the bottom of the cooker (or in a cast-iron skillet if your cooker does not have a heavy bottom). Over high heat, dry out and then toast the millet, stirring almost constantly, until the grain emits a toasted aroma resembling popcorn and begins dancing around in the pan. This may take as little as 2 to 3 minutes or as long as 8 to 10. If at any point you feel that the millet is toasting too quickly, lower the heat slightly or turn it off temporarily. (Do not be concerned if the bottom of the cooker starts to turn brown, but if the millet begins to scorch, immediately turn off the heat and stir vigorously to cool.)

TIPS & TECHNIQUES

Make sure your millet is fresh (it should smell sweet and not musty). It's worth ordering the excellent Canadian-grown millet sold by Gold Mine Natural Food Co. (see Mail-Order Sources). If buying millet in a health food store, avoid the bulk bin in favor of a well-sealed package.

Because this basic millet recipe results in a dry, fluffy grain, plan on topping it with a sauce or with a soupy dish like chili.

MAGENTA MILLET PILAF

10 minutes high pressure, 10-minute natural pressure release

This dish is as beautiful as it is delicious, and preparation time is cut by the fact that it's not necessary to peel the beets. Since the orange is critical to the taste, have at least two large ones on hand to provide sufficient peel and juice.

Serve hot, straight from the pot, or at room temperature, mounded on a bed of leafy greens. *Serves 4 to 6*

1 cup millet, rinsed and drained

1¾ to 2 cups boiling water (use higher amount in jiggle-
   top cookers)

½ pound beets, scrubbed, trimmed, and cut into ½-inch
   dice

½ teaspoon salt, or to taste

Generous pinch of ground allspice or nutmeg

3 tablespoons freshly squeezed orange juice,
   approximately

1 tablespoon freshly grated orange peel (page 23)

3 tablespoons minced fresh mint

Freshly ground pepper (optional)

Place the millet in the cooker and toast as instructed on page 167. Turn off the heat. Add the boiling water (stand back to avoid sputtering), beets, salt, and allspice.

Lock the lid in place. Set the cooker on a heated Flame Tamer. Over high heat, bring to high pressure. Lower the heat just enough to maintain high pressure and cook for 10 minutes. Allow the pressure to come down naturally for 10 minutes. Quick-release any remaining pressure. Remove the lid, tilting it away from you to allow any excess steam to escape.

Stir in enough orange juice to moisten and lightly sweeten the mixture. Then add the orange peel and mint as you fluff up the millet before serving. Add pepper to taste, if desired.

TIPS & TECHNIQUES

Any leftover millet will dry out after overnight refrigeration. Before serving again, steam it according to instructions on page 119.

VARIATION

Use parsley instead of mint. Stir in ¼ cup of dried currants after cooking.

Millet Pilaf with Mushrooms, Carrots, and Peas

10 minutes high pressure, 10-minute natural pressure release, 1 to 2 minutes simmering

A down-home approach to millet that is very pleasing to the eye as well as the taste buds. This dish is substantial enough to take center stage on the plate, with perhaps some steamed broccoli or a green salad on the side. ***Serves 4***

1 cup millet, rinsed and drained

1 tablespoon safflower or canola oil

1 cup coarsely chopped onions

2 to 2¼ cups boiling water (use higher amount in jiggle-top cookers)

2 large carrots, halved lengthwise and cut into ½-inch slices

Generous ½ cup (½ ounce) sliced, dried mushrooms (see Tips)

1 large bay leaf

1½ tablespoons dried dill

¾ teaspoon salt, or to taste

Freshly ground pepper to taste

. . . .

1 cup frozen (defrosted) peas

¼ cup thinly sliced scallion greens

Tamari soy sauce (optional)

Place the millet in the cooker and toast as directed on page 167. Transfer the toasted millet to a bowl and set aside.

Heat the oil in the cooker. Cook the onions over medium-high heat, stirring frequently, for 1 minute. (If time permits, brown the onion, stirring frequently; this will take 5 to 6 minutes.) Add the boiling water (stand back to avoid sputtering oil), and take care to scrape up any bits of onion stuck to the bottom of the cooker. Stir in the toasted millet, carrots, mushrooms, bay leaf, dill, salt, and pepper.

continued

TIPS & TECHNIQUES

My supermarket sells thinly sliced dried wild mushrooms that are quite clean and require only a quick rinsing. Other dried mushrooms, such as porcini, may be quite sandy and require soaking in boiling water for about 20 minutes. After soaking, strain the flavorful soaking water and use it to replace an equivalent amount of the cooking water. Rinse the mushrooms carefully and cut away any tough stems before slicing.

VARIATION

Use 6 ounces sliced fresh mushrooms instead of dried. Reduce the water to 1¾ cups (2 cups for jiggle-tops) and increase the dill to 2 tablespoons. This approach is likely to result in a moist millet with a stuffinglike consistency.

Lock the lid in place. Set the cooker on a heated Flame Tamer. Over high heat, bring to high pressure. Lower the heat just enough to maintain high pressure and cook for 10 minutes. Allow the pressure to come down naturally for 10 minutes. Quick-release any remaining pressure. Remove the lid, tilting it away from you to allow any excess steam to escape.

Remove the bay leaf. Stir in the peas and scallion greens. Replace (but do not lock) the lid and cook over very low heat just until the peas are warmed through, 1 to 2 minutes. Sprinkle on a bit of soy sauce to perk up the flavors, if desired.

TIPS & TECHNIQUES

In some health food stores, corn grits are sold in bulk and labeled "polenta." Make sure the grits are coarse; do not be tempted to substitute the fine cornmeal traditionally used for making polenta.

You can pour the cooked polenta into two 9-inch pie plates and allow it to cool and set. Reheat, if desired, and slice the polenta into triangles to serve. After the polenta is set in the pie plates, you can top it with ratatouille or tomato sauce or any pizza-type garnishes. Reheat before serving.

With some cookers, the polenta occasionally sticks to the bottom of the pot. If this happens, even when using the Flame Tamer, switch to the casserole polenta technique.

POLENTA WITH DRIED MUSHROOMS AND OLIVES

5 minutes high pressure, 10-minute natural pressure release

I find polenta, like pasta, the kind of comfort food I can call upon at any time to heal what ails me. Because it is made with ingredients I always have on hand, I can be enjoying this soothing dish about 20 minutes after the urge comes over me.

A mound of polenta makes a fine substitute for rice as the base for chili and other flavorful stews. See Tips for other serving ideas. Leftovers are delicious reheated in a toaster oven. *Serves 4 to 6*

Note: Owners of jiggle-top cookers *should not* attempt this recipe. Use the casserole polenta approach described on page 171.

4½ **cups water**

1 **cup yellow corn grits (so labeled in health food stores)**

1 **to 2 tablespoons olive oil**

1 **to 2 teaspoons minced garlic**

Generous ½ cup (½ ounce) sliced dried mushrooms
   (see Tips, page 169)

1 **teaspoon salt, or to taste**

1 **large bay leaf**

½ **teaspoon dried rosemary leaves**

. . . .

⅓ **cup chopped pitted green or oil-cured black olives**

Bring the water to the boil in the cooker. Sprinkle in the corn grits while stirring. Add 1 tablespoon of oil, the garlic, mushrooms, salt, bay leaf, and rosemary and stir well.

Lock the lid in place. Set the cooker on a heated Flame Tamer. Over high heat, bring to high pressure. Lower the heat just enough to maintain high pressure and cook for 5 minutes. Allow the pressure to come down naturally for 10 minutes. Quick-release any remaining pressure. Remove the lid, tilting it away from you to allow any excess steam to escape.

Remove the bay leaf. Stir vigorously to create a thick porridge as you add the olives (reserve 2 tablespoons for garnish) and the remaining tablespoon of olive oil, if desired. If you encounter lumps, mash them against the side of the cooker. If the polenta seems too thin (it will thicken considerably on standing), simmer for a few minutes, stirring frequently. Serve in small bowls, garnished with the reserved chopped olives.

Casserole Polenta

For 1 cup of yellow corn grits, use only 3½ cups water. Combine with 1 tablespoon of oil, the garlic, mushrooms, salt, bay leaf, and rosemary in a heatproof casserole. Place the rack and 2 cups of water in the cooker. Lower the uncovered casserole onto the rack with the help of a foil strip (page 9).

Lock the lid in place. Over high heat, bring to high pressure. Reduce the heat just enough to maintain high pressure and cook for 20 minutes. Allow the pressure to come down naturally for 15 minutes. Remove the lid, tilting it away from you to allow any excess steam to escape.

Remove the casserole from the cooker with the aid of the foil strip. Add the olives (reserve 2 tablespoons for garnish) and the remaining tablespoon of oil, if desired. Stir well and serve garnished with the reserved olives.

VARIATIONS

When you add the olives, stir in ½ to 1 cup diced roasted red bell peppers.

Instead of olives, add chopped oil-packed sun-dried tomatoes.

Cook the polenta with ⅛ to ¼ teaspoon crushed red pepper flakes or 1 jalapeño pepper, seeded and diced (remember to wear rubber gloves when handling chili peppers).

Substitute 6 ounces of sliced fresh mushrooms for the dried mushrooms. Decrease the water by ¼ cup.

Be sure to wash quinoa thoroughly to remove any residual saponin—the bitter coating that acts as a natural insect repellent.

Use a large, very fine-meshed strainer. Set the grains in the strainer and, using your hand to stir the grains and prevent them from overflowing, gently submerge the quinoa in a large bowl of water. Continue stirring with your hand until the water becomes quite cloudy. Lift the strainer, empty the bowl, and fill it with clean water. Repeat submerging the quinoa, stirring, and changing the water until the water is just about clear. Drain the quinoa thoroughly.

BASIC QUINOA

1 minute high pressure, 10-minute natural pressure release

In my kitchen, quinoa is in close competition with brown rice for the title of favorite grain. This tiny Andean seed has all of rice's versatility but is much quicker cooking and easier to digest. An additional bonus is that quinoa has an impressive protein profile and contains several amino acids not commonly found in grains.

Most people take to quinoa immediately if the cook follows the Tips on page 173. *Makes 4 to 5 cups*

2¼ cups vegetable stock or water
1½ cups quinoa, thoroughly washed and drained
Flavoring options (page 118)
¾ teaspoon salt, or to taste (less if using salted stock)

Bring the stock to the boil in the cooker. Stir in the quinoa, flavorings as desired, and salt.

Lock the lid in place. Over high heat, bring to high pressure. Lower the heat just enough to maintain high pressure and cook for 1 minute. Allow the pressure to come down naturally for 10 minutes. Quick-release any remaining pressure. Remove the lid, tilting it away from you to allow any excess steam to escape.

Fluff up the quinoa before serving.

QUINOA CORN CHILI

1 minute high pressure, 10-minute natural pressure release

The trio of quinoa, corn, and chili is a natural south-of-the-border alliance. Serve this attractive combo along with Black Bean Chili for a memorable feast. ***Serves 3 to 4***

2 teaspoons safflower or canola oil

¾ teaspoon whole cumin seeds

½ cup finely chopped onion

½ teaspoon minced garlic

1¼ cups water

2 cups fresh or frozen (defrosted) corn kernels

½ cup diced red bell pepper

2 teaspoons mild chili powder

1 teaspoon dried oregano leaves

¾ teaspoon salt, or to taste

1 cup quinoa, thoroughly washed (page 172) and
   drained

. . . .

¼ cup minced fresh coriander (preferred) or parsley

Heat the oil in the cooker. Sizzle the cumin seeds over medium-high heat just until they begin to pop, 5 to 10 seconds. Add the onion and garlic and cook, stirring frequently, for 2 minutes. Stir in the water (stand back to avoid sputtering oil), corn, red bell pepper, chili powder, oregano, and salt. When the water comes to the boil, stir in the quinoa.

Lock the lid in place. Over high heat, bring to high pressure. Lower the heat just enough to maintain high pressure and cook for 1 minute. Allow the pressure to come down naturally for 10 minutes. Quick-release any remaining pressure. Remove the lid, tilting it away from you to allow any excess steam to escape. If the quinoa is not quite cooked, replace (but do not lock) the lid and let steam for a few more minutes in the residual heat. (Don't leave the lid on for too long or the quinoa will turn to mush.)

If there is any unabsorbed liquid, drain off the excess, or lift the mixture out of the cooker with a slotted spoon. Fluff up the quinoa with a fork as you stir in the coriander before serving.

TIPS & TECHNIQUES

Because quinoa absorbs water quickly, don't let it soak in the rinse water or sit for long once it's wet.

Cook the quinoa in a minimal amount of liquid to create a fluffy grain (somewhat like couscous) that has a bit of crunch.

Some strains of quinoa have a slightly grassy taste, which is not noticeable if you include seasonings, such as dried herbs or a thinly sliced clove of garlic. Alternatively, cook the quinoa in vegetable stock rather than water.

When quinoa is properly cooked, most of the grains will sport a little white tail.

Rather than cook the quinoa with salt, I often add tamari soy sauce to taste after it's cooked.

VARIATIONS

Cook with 1 to 2 jalapeño peppers that have been seeded and diced (remember to wear rubber gloves when handling chili peppers).

Instead of cooking the quinoa with red bell pepper, after cooking, stir in 1 roasted red bell pepper that has been seeded and diced.

After cooking, stir in ½ to ¾ cup cooked black beans. You may need to add a bit more salt or coriander.

CURRIED QUINOA PILAF

1 minute high pressure, 10-minute natural pressure release, 1 minute simmering

TIPS & TECHNIQUES

For best results, make sure that your curry powder is fresh (it should not taste bitter) and not too hot for your taste. To make a mild curry powder, see page 20.

The rich golden color of this pilaf is the dramatic backdrop for bright green dots of peas. You can serve it as part of a medley of Indian dishes or consider it an entree, accompanied by something hearty, like Split Pea Dal with Apple and Coconut. *Serves 4 to 6*

2 teaspoons safflower or canola oil

1 teaspoon finely minced garlic

2¼ cups boiling water

1 medium carrot, halved lengthwise and thinly sliced

1 tablespoon finely minced fresh ginger

2½ teaspoons mild curry powder

2 teaspoons ground coriander seeds

1 teaspoon salt, or to taste

1½ cups quinoa, thoroughly washed (page 172) and drained

. . . .

1 cup cooked or frozen (defrosted) green peas (petit pois are an elegant choice)

Heat the oil in the cooker. Cook the garlic over medium-high heat, stirring constantly, until it begins to turn golden, about 1 minute. Add the water (stand back to avoid sputtering oil), carrot, ginger, curry powder, coriander, salt, and quinoa.

Over high heat, bring to high pressure. Lower the heat just enough to maintain high pressure and cook for 1 minute. Allow the pressure to come down naturally for 10 minutes. Quick-release any remaining pressure. Remove the lid, tilting it away from you to allow any excess steam to escape.

Stir in the peas, replace (but do not lock) the lid, and cook over very low heat just until the peas are heated through, about 1 minute. (Don't overcook or the peas will lose their bright green color.) If there is any unabsorbed liquid, drain off the excess, or lift the pilaf out of the cooker with a slotted spoon. Fluff up the quinoa before serving.

Quinoa with Currants and Pine Nuts

Omit the garlic and oil and cook the quinoa with ⅓ cup dried currants (or raisins). After cooking, instead of peas, stir in ¼ cup toasted pine nuts or slivered, toasted almonds.

If you wish, stir in 2 tablespoons of minced parsley for some flecks of vibrant color.

QUINOA WITH GREEN BEANS, TOMATOES, AND BASIL

1 minute high pressure, 10-minute natural pressure release

A lovely dish to prepare in the summer, when beans, tomatoes, and fresh basil are plentiful. It's good straight out of the pot but also makes a lovely main-dish salad when served at room temperature with an extra drizzle of lemon juice.
Serves 4

TIPS & TECHNIQUES

I've called for less than the usual amount of water because the tomatoes release considerable liquid while cooking.

1 cup water
1 cup quinoa, thoroughly washed (page 172) and
   drained
¾ pound fresh green beans, trimmed and cut into
   ½-inch pieces
1 cup seeded and diced fresh plum tomatoes
½ teaspoon minced garlic
¾ teaspoon salt, or to taste
. . . .
1 tablespoon olive oil
½ cup minced fresh basil
1 to 2 tablespoons freshly squeezed lemon juice

Bring the water to the boil in the cooker. Add the quinoa, green beans, tomatoes, garlic, and salt.

Lock the lid in place. Over high heat, bring to high pressure. Lower the heat just enough to maintain high pressure and cook for 1 minute. Allow the pressure to come down naturally for 10 minutes. Quick-release any remaining pressure. Remove the lid, tilting it away from you to allow any excess steam to escape.

Stir in the olive oil and basil. Add the lemon juice and fluff up the quinoa just before serving. Serve hot or at room temperature.

GRAIN SALADS
AND SUSHI ROLLS

Unless otherwise noted, these salads are substantial enough to serve as entrees for lunch or a light dinner. If your grains are not freshly cooked, and have had a sojourn in the refrigerator, you will probably need to rehydrate them as directed on page 119.

GUACAMOLE RICE SALAD

This salad works beautifully with brown rice or a mixture of brown rice and barley. When I know I'll be making Guacamole Rice Salad, I cook the rice with 1 teaspoon of minced garlic, a pinch of crushed red pepper flakes, and salt. Since avocados are so rich, I don't add any oil to this salad.
Serves 4 to 6

VARIATION

Instead of green bell pepper, use an equivalent amount of roasted red bell pepper.

3 to 4 cups cooked grains, cooled to room temperature
2 ripe but firm avocados, preferably Haas variety,
    peeled, pitted, and cut into ½-inch dice
1 cup peeled, seeded, diced cucumber
½ pound fresh plum tomatoes, coarsely chopped
½ cup diced green bell pepper
1 jalapeño pepper, seeded and diced (optional; wear
    rubber gloves when handling chili peppers)
¼ cup finely chopped red onion
3 to 4 tablespoons freshly squeezed lime juice
⅓ to ½ cup minced fresh coriander (preferred) or
    ¼ cup minced fresh parsley
Salt and freshly ground pepper to taste
Watercress or radicchio (optional)

In a large bowl, combine all the ingredients except the watercress. Adjust the seasonings to taste. To serve, set on a bed of watercress or radicchio.

QUINOA *SALPICÓN*

This recipe was inspired by numerous visits to The Ballroom, a restaurant in Manhattan made famous by the late chef Felipe Rojas-Lombardi. Chef Felipe's love of bold flavors is nowhere more apparent than in this colorful salad based on quinoa, the staple grain of his native Peru.

One way to describe *salpicón* would be to call it a South American version of tabbouleh. I've adapted the recipe from Felipe's fine volume *The Art of South American Cooking* (Harper-Collins, 1991).

When I know I'll be making *salpicón*, I usually cook the quinoa with a clove or two of minced garlic. ***Serves 4***

VARIATION

Instead of using the avocado for garnish, dice it and toss it into the *salpicón*.

4 cups cooked quinoa (page 172), fluffed and cooled slightly

1 cup peeled, seeded, and diced cucumber (Kirbys are nice)

1 cup finely chopped fresh plum tomatoes

1 to 2 jalapeño peppers, seeded and diced (wear rubber gloves when handling chili peppers)

¼ cup thinly sliced scallions (use only the scallion greens if you prefer a milder taste)

⅔ cup tightly packed minced fresh parsley

⅓ cup tightly packed fresh mint or additional parsley

3 tablespoons full-flavored olive oil

3 tablespoons freshly squeezed lime juice, approximately (resist any temptation to substitute lemon juice)

½ teaspoon salt, or to taste

⅛ teaspoon ground pepper

8 large radicchio or lettuce leaves

1 ripe avocado, preferably Haas variety, peeled, pitted, and sliced

In a large bowl, combine the quinoa, cucumber, tomatoes, jalapeño, scallions, parsley, and mint.

In a blender, food processor, or small jar, blend together the oil, lime juice, salt, and pepper. Pour the dressing over the quinoa mixture and toss to coat the grains and vegetables thoroughly.

Taste and add more lime juice or salt as needed. (The salad should be assertively seasoned.) Serve on individual platters mounded into radicchio cups and garnished with avocado slices.

WHOLE GRAIN TABBOULEH SALAD

VARIATIONS

Add 1 cup cooked corn kernels.

Add 2 tablespoons drained capers.

Tabbouleh is traditionally made with bulgur, a refined form of the wheat berry. I thought it would be fun to try a similar preparation with wheat berries and was pleased with the results. You can use any form of whole grain in this salad — quinoa, kamut, barley, and spelt are good possibilities. The texture is best when the grains are freshly cooked.

Serve the tabbouleh with Split Pea Hummus, some good oil-cured or Greek calamata olives, and triangles of pita bread. ***Serves 4 to 6***

4 cups cooked whole grains
1 cup diced zucchini
¼ to ½ cup minced red onion
1 cup finely chopped fresh plum tomatoes
½ cup diced red bell pepper
¾ cup minced fresh parsley
¼ cup minced fresh mint
3 tablespoons olive oil
¼ cup freshly squeezed lemon juice
Salt to taste
Assorted salad greens
Carrot sticks or orange segments
Olives (a mixture of black and green is nice)

In a large bowl, combine the grains, zucchini, onion, tomatoes, red bell pepper, parsley, and mint. Drizzle the olive oil and lemon juice onto the mixture while stirring. Add the salt.

Create a bed of greens on a platter. Mound the tabbouleh salad on the greens. Arrange the carrot sticks or orange segments decoratively — perhaps like spokes of a wheel — on top. Place the olives on top and around the sides.

DOUBLE SESAME GRAIN SALAD

This is a very pretty and sophisticated salad with a Chinese accent. Grain salads absorb flavors quickly and should be assembled just before serving. Leftovers are likely to need perking up with a drizzle of rice vinegar and tamari soy sauce. *Serves 6*

5 to 6 cups cooked grains (Tamari Brown Rice with
Barley is especially nice)
1 pound fresh asparagus, trimmed
2 tablespoons toasted (Oriental) sesame oil
1 to 2 tablespoons brown or white rice vinegar
1 to 4 teaspoons tamari soy sauce
½ cup finely chopped carrot or red cabbage
½ cup thinly sliced scallions (for a milder taste, use
only the scallion greens)
2 tablespoons toasted sesame seeds

Place the cooked grains in a large bowl or storage container.

Steam the asparagus over high heat in about ½ inch of water in a large, shallow covered pan until tender-crisp, 2 to 3 minutes. Refresh under cold water and drain. Cut into ½-inch pieces. Set aside.

In a small jar, combine the sesame oil, 1 tablespoon rice vinegar, and 1 teaspoon soy sauce. Cover and shake well to blend.

Just before serving, pour the dressing over the grains and toss to coat. Add the asparagus, carrot, scallions, and sesame seeds and stir to distribute all ingredients evenly. Add extra rice vinegar and soy sauce to taste. (You will probably need at least 1 tablespoon more soy sauce if you are using unsalted grains.)

TIPS & TECHNIQUES

If you are using Tamari Brown Rice with Barley, you may need to break up clumps with a fork as you toss in the dressing.

Brown rice vinegar is available in health food stores and does not contain sugar. The rice vinegar sold in most supermarkets is what I'm referring to as "white." It has added sugar and therefore will contribute a sweet edge to the salad.

VARIATIONS

For a more complex salad, add miniature corn (available in gourmet shops and Oriental groceries) or seasoned, baked tofu (available in health food stores), cut into cubes.

If a small handful of the salad is moist enough to hold its shape when squeezed in your palm, try making sushi by rolling leftovers in sheets of nori (see page 180).

BROWN RICE SUSHI ROLLS

TIPS & TECHNIQUES
. . . .
Do not refrigerate the nori rolls as the rice will get hard and dry out.

VARIATION
. . . .
Add 1 slender spear of steamed asparagus per roll.

A favorite snack and travel food, these rolls are made by stuffing sheets of nori with soft-cooked sushi brown rice. I eat them whole, out of hand, but you can cut them into 1-inch pieces.

When the rolls are eaten as soon as they are prepared, the nori is crisp. When they are allowed to sit for an hour or two, or are prepared with freshly cooked, warm rice, the nori becomes soft and chewy. Either way, they're satisfying and delicious.

Toasted nori is available in health food stores and Oriental markets. ***Makes 4 rolls***

> 4 sheets toasted sushi nori
> 1 teaspoon umeboshi plum paste, wasabi, or prepared
>   mustard, approximately
> 1½ cups sushi brown rice, approximately (page 122)
> ½ ripe avocado, preferably Haas variety, peeled and cut
>   into thin slices
> 4 tablespoons chopped scallion greens
> 12 thin slivers pickled ginger (available in health food
>   stores)
> 4 teaspoons toasted sesame seeds

For each roll: Place a sheet of nori on a flat work surface. Cover the bottom third of the sheet with a very thin layer (about ¼ teaspoon) of plum paste, wasabi, or mustard.

Spread about ⅓ cup of rice on top of the plum paste, leaving about an inch uncovered along the bottom edge. Distribute one quarter of each of the remaining ingredients on top of the rice.

Wet your middle fingers in a small bowl of water and use them to moisten the top edge of the nori sheet. Lift the bottom edge (nearest the filling) and press it gently into the rice, rolling the rice into the nori as you would a jelly roll, until it is folded over to the top edge. Press gently to seal. (The moistened nori should adhere nicely.) Let the rolled nori sit, seam side down, while you are preparing the remainder. Store in a cool place for up to 6 hours.

Eat whole, out of hand, or cut into 1-inch slices with a sharp knife and place decoratively on a platter, cut side up.

BEANS

Beans play an important part in my diet and in my culinary imagination. Perhaps it's their infinite shapes and colors. Perhaps it's their subtle range in taste, a mellow backdrop that invites a wide variety of treatments and seasonings. Then again, it might be the deep sense of nourishment and satiety I experience after eating a bowlful.

But aside from a few of the quick-cooking varieties, such as lentils and split peas, bean cooking normally requires more time than most people are willing or able to spend.

Enter the pressure cooker, which performs some of its most amazing magic with beans. Think of a lentil stew emerging from the pot in 9 minutes, or flavor-infused Boston "baked" beans ready to eat in under half an hour. The pressure cooker makes it possible to think of economical, nutrition-packed beans as everyday fare.

Because we can never know the precise age of the beans nor if our batch is an amalgamation from different harvests, bean cooking is not an exact science. Add to that the fact that growing and storing conditions vary and you can understand why bean cooking cannot be precisely timed.

My approach to this challenge is to count on the pressure cooker to do about 90 percent of the cooking and then to finish off the beans by stove-top simmering. This way I can keep a steady eye on the beans and take them off the heat at the precise moment of tenderness.

For cooks in a real rush, a viable alternative is to pressure cook the beans to the maximum and accept the fact that they may be slightly overcooked. There are far greater tragedies in life than a bowl of meltingly soft beans.

Heirloom Beans

The growing availability of heirloom beans is bringing more interest and excitement to the bean pot. Heirloom beans are generally grown in small quantities by dedicated farmers who appreciate the value of their enhanced taste, texture, and appearance. Any bean variety that is not typically sold on a large scale may automatically be considered an heirloom bean. (Often these select beans are referred to as "boutique" or "designer" beans.) Happily, an astonishing variety of heirloom beans is now available by mail. They have fetching names like Christmas Limas, Black Valentines, Scarlet Runners, or Madeiras.

To bean cognoscenti, eating supermarket beans of unknown age and origin is the equivalent of choosing canned asparagus over fresh. Although this analogy may be somewhat exaggerated, anyone who has experienced the flavor and texture of organically grown heirloom beans is unlikely to voluntarily return to supermarket brands.

Despite the splendid assortment of colors and shapes, beans have only subtle variations in taste. Some are slightly sweet. Others have vague overtones of chestnut. A few are faintly smoky.

Because of their mild taste, beans offer a blank canvas to the cook who likes to paint with bold flavors. Because they absorb seasonings like a sponge, it's a simple matter to infuse them with the flavors of a particular country or douse them with a quick dressing of fruity olive oil, balsamic vinegar, and minced fresh herbs.

When it comes to texture, beans bring to mind the same vocabulary we might use to describe potatoes. In my opinion, the best beans are creamy, velvety, or buttery, while less desirable ones are starchy, grainy, or mealy. Because of their textural variety, some beans lend themselves better to thick soups and purées while others work better in salads and side dishes.

Some Personal Favorites

Adzukis: Long prized by the Japanese, these small brownish-red beans have a characteristic white stripe. Mild and earthy, they marry well with Oriental condiments such as ginger, tamari soy sauce, and toasted sesame oil.

Black Soybeans: Round and plump, these are the king of soybeans, with a sweet and nutty taste and a silken texture. Toss them with a little tamari soy sauce and some chopped scallion greens for an elegant treat.

Black Valentines: A large, bold ebony-colored bean with a potatolike flavor and texture. Striking in salads.

Cannellinis: Italians love this white kidney-shaped bean for its creaminess. Great in soups and purées, seasoned with olive oil, balsamic vinegar, and basil or rosemary.

China Yellows: Despite the name, this small, roundish bean is a longtime New England favorite, with a mild flavor and silken texture. Great for purées.

Christmas Limas: Perhaps the most "chestnutty" of all beans, these have the characteristic shape of large limas but sport handsome brown spots. They are striking enough to serve on their own, with a light sprinkling of fresh sage.

Jacob's Cattle: A New England classic, these speckled maroon and ivory beans are also known as Trout beans. Try them with your favorite recipe for baked beans.

Lentils le Puy: These diminutive French green lentils with their blackish freckles are full-flavored but not as peppery as domestic brown lentils. They have the great advantage of holding their shape well, making them excellent candidates for lentil salads.

Spanish Tolosanas: A smallish purple and tan speckled bean that works beautifully in chili.

Scarlet Runners: Gorgeous large beans of deep rose and black that hold their shape and color very well. Ideal for serving on their own with a drizzle of olive oil, and great in salads.

General Tips and Techniques

Shopping for Beans: Because dried beans have long keeping ability, we tend to overlook the value of freshness. Experience has taught me that "fresh" dried beans—those harvested within the last year or so—not only cook more quickly, but have more vibrant taste. I also find that organically grown beans have considerably better flavor and are worth the higher price they usually command. An excellent mail-order source of high-quality organic beans is Bean Bag (see Mail-Order Sources).

You will also find a good selection of organic beans in most health food stores. Look for beans of uniform size and rich color; fading indicates that they have been around for a while. Avoid beans that are split or broken, indicating rough handling or delayed harvesting. Once a bean is skinless, its flavor and the quality of its proteins and fats gradually diminish.

Beans purchased from bulk bins are generally less expensive than packaged beans, but at times I have found the reverse to be true. It always pays to compare price and quality.

Storing Beans: Store beans in a cool, dry place. Try to use them within 6 months. As a bean ages, it becomes drier and harder. For this reason, it's best to avoid mixing batches of the same variety, which may result in uneven cooking.

Cleaning Beans: Inspect the beans for stones and grit. Rinse them thoroughly before soaking or cooking.

Soaking Beans Overnight: For more even cooking and to eliminate water-soluble, gas-producing sugars, I *strongly recommend* soaking beans. To request that beans be soaked overnight is a shorthand way of saying that they should be soaked until the water penetrates to their center. Depending upon the age and size of the bean, this can take from 4 to 8 hours. For even cooking, I prefer this slow, time-tested method, but it does require planning.

To determine if a batch of beans is thoroughly soaked, I use a technique shared by my colleague Carol Gelles. Slice a bean in half with a sharp paring knife. If there is an opaque spot in the center, the beans require more soaking. Once the beans are thoroughly soaked, drain and rinse them. If you're not cooking them at that point, you can store them in a tightly sealed container in the refrigerator for up to 2 days.

Speed-soaking Beans

If you haven't soaked the beans in advance, use this 20-minute speed soak technique.

Use 3 cups of water for the first cup of dried beans and 2 cups of water per additional cup of beans. Place the beans and water in the cooker. (Owners of jiggle-top cookers should add 1 tablespoon of oil per 1 cup of dried beans.) Lock the lid in place. Over high heat, bring to high pressure.

For small beans (such as navy or adzuki): As soon as high pressure is reached, turn off the heat and allow the pressure to come down naturally for 10 minutes. Release any remaining pressure with a quick-release method.

For medium beans (such as red kidney or pinto): Cook for 1 minute under high pressure. Turn off the heat and allow the pressure to come down naturally, 10 to 15 minutes.

For very large beans (such as chickpeas or Black Valentine): Cook for 2 to 3 minutes under high pressure. Turn off the heat and allow the pressure to come down naturally, 10 to 15 minutes.

With a slotted spoon, remove a few beans from the pot. Slice them in half with a sharp paring knife. If there is an opaque spot in the center of each bean, you can do one of three things:

1. Return to high pressure for another 1 to 2 minutes and again let the pressure come down naturally.
2. If time permits, replace (but do not lock) the lid and let the beans soak until the insides of the beans are all one color.
3. Rinse and drain the beans. Proceed with preparing the dish, using your judgment to increase the cooking time by 1 to 5 minutes under high pressure. Alternatively, use the cooking time indicated and be prepared to do some stove-top simmering as needed. The latter is a safer way to go, but may take more time.

Under all circumstances, discard the bean soaking liquid and use fresh water or stock as directed in the recipe.

Pressure Cooking Beans

Here are a few general rules to follow:

Do not fill the cooker more than halfway.

For even cooking, be sure the beans are covered with water or stock.

Add 1 tablespoon of oil per 1 cup of dried beans. The oil subdues foaming, which might catapult a bean skin into the vent. With a few exceptions (namely large limas and soybeans), I consider the oil optional when using a second-generation cooker, but *mandatory* with jiggle-tops. When cooking beans in a jiggle-top, if you hear loud sputtering, immediately turn off the heat and place the cooker under cold running water to bring down the pressure. Remove and clean the lid, vent, and rubber gasket. Discard any free-floating bean skins. Add another tablespoon of oil, lock the lid back in place, and proceed with cooking. These rules hold true when cooking bean recipes as well as plain beans.

Cook beans for the time indicated on the cooking chart (page 188). Please keep in mind that timings are approximate and that I purposely err on the side of undercooking. If it's important that the beans hold their shape, cook for the minimum time indicated and complete cooking as needed by simmering. For soups or purées, choose the maximum time.

For specialty beans not on the cooking chart, use the timing for a bean of approximately the same shape and size. If you are feeling very cautious, you can cook a small handful of the beans in a trial run to determine more precise timing.

If time permits, use a natural pressure release rather than a quick-release method, as the latter often causes bean skins to burst. The natural pressure release is equivalent to about 4 minutes of cooking under pressure. In recipes where I request a natural pressure release, I have calculated in this additional cooking time. In recipes where I offer an optional natural pressure release, I don't feel concerned about overcooking and prefer this technique if the extra time is available.

Once the pressure is down, if the beans require more cooking, it's best to finish them off by stove-top simmering, tasting frequently until they are just right. However, if the beans are quite undercooked and timing is of the essence, return them to high pressure for a few more minutes and let the pressure come down naturally again.

When the beans are tender (they should be soft enough to mash against your hard palate with very little pressure), drain them. If you like, reserve the cooking liquid and use it for stock. Alternatively, let the beans cool in the cooking liquid, which in most cases will thicken into a nice sauce.

To Salt or Not to Salt

Adding salt or any acid (like vinegar, molasses, or tomatoes) to beans hardens their skins and prevents them from absorbing water properly. At best, cooking time will be retarded; at worst, the beans will never become tender no matter how long you cook them.

There are two exceptions to this rule:

1. When cooking beans with exceptionally delicate skins, such as large limas and black soybeans, a teaspoon of salt in the soaking and then the cooking water is necessary to keep the bean skins intact.
2. When pressure cooking soups and stews, adding a small quantity of tomatoes or using a lightly salted stock may lengthen cooking time slightly but does not prevent the beans from softening.

However, as a general rule, add salt and acidic ingredients at the end of cooking.

FLAVORINGS OPTIONS

Here are some nice things to add to the pot per cupful of dried beans:

1 to 2 smashed, peeled cloves of garlic
1 large bay leaf
½ to 1 teaspoon dried herbs such as sage, oregano, thyme, and tarragon
One 3-inch strip kombu sea vegetable (adds minerals and is thought to make the beans more digestible and enhance flavor)

Bean Cooking Times at a Glance

For instructions on cooking beans, see pages 184–187.

Approximate Minutes Under High Pressure

Beans (1 Cup Dry)	Soaked Natural Pressure Release°	Soaked Quick-Release	Unsoaked Quick-Release	Yield in Cups
Adzuki	2–3	5–9	14–20	2½
Anasazi	1–2	4–7	20–22	2¼
Black (turtle)	3–6	5–9	18–25	2
Black-eyed peas	—	—	10–11	2¼
Cannellini	5–8	9–12	22–25	2
Chickpeas (garbanzos)	9–14	13–18	30–40	2½
Christmas Lima	4–6	8–10	16–18	1¼
Cranberry (borlotto)	5–8	9–12	30–34	2¼
Fava[†]	8–14	12–18	22–28	2
Flageolet	6–10	10–14	17–22	2
Great Northern	4–8	8–12	25–30	2¼
Lentils (brown)	—	—	8–10	2
Lentils (French)	—	—	10–12	2
Lentils (red)	—	—	4–6	2
Lima (large)[‡]	1–3	4–7	12–16	2
Lima (baby)	2–3	5–7	12–15	2½
Mung	—	—	10–12	2
Navy (pea)	3–4	6–8	16–25	2
Peas (split, green or yellow)	—	—	6–10	2
Peas (whole, green)	4–6	8–10	16–18	2
Pigeon peas (gandules)	2–5	6–9	20–25	3
Pinto	1–3	4–6	22–25	2¼
Red kidney	5–8	10–12	20–25	2
Scarlet Runner	8–10	12–14	17–20	1¼
Soy beans (beige)[‡]	5–8	9–12	28–35	2¼
Soy beans (black)[‡]	16–18	20–22	35–40	2½

NOTE: Do not fill the cooker more than halfway. Owners of jiggle-top cookers should add 1 tablespoon of oil per cup of dried beans to control foaming.

° Use the timing in this column if you intend to let the pressure come down naturally, about 10 minutes. This is the preferred technique.

[†] Skins remain leathery after cooking and must be removed before serving unless the beans are puréed.

[‡] Requires 2 tablespoons of oil per cup of dried beans. Add ½ teaspoon salt when soaking/cooking large limas and black soy beans. Remove any floating bean skins before cooking.

GINGERED ADZUKI-SQUASH STEW

5 minutes high pressure, 10-minute natural pressure release

Adzuki beans, with their rich flavor and reputed healing properties, are highly esteemed in the Japanese kitchen. Adzukis and squash are a traditional pairing in that country, and my addition of shiitake mushrooms and ginger seemed a natural way to go.

The squash becomes quite soft and, when you stir the cooked dish, lends much of its flesh to thickening the stew. The scallion greens mixed in at the end add a vibrant punch of flavor and color. Serve the stew over brown rice or millet for a wholesome entree. ***Serves 4 to 6***

1 cup dried adzuki beans, picked over and rinsed, soaked overnight in ample water to cover or speed-soaked (page 185)

8 large or 12 medium dried shiitake mushrooms (about 1 ounce total), soaked in 1½ cups boiling water in a covered bowl for 10 minutes

1 tablespoon light sesame oil or canola oil

1½ cups coarsely chopped onions

2 tablespoons finely minced fresh ginger

1 cup boiling water, approximately

1 pound kabocha, delicata, or butternut squash, seeded and cut into 1-inch chunks (peeling not necessary, especially if organic)

. . . .

½ cup thinly sliced scallions (use only the scallion greens for a milder taste)

Tamari soy sauce to taste

2 to 3 tablespoons toasted sesame seeds or ¼ cup toasted pumpkin seeds (optional)

continued

TIPS & TECHNIQUES

If you don't like a strong, spicy ginger flavor, reduce the amount of minced fresh ginger to 1 tablespoon.

In addition to tamari soy sauce, a bit of umeboshi plum vinegar (available in health food stores) brings out the flavors nicely.

The pressure cooker does a nice job of tenderizing squash skins, rendering peeling optional. However, any tough, crusty spots should be pared off.

Drain and rinse the adzukis. Set aside

Lift the shiitakes out of the water with a slotted spoon. Reserve the soaking water. Cut off the mushroom stems and save for stock or discard. Slice the caps into ¼-inch slivers. Set aside.

Heat the oil in the cooker. Cook the onions over medium-high heat, stirring frequently, for 2 minutes. Stir in the ginger and the reserved adzukis and mushrooms. Add the mushroom soaking water (stand back to avoid sputtering oil) plus enough boiling water to just cover the adzukis. Set the squash on top.

Lock the lid in place. Over high heat, bring to high pressure. Lower the heat just enough to maintain high pressure and cook for 5 minutes. Allow the pressure to come down naturally for 10 minutes. Quick-release any remaining pressure. Remove the lid, tilting it away from you to allow any excess steam to escape. If the adzukis are not tender, replace (but do not lock) the lid and simmer until the beans are done. Add a bit more boiling water in the unlikely event that the mixture seems dry.

Stir well to distribute the squash. (I like to cut each piece of squash in half as I do this.) Stir in the scallions and add soy sauce to taste. Garnish the bowlful or individual servings with toasted sesame or pumpkin seeds, if desired.

BABY LIMAS WITH SPINACH AND DILL

4 minutes high pressure, 10-minute natural pressure release, 2 to 3 minutes simmering

Although very low-fat and cholesterol-free, this combination is remarkably reminiscent of creamed spinach. You can serve it in small bowls as a vegetable side dish or toss it with pasta. (Try it over Eden-brand tricolored spiral pasta — available in health food stores — for a very pretty dish.)

Note that this recipe calls for baby limas, which have different cooking requirements from large ones. *Serves 6*

1½ cups dried baby limas, picked over and rinsed, soaked overnight in ample water to cover or speed-soaked (page 185)

1 tablespoon safflower or canola oil

1 cup coarsely chopped onions

2 cups boiling water

1 bay leaf

2½ teaspoons dried dill

. . . .

5 ounces frozen (defrosted) chopped spinach (squeeze between two plates and tip off excess water)

1 teaspoon salt, or to taste

1 to 2 tablespoons freshly squeezed lemon juice

Drain and rinse the limas. Set aside.

Heat the oil in the cooker. Cook the onion over medium-high heat, stirring frequently, for 1 minute. Add the water (stand back to avoid sputtering oil), bay leaf, dill, and reserved limas.

Lock the lid in place. Over high heat, bring to high pressure. Lower the heat just enough to maintain high pressure and cook for 4 minutes. Allow the pressure to come down naturally for 10 minutes. Quick-release any remaining presure. Remove the lid, tilting it away from you to allow any excess steam to escape. If the limas are not quite tender, replace (but do not lock) the lid and simmer until the beans are done.

Remove the bay leaf. If you are serving the dish immediately, with a slotted spoon, transfer about a cupful of the limas to a food processor or blender, and purée. Stir the purée back into the beans to create a thick sauce. Otherwise, let the limas sit in the cooker for a few hours at room temperature with the lid slightly ajar. (During this time the limas will absorb much of the cooking liquid.)

Shortly before serving, stir in the spinach and salt to taste. Simmer until the spinach is heated, 2 to 3 minutes. Add lemon juice to taste just before serving.

This dish thickens considerably with overnight refrigeration. Thin it as needed with milk (soy or dairy) when you reheat leftovers.

VARIATION
. . . .
To make a dish even more reminiscent of creamed spinach, add 10 ounces instead of 5 ounces of spinach. Purée the entire mixture by pulsing in a food processor. (Do not overwork, or the mixture will become pasty.) Omit the lemon juice and add nutmeg to taste, if desired.

BLACK BEAN CHILI

12 minutes high pressure

TIPS & TECHNIQUES
. . . .

Be sure to use a fine-quality blend of chili powder — one whose flavor you truly enjoy. (Or see page 18 for a mild homemade blend.)

My most memorable results have come from using either my own or the Frontier blend of chili powder plus 1 dried chipotle pepper, which lends some heat and a delightful smokiness. For a more incendiary chili, you can include some of the chipotle's seeds. Both the chili powder and the chipotle are available through the mail-order sources listed at the back of the book.

If you have a yen for chili but have no chipotles in the cupboard, try adding a drizzle of liquid smoke flavoring after cooking.

Although most traditional chilies are made with red kidney or pinto beans, I have found that using black beans as the base creates superb results. This recipe receives rave reviews from my testers and makes a wonderful entree for vegetarians and nonvegetarians alike.

For a terrific alternative, serve the chili over polenta rather than rice. Another good accompaniment is Mexican Green Rice with Corn. ***Serves 6 to 8***

2 cups dried black beans, picked over and rinsed, soaked overnight in ample water to cover or speed-soaked (page 185)

1 tablespoon olive oil

1 teaspoon whole cumin seeds

2 cups coarsely chopped onions

1 tablespoon finely minced garlic

1 large red bell pepper, seeded and diced

1 to 2 dried chipotle peppers, stemmed, seeded, and snipped into bits, or 2 jalapeño peppers, seeded and thinly sliced (wear rubber gloves when handling chili peppers)

1½ to 2 tablespoons mild chili powder

1½ teaspoons dried oregano leaves

½ teaspoon whole fennel seeds

¼ teaspoon ground cinnamon

3 cups boiling water, approximately

. . . .

Salt and freshly ground pepper to taste

2 cups finely chopped fresh or canned (drained) plum tomatoes

½ cup tightly packed minced fresh coriander or parsley

1 ripe avocado, preferably Haas variety, peeled, pitted, and thinly sliced

1 lime, cut into 6 to 8 wedges

Drain and rinse the beans. Set aside.

Heat the oil in the cooker. Sizzle the cumin seeds over medium-high heat just until they begin to pop, 5 to 10 seconds.

Stir in the onions, garlic, and red bell pepper and cook, stirring constantly, for 1 minute. Add the reserved beans, chipotle pepper(s), chili powder, oregano, fennel, cinnamon, and enough boiling water (stand back to avoid sputtering oil) to just cover the mixture. Stir well.

Lock the lid in place. Over high heat, bring to high pressure. Lower the heat just enough to maintain high pressure and cook for 12 minutes. Reduce the pressure with a quick-release method. Remove the lid, tilting it away from you to allow any excess steam to escape. If the beans are not quite tender, replace (but do not lock) the lid and simmer until the beans are done. Stir in the salt and pepper and the tomatoes.

The chili should be fairly thick. If time permits, let the chili sit in the cooker at room temperature with the lid slightly ajar for a few hours to thicken. If it's still too thin, or if you are serving it immediately, with a slotted spoon, transfer 1 cup of the beans to a food processor or blender, and purée. Stir the purée back into the chili.

Just before serving, stir in all but about 2 tablespoons of the coriander. Reheat, if necessary. Transfer to a casserole or individual plates and garnish with decoratively arranged avocado slices, lime wedges, and the remaining coriander.

CUBAN BLACK BEANS

12 minutes high pressure

Among the commonly available beans, I am probably most partial to the taste and looks of black (turtle) beans. I know that I share that appreciation with thousands of cooks around the world.

Here is a robust version of a classic Caribbean approach to black beans, especially striking when served over steamed white or brown rice with a garnish of olives and fried plantains. And don't forget to pass the hot sauce. *Serves 5 to 6*

1½ cups dried black beans, picked over and rinsed, soaked overnight in ample water to cover or speed-soaked (page 185)
1 tablespoon olive oil
2 teaspoons minced garlic
1 cup coarsely chopped onions
2 cups boiling water, approximately
1 large red bell pepper, seeded and cut into strips about ½ inch wide and 3 inches long
1 large green bell pepper, seeded and cut into strips about ½ inch wide and 3 inches long
1 large bay leaf
2 teaspoons dried oregano leaves

. . . .

2 to 3 teaspoons red wine vinegar
Salt to taste
¼ cup minced fresh parsley (optional)
⅓ cup minced pimiento-stuffed olives
1 to 2 very ripe plantains, peeled, cut on the diagonal into thin slices, and fried in a heavy skillet lightly brushed with oil

Drain and rinse the beans. Set aside.

Heat the oil in the cooker. Cook the garlic over medium-high heat, stirring constantly, until lightly browned. Add the onions and continue cooking, stirring frequently, for 1 minute. Add the reserved beans, just enough boiling water to cover (stand back to avoid sputtering oil), and the red and green bell peppers, bay leaf, and oregano.

VARIATIONS
. . . .

Add 1 cup seeded, finely chopped fresh plum tomatoes when you add the vinegar.

Stir in ⅓ cup thinly sliced scallion greens after cooking.

Sliced avocado (preferably Haas variety) also makes a wonderful garnish.

Leftovers are great rewarmed and stuffed into a whole-wheat or corn tortilla or a pita.

Lock the lid in place. Over high heat, bring to high pressure. Lower the heat just enough to maintain high pressure and cook for 12 minutes. Allow the pressure to come down naturally or use a quick-release method. Remove the lid, tilting it away from you to allow any excess steam to escape. If the beans are not quite tender, replace (but do not lock) the lid and simmer until the beans are done.

Remove the bay leaf and stir in the vinegar and salt. If the mixture is too soupy, with a slotted spoon, transfer about a cupful of the beans to a food processor or blender, and purée. Stir the purée back into the beans to create a thick sauce. Alternatively, if time permits, allow the dish to sit in the cooker at room temperature with the lid slightly ajar for about 2 hours, during which time much of the liquid will be absorbed.

Reheat, if necessary, and stir in the parsley just before serving. Serve on steamed white or brown rice garnished with olives and fried plantains.

Last-Minute Black-eyed Pea Chili

11 minutes high pressure, 2 to 3 minutes simmering

Because black-eyed peas are quick-cooking (without soaking), they make a great base for an impromptu quick and economical chili. For a more complex taste, some flavorful bottled salsa may be stirred in at the end.

This is a hearty chili. Serve it in shallow bowls over polenta or rice, accompanied by warm tortillas and a green salad.
Serves 6 to 8

1 tablespoon safflower or canola oil

1 to 2 tablespoons coarsely chopped garlic

1 teaspoon whole cumin seeds

2 cups coarsely chopped onions

1 teaspoon dried oregano leaves

¼ teaspoon ground cinnamon

1 cup diced green bell pepper

2½ cups dried black-eyed peas, picked over and rinsed

4 cups boiling water

2 to 3 tablespoons mild chili powder

. . . .

One 15-ounce bottle mild or hot salsa (optional)

Salt to taste

¼ cup minced fresh coriander or parsley

Heat the oil in the cooker. Cook the garlic over medium-high heat, stirring frequently, until lightly browned. Add the cumin seeds and continue stirring for about 5 more seconds. Add the onions, oregano, cinnamon, green bell pepper, black-eyed peas, water (stand back to avoid sputtering oil), and 2 tablespoons of chili powder. Taste the liquid and add more chili powder if the chili flavor isn't fairly intense.

Lock the lid in place. Over high heat, bring to high pressure. Lower the heat just enough to maintain high pressure and cook for 11 minutes. Allow the pressure to come down naturally or use a quick-release method. Remove the lid, tilting it away from you to allow any excess steam to escape. The beans should be tender. If they are not, either return to high pressure for a few more minutes or replace (but do not lock)

the lid and simmer until the black-eyed peas are done. If the mixture is too soupy, puree about a cupful of peas and stir the puree back into the chili.

Stir in salsa to taste (if using) and salt. Simmer for a few minutes to allow the beans to pick up some of the salsa flavor. Stir in the coriander just before serving.

BLACK-EYED PEA GUMBO

11 minutes high pressure, 2 to 3 minutes simmering

Here's a quick and attractive way to bring the bold flavors of New Orleans to your table. Delicious over Bulgur and Brown Rice with a side of Collard Spaghetti and perhaps some corn bread. And have the Tabasco close at hand. *Serves 6*

1 tablespoon olive or canola oil

2 teaspoons finely minced garlic

2 cups coarsely chopped onions

2 large celery ribs, cut into ½-inch slices

1 large red or green bell pepper, seeded and coarsely chopped

1 to 3 jalapeño peppers, seeded and thinly sliced (wear rubber gloves when handling chili peppers), or a generous pinch of crushed red pepper flakes

2 cups dried black-eyed peas, picked over and rinsed

3 cups boiling water

1 large bay leaf

1 teaspoon dried oregano leaves

½ teaspoon dried thyme leaves

Generous pinch of dried sage leaves

. . . .

2 cups chopped fresh or canned (drained) plum tomatoes

10 ounces frozen (defrosted) sliced okra

1 teaspoon salt, or to taste

Freshly ground pepper to taste

2 to 4 teaspoons red wine vinegar (optional)

TIPS & TECHNIQUES
. . . .
If you know that your guests or family expect gumbo to be fire-alarm hot, include some of the jalapeño pepper seeds.

VARIATION
. . . .
To impart the scent of hickory, stir in a bit of liquid smoke flavoring at the end.

continued

Heat the oil in the cooker. Add the garlic, onions, celery, bell pepper, and Jalapeno and cook over medium-high heat, stirring frequently, for 2 minutes. Add the black-eyed peas, water (stand back to avoid sputtering oil), bay leaf, oregano, thyme, and sage.

Lock the lid in place. Over high heat, bring to high pressure. Lower the heat just enough to maintain high pressure and cook for 11 minutes. Allow the pressure to come down naturally or use a quick-release method. Remove the lid, tilting it away from you to allow any excess steam to escape. If the beans are not tender, replace (but do not lock) the lid and simmer until they are done.

Remove the bay leaf. Stir in the tomatoes, okra, and salt and pepper and simmer until the okra is tender, 2 to 3 minutes. Add a splash of vinegar, if desired, to perk up the flavors.

THAI CHICKPEAS

18 minutes high pressure

"It's the best chickpea dish I've ever eaten," say some vegetarian friends who have tasted their way around the world of chickpeas. The inspiration for this most delicious dish comes from a wonderful cookbook called *Thai Vegetarian Cooking* by Vatcharin Bhumichitr (Clarkson Potter, 1991). I was intrigued to learn that this dish is unusual even in Thailand, where eating beans is not commonplace. The author discovered this dish in a forest monastery west of Bangkok. I have altered the quantities and proportions and substituted sweet potatoes for white — with exciting results.

This dish makes a luscious main course when served over white rice. ***Serves 4 to 6***

TIPS & TECHNIQUES

If using the speed-soak technique, before you begin cooking, cut a few chickpeas in half to be sure they are one color throughout (page 185).

1½ cups dried chickpeas, picked over and rinsed, soaked overnight in ample water to cover or speed-soaked (page 185)

3 cups coconut milk (page 19)

1 teaspoon minced garlic

¾ pound sweet potatoes, peeled and cut into 1-inch chunks

1 cup coarsely chopped fresh or canned (drained) plum tomatoes

1 tablespoon mild curry powder

¼ cup minced fresh coriander

. . . .

½ cup minced fresh basil

1 to 2 tablespoons tamari soy sauce

Drain and rinse the chickpeas. In the cooker, combine the chickpeas, coconut milk, garlic, sweet potatoes, tomatoes, curry powder, and coriander.

Lock the lid in place. Over high heat, bring to high pressure. Lower the heat just enough to maintain high pressure and cook for 18 minutes. Allow the pressure to come down naturally or use a quick-release method. Remove the lid, tilting it away from you to allow any excess steam to escape. If the chickpeas are not tender, either return to high pressure for a few more minutes or replace (but do not lock) the lid and simmer until the chickpeas are done.

Add the basil and soy sauce to taste as you break up the sweet potatoes and stir to create a thick sauce.

VARIATION

If fresh basil is not available, cook the chickpeas with 2 teaspoons of dried basil leaves and stir in the ¼ cup of fresh coriander at the end.

CHICKPEA STEW WITH SWEET ONIONS

18 minutes high pressure

I am always on the lookout for interesting chickpea recipes that can be adapted for the pressure cooker, so when my eye fell on this approach in *Please to the Table* by Anya von Bremzen and John Welchman (Workman, 1990), I took special note.

According to the authors, this recipe is from Tadzhikistan, a region in the former Soviet Union famous for having the largest and sweetest onions in the country. I have taken considerable liberties with the proportions, but all the traditional seasonings are included.

This stew is delicious served in bowls on its own or over parsley or spinach fettuccine. **Serves 4 to 6**

1½ **cups dried chickpeas, picked over and rinsed, soaked overnight in ample water to cover or speed-soaked (page 185)**
1 **tablespoon safflower or canola oil**
2 **teaspoons whole cumin seeds**
2 **cups vegetable stock**
1 **tablespoon ground coriander seeds**
2 **teaspoons sweet paprika**
¼ **teaspoon saffron threads**
Generous pinch of crushed red pepper flakes
Generous pinch of ground cinnamon
2 **pounds red, Bermuda, or Vidalia onions, peeled and thinly sliced (6 to 7 cups loosely packed)**
1 **cup finely chopped fresh or canned (drained) plum tomatoes**

. . . .

Salt to taste

Drain and rinse the chickpeas. Set aside.

Heat the oil in the cooker. Sizzle the cumin seeds over medium-high heat just until they begin to pop, 5 to 10 seconds. Add the stock (stand back to avoid sputtering oil), coriander, paprika, saffron, red pepper flakes, cinnamon, and reserved

TIPS & TECHNIQUES
. . . .
Do not be concerned if the onions and tomatoes come to the top of the cooker. They will shrink as the cooker comes up to pressure.

If using canned tomatoes, do not include the juice as it will interfere with the cooking of the chickpeas.

An alternative to puréeing the chickpeas is to mash some against the side of the pot.

chickpeas. Set the onions on top of the chickpeas and the to-matoes on top of the onions. (Do not stir at this point.)

Lock the lid in place. Over high heat, bring to high pressure. Lower the heat just enough to maintain high pressure and cook for 18 minutes. Allow the pressure to come down naturally or use a quick-release method. Remove the lid, tilting it away from you to allow any excess steam to escape. If the chickpeas are not fairly tender (they should hold their shape but be quite soft), return to high pressure for a few more minutes or replace (but do not lock) the lid and simmer until the chickpeas are done.

With a slotted spoon, transfer a cup of the chickpeas (and onions) to a food processor or blender, and purée. Stir the purée back into the stew to create a thick sauce. Add salt before serving.

LEB LEBI

TUNISIAN CHICKPEA STEW

18 minutes high pressure

I was introduced to this unforgettable chickpea-bread stew during a recent trip to Tunisia, where it is a favorite breakfast food. First thing in the morning, I'm not ready for the variety of tastes and textures presented in this dish, but on a cold winter's evening, there is nothing like *leb lebi* to make all seem right with the world.

The basis of *leb lebi* is a thin, flavorful broth studded with chickpeas. The hot liquid is spooned over torn bread, and a variety of flavor-packed ingredients and seasonings are added to taste. I've offered suggested amounts as guidelines.

Leb lebi is a great dish to serve at an informal dinner party. You can set out the olives, capers, and *harissa* in small bowls and invite each guest to create his own combination.

Serves 5 to 6

For the soup

> 1½ cups dried chickpeas, picked over and rinsed, soaked overnight in ample water to cover or speed-soaked (page 185)
>
> 6 cups vegetable stock (page 68) or garlic-parsley stock (page 71)
>
> 2 cups coarsely chopped onions
>
> 1 tablespoon olive oil
>
> 1½ teaspoons ground caraway seeds
>
> Salt to taste

For each portion of leb lebi

> One 1-inch wedge of a fresh peasant loaf, crust removed, torn into 4 to 6 pieces
>
> ¼ teaspoon ground cumin seeds (freshly ground, if possible)
>
> ½ tablespoon fruity olive oil
>
> 1 to 2 tablespoons chopped pitted black olives
>
> 1 to 2 teaspoons drained capers
>
> *Harissa* (hot chili paste) or hot sauce to taste

To prepare the soup, rinse and drain the chickpeas. Place the chickpeas, stock, onions, oil, and caraway in the cooker.

Lock the lid in place. Over high heat, bring to high pressure. Lower the heat just enough to maintain high pressure and cook for 18 minutes. Allow the pressure to come down naturally or use a quick-release method. Remove the lid, tilting it away from you to allow any excess steam to escape. If the chickpeas are not meltingly soft, either return to high pressure for a few more minutes or replace (but do not lock) the lid and simmer until the chickpeas are done. Add salt.

To assemble each portion of *leb lebi:* Place the bread in a large soup bowl. Sprinkle the cumin on top. Ladle enough stock and chickpeas over the bread to thoroughly soften it. Stir in olive oil, olives, capers, and *harissa* before serving.

GEORGIAN KIDNEY BEANS WITH WALNUT-CORIANDER SAUCE

6 minutes high pressure, 10-minute natural pressure release

For years I have come across this combination of kidney beans with walnuts in Russian cookbooks, and it has always intrigued me. Finally I got around to trying it out and am glad to report that I was not disappointed.

This dish is rich and filling, so plan on smaller-than-average portions even when you're serving it as an entree. I'd suggest simple accompaniments, such as steamed corn and a marinated green bean salad. *Serves 6*

1½ cups dried red kidney beans, picked over and rinsed, soaked overnight in ample water to cover or speed-soaked (page 185)

2 to 3 cups boiling water

2 teaspoons ground coriander seeds

¼ teaspoon ground cinnamon

1 tablespoon safflower or canola oil (optional, except for owners of jiggle-top cookers)

For the sauce

⅓ cup bean cooking liquid, approximately

3 large cloves of roasted garlic (page 20)

⅓ cup chopped walnuts

2 tablespoons white wine vinegar

1 teaspoon salt, or to taste

1 cup tightly packed fresh coriander

Assorted salad greens (optional)

Tomatoes wedges (optional)

Drain and rinse the beans. Place them in the pressure cooker with just enough water to cover, the ground coriander, cinnamon, and oil (if needed).

Lock the lid in place. Over high heat, bring to high pressure. Lower the heat just enough to maintain high pressure and cook for 6 minutes. Allow the pressure to come down

TIPS & TECHNIQUES

In many traditional recipes, the beans are tossed with a pestolike paste containing walnuts, fresh coriander, and raw garlic, but I much prefer the taste of roasted garlic.

Because the beans quickly absorb the sauce, it's best to dress them just before serving. Serve this dish warm or at room temperature.

For optimum taste and freshness, shell the walnuts yourself. Store any leftovers (shelled or unshelled) in the freezer.

Leftover bean cooking liquid can be used for cooking grains.

VARIATIONS

Before adding the dressing, toss the beans with any of the following:

¼ cup finely chopped red or Vidalia onion

½ cup peeled, seeded, diced cucumber

½ cup thinly sliced celery

naturally. Remove the lid, tilting it away from you to allow any excess steam to escape. If the beans are not quite tender (they should retain their shape but be quite soft when you bite into them), replace (but do not lock) the lid and simmer until they are done. Drain the beans, reserving the cooking liquid, and set aside.

Prepare the sauce by combining ⅓ cup slightly cooled cooking liquid, the roasted garlic, walnuts, vinegar, salt, and coriander in a food processor or blender to create a thick but pourable sauce. Add a bit more of the cooking liquid, if necessary.

Just before serving, toss the beans with the sauce. Mound the beans on a bed of greens surrounded by tomato wedges, if desired.

LENTILS WITH SQUASH

9 minutes high pressure

This recipe is extremely satisfying in the way that simple dishes with a few high-quality ingredients can be. I've offered a range of sage and recommend the smaller quantity to those of you not as committed to its particular flavor as I am.

This is a great weekday dish that requires very little prep. Serve it over whole-wheat couscous accompanied by a salad for a complete meal. *Serves 4 to 6*

1 tablespoon safflower or canola oil

1½ cups coarsely chopped onions

2¾ cups boiling water

1 cup dried lentils, picked over and rinsed

1 pound butternut, kabocha, or delicata squash, seeded and cut into 1-inch chunks (peeling not necessary)

½ to 1½ teaspoon(s) dried sage leaves

. . . .

Salt and freshly ground pepper to taste

1 to 3 teaspoons balsamic vinegar (optional)

¼ cup minced fresh parsley

Heat the oil in the cooker. Cook the onions over medium-high heat, stirring frequently, until they just begin to brown, 2 to 3 minutes. Add the water (stand back to avoid sputtering oil), lentils, squash, and sage.

Lock the lid in place. Over high heat, bring to high pressure. Lower the heat just enough to maintain high pressure and cook for 9 minutes. Release the pressure with a quick-release method. Remove the lid, tilting it away from you to allow any excess steam to escape. If the lentils are not quite tender, replace (but do not lock) the lid and simmer until they are done. (Depending upon the age of the lentils, the mixture may be soupy or a bit dry; add boiling water as needed to create a stewlike consistency.)

Add salt and pepper and stir well. Add a bit of vinegar, if desired, to perk up the flavors. Serve in small bowls garnished with parsley.

Lentils with Sweet Potatoes

Substitute an equal amount of peeled sweet potatoes, cut into chunks, for the squash. Instead of sage, use 2½ teaspoons

This dish is especially good when prepared with a full-flavored squash, such as kabocha or delicata. The bright green, yellow, or orange of the squash skin adds a welcome splash of color.

I once prepared this dish with Spanish Pardina lentils, which have a pinkish hue and are slightly smaller than brown lentils. While the latter are often peppery, Pardina lentils have a delightful nuttiness. They are worth ordering by mail from Bean Bag (see Mail-Order Sources) — and while you're at it, consider asking for some French lentils le Puy as well. You won't regret it. (Add 2 more minutes under high pressure when cooking Spanish or French lentils.)

Depending on how much cooking the lentils require, the squash may begin to break down into a purée. If you prefer to keep the squash intact, you can cut it into larger chunks and stir more carefully when you are adding the salt.

ground coriander seeds and ⅛ to ¼ teaspoon ground cardamom seeds. If desired, stir in 1 tablespoon of minced orange peel at the end. The sweet potatoes become very soft and turn into a purée when stirred. This variation results in a sweeter and starchier dish.

LENTIL STEW WITH SPICY GREENS

9 minutes high pressure, 2 to 3 minutes simmering

Here is a pretty stew with its bright flecks of green against an earthy foreground of lentils. Full of flavor surprises and rich in taste straight from the pot, but even better the next day.

Taste the greens before adding to make sure they are not too bitter or spicy for you. Serve the lentils over rice, bulgur, or couscous and accompany with a steamed vegetable or green salad. *Serves 3 to 4*

1 tablespoon safflower or canola oil
1 cup coarsely chopped onions
1 cup diced carrots
2 teaspoons ground coriander seeds
1½ teaspoons ground cinnamon
½ teaspoon ground allspice
4 cups boiling water
1½ cups dried lentils, picked over and rinsed

. . . .

4 to 6 cups coarsely chopped fresh quick-cooking greens
    such as arugula, watercress, or young mustard greens
    (trim off any thick stems)
¾ teaspoon salt, or to taste
Freshly squeezed lemon juice or balsamic vinegar
    (optional)

continued

TIPS & TECHNIQUES

For best visual effect, add the greens only to that portion of stew you plan to eat. When reheating any leftovers, cook the remaining greens at that time.

Alternatively, if the mixture is fairly thick, use leftovers to make a nice pâté. Add all the greens when you prepare the dish. Place leftovers in a small loaf pan. Press ⅓ cup coarsely chopped walnuts into the top and refrigerate. Next day, serve in slices as a pâté.

....

Use 5 ounces of frozen (defrosted) chopped spinach instead of the greens.

Use chopped beet greens or Swiss chard instead of spicy greens.

Add ⅓ cup coarsely chopped walnuts just before serving.

Heat the oil in the cooker. Cook the onions and carrots over medium-high heat, stirring frequently, for 1 minute. Stir in the coriander, cinnamon, and allspice and cook an additional 20 seconds. Add the water (stand back to avoid sputtering oil) and lentils.

Lock the lid in place. Over high heat, bring to high pressure. Lower the heat just enough to maintain high pressure and cook for 9 minutes. Reduce the pressure with a quick-release method. Remove the lid, tilting it away from you to allow any excess steam to escape. If the lentils are not quite tender, replace (but do not lock) the lid and simmer until they are done. Add ¼ to ½ cup extra boiling water if the mixture seems dry.

Stir in the greens and salt. Cook over medium heat until the greens are tender, 2 to 3 minutes. Stir in lemon juice just before serving, if desired, to sharpen the flavors. Serve in shallow bowls.

PHILIPPINE MONGO
MUNG BEAN STEW

10 minutes high pressure

....

For a mellower version, replace the arugula with 10 ounces frozen (defrosted) chopped spinach, squeezed between two plates to release excess water. Simmer until the spinach is heated through.

Use lentils instead of mung beans. Cook under pressure for 9 minutes.

This tasty dish was suggested to me by my Philippine friend and colleague Reynaldo Alejandro, author of *The Philippine Cookbook* (Coward-McCann, 1982). He thought that arugula would be a good choice to replace his country's bitter melon leaves and that lime juice would be a nice stand-in for the citruslike calamansi. I've added some diced red bell pepper for a splash of color.

Since mung beans are quick-cooking and require no soaking, *mongo* is a good choice for last-minute suppers. The beans don't hold their shape, so this recipe results in a thick pottage best served as a side dish in bowls. It's also great over rice, pasta, or polenta. (You may need to thin it slightly.) Refrigerated leftovers often become thick enough to serve in slices as a pâté.

Taste the arugula or watercress first to be sure it is not too spicy for you. ***Serves 4 to 6***

1 tablespoon olive oil

1 tablespoon minced garlic

2 cups coarsely chopped onions

½ cup diced red bell pepper

1½ cups dried mung beans, picked over and rinsed

3 cups boiling water

. . . .

3 to 4 cups chopped arugula or watercress leaves

2 to 3 tablespoons freshly squeezed lime juice

Salt to taste

Heat the oil in the cooker. Cook the garlic over medium-high heat, stirring constantly, until lightly browned. Immediately add the onions and red bell pepper and continue cooking, stirring frequently, for 1 minute. Add the mung beans and water (stand back to avoid sputtering oil).

Lock the lid in place. If your cooker has a thin bottom, set it on a heated Flame Tamer. Over high heat, bring to high pressure. Lower the heat just enough to maintain high pressure and cook for 10 minutes. Allow the pressure to come down naturally or use a quick-release method. Remove the lid, tilting it away from you to allow any excess steam to escape. If the mung beans are not quite tender, replace (but do not lock) the lid and simmer until they are done. Add a bit more boiling water if the mixture seems dry.

Just before serving, stir in the arugula, lime juice, and salt. Serve in shallow bowls.

LOUISIANA RED BEANS

12 minutes high pressure

I've never managed to taste the famous red beans at Buster Holmes's restaurant in New Orleans, but I suspect that natives of that town might be surprised at how flavorful a vegetarian version can be. Serve the red beans over Basic Casserole Brown Rice with a side of Creole Okra Stew. And don't forget to pass the Tabasco.

I hope Creole cooks will forgive me for mentioning that leftover beans taste great reheated and rolled into a flour tortilla with slivers of avocado and a sprinkling of additional chopped scallions. *Serves 6*

1½ cups dried red kidney beans, picked over and rinsed, soaked overnight in ample water to cover or speed-soaked (page 185)

1 tablespoon olive oil

1 tablespoon coarsely chopped garlic

1½ cups coarsely chopped onions

2 to 3 cups boiling water

1 large red or green bell pepper, seeded and diced

2 teaspoons dried oregano leaves

½ teaspoon dried thyme leaves

1 teaspoon dried sage leaves

2 large bay leaves

⅛ to ¼ teaspoon crushed red pepper flakes or a generous pinch of cayenne (optional)

. . . .

½ cup thinly sliced scallion greens

2 to 4 teaspoons apple cider or balsamic vinegar

Salt and freshly ground pepper to taste

Liquid smoke flavoring to taste (optional)

Tabasco sauce to taste

Drain and rinse the beans. Set aside.

Heat the oil in the cooker. Cook the garlic over medium-high heat, stirring constantly, until lightly browned. Immediately add the onions and continue to cook, stirring frequently, for 1 minute. Add the reserved beans and just enough water to cover (stand back to avoid sputtering oil). Stir in the bell

If you find the dish too soupy, before adding the scallion greens and seasonings, you may either lift out all of the beans with a slotted spoon and serve, or purée about a cupful of the beans in a food processor or blender and stir them back in to thicken. Alternatively, if time permits, allow the dish to sit in the cooker at room temperature with the lid slightly ajar for about 2 hours, during which time much of the liquid will be absorbed by the beans.

pepper, oregano, thyme, sage, bay leaves, and red pepper flakes (if using).

Lock the lid in place. Over high heat, bring to high pressure. Lower the heat just enough to maintain high pressure and cook for 12 minutes. Allow the pressure to come down naturally (preferred) or use a quick-release method. Remove the lid, tilting it away from you to allow any excess steam to escape. If the beans are not quite tender, replace (but do not lock) the lid and simmer until they are done.

Remove the bay leaves. Stir in the scallion greens and the vinegar, salt and pepper, and liquid smoke (if using) to taste. Serve over a mound of steamed brown or white rice, and pass the Tabasco on the side.

Split Pea Dal
with Apple and Coconut

6 minutes high pressure

This enchanting souplike dal is a magic carpet ride to India. It has a very exotic flavor and a fetching burnished-gold hue. The recipe was inspired by a similar preparation in Yamuna Devi's fascinating cookbook, *Lord Krishna's Cuisine* (Dutton, 1987).

Serve the dal in small bowls as part of an Indian menu. Or try it as the soup course to begin a meal. The dal thickens on standing, so plan to thin it as needed with a bit of water or vegetable stock. *Serves 4 to 6*

1 tablespoon safflower or canola oil

2 teaspoons whole cumin seeds

1 to 2 jalapeño peppers, seeded and diced (wear rubber gloves when handling chili peppers), or a generous pinch of crushed red pepper flakes

1½ tablespoons finely minced fresh ginger

4 cups boiling water

1½ cups dried yellow split peas, picked over and rinsed

⅓ cup dried, grated, unsweetened coconut

1 teaspoon ground turmeric

½ teaspoon ground cinnamon

⅛ teaspoon ground cloves

⅛ teaspoon freshly ground pepper

1 large Granny Smith apple, peeled, cored, and cut into about 8 chunks

Salt to taste

¼ cup minced fresh coriander or parsley

Heat the oil in the cooker. Sizzle the cumin seeds over medium-high heat just until they begin to pop, 5 to 10 seconds. Immediately stir in the jalapeño and ginger and cook, stirring constantly, an additional 20 seconds. Add the water (stand back to avoid sputtering oil), split peas, coconut, turmeric, cinnamon, cloves, pepper, and apple.

TIPS & TECHNIQUES

Take care to add the cumin before the oil reaches its smoking point. If smoking occurs, turn off the heat, sop up the oil with a paper towel, and begin again.

VARIATION

Use red lentils instead of split peas. Cooking time remains the same.

Lock the lid in place. Over high heat, bring to high pressure. Lower the heat just enough to maintain high pressure and cook for 6 minutes. Allow the pressure to come down naturally or use a quick-release method. Remove the lid, tilting it away from you to allow any excess steam to escape.

Stir well as you add salt and the fresh coriander. If the dal is too thick, stir in a bit of boiling water or vegetable stock.

SPLIT PEA HUMMUS

8 minutes high pressure

Here is an easy hummus to prepare from quick-cooking yellow split peas instead of the longer cooking chickpeas. It is also an unconventionally low-fat hummus in that no sesame tahini is included. However, given the creaminess of the split peas, I don't think you'll be disappointed. And it even gets better as it ages under refrigeration. The inspiration for this recipe comes from the USA Dry Peas and Lentil Council.

For a Middle Eastern meal, try pairing the hummus with Whole Grain Tabbouleh Salad and pita triangles. It's nice to start out the meal with Herbed Tomato-Cauliflower Soup or Ratatouille Soup. ***Makes about 2 cups***

1 tablespoon safflower or canola oil

2 to 3 teaspoons finely minced garlic

1 teaspoon whole cumin seeds

½ cup finely chopped onion

1 cup dried yellow split peas, picked over and rinsed

2½ cups boiling water

2 teaspoons ground coriander seeds

. . . .

Salt to taste

2 to 3 tablespoons freshly squeezed lemon juice

¼ cup minced fresh parsley

Green or black olives

Sweet paprika

continued

TIPS & TECHNIQUES
. . . .
The hummus thickens and sometimes becomes quite hard when refrigerated. You may need to vigorously stir in a tablespoon or two of warm water before serving. Add more fresh lemon juice, if needed.

Heat the oil in the cooker. Cook the garlic over medium-high heat, stirring constantly, just until it begins to brown. Add the cumin seeds and continue stirring for about 5 more seconds. Immediately add the onion and cook, stirring frequently, for 1 additional minute. Add the split peas, water (stand back to avoid sputtering oil), and coriander.

Lock the lid in place. Over high heat, bring to high pressure. Lower the heat just enough to maintain high pressure and cook for 8 minutes. Allow the pressure to come down naturally or use a quick-release method. Remove the lid, tilting it away from you to allow any excess steam to escape.

Stir in the salt and transfer to a serving bowl to cool and thicken. Cover with a plate to prevent a crust from forming on top. Just before serving, stir in the lemon juice and parsley. Garnish with olives and a sprinkling of paprika.

SWEDISH BROWN BEANS WITH PEARS

6 minutes high pressure, 10-minute natural pressure release

I became smitten with a Swiss recipe for potatoes and pears that appeared in the late Jane Grigson's wonderful *Vegetable Book* (Atheneum, 1979). It seemed like a good idea to try substituting beans for the potatoes. If you enjoy adding a bit of fruity sweetness to foods that are normally classified as savory, I think you'll like this approach just fine.

I know that Swedish brown beans are probably not available at your local grocery or health food store, but I wanted you to know about them. They are a smallish brown bean with a creamy texture and full flavor. You can order them from Bean Bag (see Mail-Order Sources), or you can substitute navy beans in this recipe.

This dish goes nicely with Millet Pilaf with Mushrooms, Carrots, and Peas. *Serves 4 to 6*

TIPS & TECHNIQUES

The dried pears are often quite leathery. You might find it easier to snip them with kitchen shears rather than chop them.

Use the smaller amount of pears to reduce the sweetness of this dish.

VARIATION

Substitute chopped dried apricots or pitted prunes for the pears.

1½ cups dried Swedish brown or navy (pea) beans,
    picked over and rinsed, soaked overnight in ample
    water to cover or speed-soaked (page 185)
1 tablespoon safflower or canola oil
1 cup coarsely chopped onions
2 cups boiling water, approximately
½ to ¾ cup coarsely chopped dried pears
Scant ½ teaspoon ground cardamom

. . . .

1 to 2 tablespoons finely chopped fresh parsley
Salt and freshly ground pepper to taste

Drain and rinse the beans. Set aside.

Heat the oil in the cooker. Cook the onion over medium-high heat, stirring frequently, for 1 minute. Add the reserved beans and just enough water to cover (stand back to avoid sputtering oil). Stir in the pears and cardamom.

Lock the lid in place. Over high heat, bring to high pressure. Lower the heat just enough to maintain high pressure and cook for 6 minutes. Allow the pressure to come down naturally for 10 minutes. Quick-release any remaining pressure. Remove the lid, tilting it away from you to allow any excess steam to escape. If the beans are not quite tender, replace (but do not lock) the lid and simmer until they are done.

Stir in the parsley and the salt and pepper. If you have time to let the beans stand for an hour or so, the sauce will thicken. If you are serving them immediately, with a slotted spoon, transfer about a cupful of the beans to a food processor or blender, and purée. Stir the purée back into the pot.

TUSCAN WHITE BEANS WITH SAGE

8 to 9 minutes high pressure, 10-minute natural pressure release

The next time your heart aches to be in a small hill town in Tuscany, do the next best thing and transport your taste buds there with a portion of white beans and sage. This is one of those dishes that reminds me of the deep satisfaction afforded by life's simple pleasures.

Serve the beans with a steamed vegetable or a side of polenta and a colorful salad of greens and radicchio drizzled with a balsamic vinaigrette. ***Serves 4***

> 1½ cups dried cannellini or navy (pea) beans, picked over and rinsed, soaked overnight in ample water to cover or speed-soaked (page 185)
>
> 2 tablespoons olive oil
>
> 2 teaspoons coarsely chopped garlic
>
> 1½ to 2 teaspoons dried sage leaves (depending upon your love of sage)
>
> 2 cups boiling water, approximately
>
> . . . .
>
> Salt and freshly ground pepper to taste

Drain and rinse the beans. Set aside.

Heat 1 tablespoon of oil in the cooker. Cook the garlic over medium-high heat, stirring constantly, until lightly browned. Add the reserved beans, the sage, and just enough water to cover the beans (stand back to avoid sputtering oil).

Lock the lid in place. Over high heat, bring to high pressure. Lower the heat just enough to maintain high pressure and cook for 8 minutes (navy beans) or 9 minutes (cannellini beans). Allow the pressure to come down naturally for 10 minutes. Quick-release any remaining pressure. Remove the lid, tilting it away from you to allow any excess steam to escape. If the beans are not tender, replace (but do not lock) the lid and simmer until they are done.

Stir in the additional tablespoon of olive oil and the salt and pepper. To thicken the cooking liquid, either let the beans sit in the cooker at room temperature with the lid slightly ajar for 1 to 2 hours or, with a slotted spoon, transfer about 1 cup

TIPS & TECHNIQUES

A cautionary tale: I am one of those people who can't resist trying to make even the best foods taste better. Such was the case recently when I made these Tuscan beans and a bottle of fine-quality balsamic vinegar was standing nearby. "Why not?" said I to myself, and in went a scant ¼ teaspoon. Mistake. The simplicity vanished. Sometimes less is more.

When adding the sage leaves, rub them between your palms to release their essential oils.

VARIATION

Use 1 tablespoon dried basil leaves or *herbes de provence* (a commercial blend) instead of the sage.

of the beans to a food processor or blender, and purée. Stir the purée back in. Serve hot or at room temperature.

INDONESIAN-STYLE TEMPEH

3 minutes high pressure

The fermented soybean cake known as tempeh is a staple in the Indonesian kitchen, so I thought it was time I got around to using that country's culinary approach for its preparation.

If you have been looking for a recipe that shows tempeh off at its best, this may well be it. It's great over steamed white or brown rice. And I also like to use it as a sauce for spiral pasta. *Serves 4 to 6*

3 cups coconut milk (page 19)

2 teaspoons minced garlic

1½ cups coarsely chopped onions

1 large red bell pepper, seeded and cut into thin strips

½ pound fresh green beans, trimmed and cut into thirds

1 jalapeño pepper, seeded and thinly sliced (wear rubber gloves when handling chili peppers), or a generous pinch of crushed red pepper flakes (optional)

1 pound tempeh (two 8-ounce packages), cut into ½-inch dice

2 to 3 tablespoons tamari soy sauce

2 to 3 tablespoons freshly squeezed lime juice

¼ cup thinly sliced scallion greens or chopped chives

Place the coconut milk, garlic, onions, red bell pepper, green beans, jalapeño (if using), tempeh, and 2 tablespoons of the soy sauce in the cooker.

Lock the lid in place. Over high heat, bring to high pressure. Lower the heat just enough to maintain high pressure and cook for 3 minutes. Reduce the pressure with a quick-release method. Remove the lid, tilting it away from you to allow any excess steam to escape.

With a slotted spoon, transfer about 1 cup of the tempeh and vegetables to a food processor or blender and purée. Stir the purée back into the pot to create a thick sauce. Add soy sauce and lime juice to taste. Garnish with scallions.

PASTA E FAGIOLI

12 minutes high pressure (approximately), 7 to 8 minutes additional cooking

TIPS & TECHNIQUES

If you're in a hurry, you can precook the pasta and add it at the end. The stew will not initially be as thick, but it will thicken and the pasta will swell upon standing.

Although it's traditional to make this hearty winter soup with cannellini, I like to make it with mixed beans—a good way to use up odd bits that are left over. It's nice to include some red kidney beans for their rich color.

Just cook this dish the length of time required for the longest-cooking bean. Some of the other beans may become a bit mushy, but that creates an appealing creamy thickness.

Plan to serve the Pasta e Fagioli in bowls. A meal in itself with some crunchy bread sticks or foccaccia and a large green salad. *Serves 6*

1½ cups dried mixed beans, cannellini, or navy (pea) beans, soaked overnight in ample water to cover or speed-soaked (page 185)

1 to 2 tablespoons olive oil

1 tablespoon coarsely chopped garlic

2 cups coarsely chopped onions

2 large celery ribs, diced

2 large carrots, halved lengthwise and cut into ½-inch slices

1 large bay leaf

1½ teaspoons dried basil leaves

1 teaspoon dried rosemary leaves

¼ teaspoon crushed red pepper flakes (optional)

5 cups boiling water

. . . .

3 tablespoons tomato paste

1 cup small or medium dry pasta (such as orzo or spirals)

2 to 3 teaspoons balsamic vinegar

1 teaspoon salt, or to taste

Freshly grated Parmesan cheese (optional)

Drain and rinse the beans. Set aside.

Heat 1 tablespoon of the oil in the cooker. Cook the garlic over medium-high heat, stirring frequently, until lightly browned. Stir in the onions and continue cooking, stirring occasionally, for 1 minute. Add the celery, carrots, bay leaf, basil, rosemary, red pepper flakes (if using), reserved beans, and water (stand back to avoid sputtering oil).

Lock the lid in place. Over high heat, bring to high pressure. Lower the heat just enough to maintain high pressure and cook for the length of time indicated for the longest cooking beans (check the bean cooking chart on page 188). Allow the pressure to come down naturally or use a quick-release method. Remove the lid, tilting it away from you to allow any excess steam to escape. If the beans are still quite hard, return to high pressure for a few more minutes or replace (but do not lock) the lid and simmer until they are just about tender. (Remember that they will be cooking 7 to 8 additional minutes with the pasta.)

Remove the bay leaf and stir in the tomato paste and pasta. Continue cooking over medium-high heat, stirring occasionally, until the pasta is tender, about 7 minutes. Stir in the vinegar, additional tablespoon of olive oil (if using), and salt. Garnish individual portions with Parmesan cheese, if desired.

Boston "Baked" Beans

5 minutes high pressure (divided), two 10-minute natural pressure releases

TIPS & TECHNIQUES

Because the acid in the molasses, tomato paste, and mustard toughens the bean skins and prevents the beans from cooking properly, these ingredients are added after the beans are thoroughly cooked. The final minute under pressure is critical for infusing them with flavor.

VARIATION

Add a few sliced tofu pups for a vegetarian version of franks and beans.

The pressure cooker achieves in a flash the mellow flavor and texture of long-baked beans. I think the Puritans would have been delighted with this adaptation (although they might have been shocked by the garlic).

In this recipe, the soaked beans are pressure cooked until just about tender. Then the flavorings are infused in a final minute under pressure. If you wish, add the red bell pepper for a touch of color.

Serve the beans with Red Flannel Hash, Coleslaw, and Revisionist Boston Brown Bread (recipe follows). ***Serves 4***

1½ cups dried navy (pea) beans, picked over and rinsed, soaked overnight in ample water to cover or speed-soaked (page 185)

1 to 2 teaspoons minced garlic

2 cups boiling water, approximately

1 tablespoon safflower or canola oil (optional, except for owners of jiggle-top cookers)

. . . .

2 to 3 tablespoons molasses

3 tablespoons tomato paste

2 tablespoons prepared mustard (coarse-grained is nice)

½ cup diced red bell pepper (optional)

. . . .

Salt to taste

1 to 3 teaspoons apple cider vinegar (optional)

Rinse and drain the beans. Set the beans, garlic, just enough water to cover, and the oil (if needed) in the cooker.

Lock the lid in place. Over high heat, bring to high pressure. Reduce the heat just enough to maintain high pressure and cook for 4 minutes. Allow the pressure to come down naturally for 10 minutes. Quick-release any remaining pressure. Remove the lid, tilting it away from you to allow any excess steam to escape. The beans should be tender enough to eat (see Tips). If they are not sufficiently soft, replace (but do not lock) the lid and simmer until they are done.

Stir in the molasses, tomato paste, mustard, and red bell pepper (if using). Lock the lid in place. Over high heat, bring to high pressure. Lower the heat just enough to maintain high pressure and cook for 1 minute. Again allow the pressure to come down naturally for 10 minutes. Quick-release any remaining pressure. Remove the lid, tilting it away from you to allow any excess steam to escape. Add salt to taste. At this point, the beans should be quite soft and infused with flavor. If not, simmer with the cover slightly ajar until the beans are done.

If the dish is too soupy, allow it to sit in the cooker at room temperature with the lid slightly ajar for an hour, or until most of the liquid is absorbed. Alternatively, with a slotted spoon, transfer about a cupful of the beans to a food processor or blender, and purée. Stir the purée back into the pot. Add a bit of vinegar, if desired, to perk up the flavors. Serve in shallow bowls.

REVISIONIST
BOSTON BROWN BREAD

20 to 25 minutes high pressure, 10-minute natural pressure release

H ere's a quick and appealing way to make this New England favorite. The batter is steamed in three 15-ounce cans (see Tips) and then unmolded before serving. ***Makes 3 mini-loaves***

1 cup yellow cornmeal

1 cup rye flour

1 cup whole-wheat pastry flour

1½ teaspoons baking soda

½ teaspoon salt

¾ cup raisins

1¼ cups prune juice

⅓ cup molasses

In a large bowl, combine the cornmeal and the rye and pastry flours. (Sifting is not necessary.) Stir in the baking soda, salt, and raisins. In a liquid measuring cup, stir together the prune juice and molasses. Stir this liquid into the dry ingredients just until it is absorbed.

Divide the mixture among three 15-ounce cans (they will each be about three quarters full). Cover each securely with a piece of aluminum foil large enough so that the ends reach under the bottom of the can.

Place the rack and 6 cups of boiling water in the cooker. Set the cans on the rack.

Lock the lid in place. Over high heat, bring to high pressure. Lower the heat just enough to maintain high pressure and cook for 20 minutes. Allow the pressure to come down naturally for 10 minutes. Quick-release any remaining pressure. Remove the lid, tilting it away from you to allow any excess steam to escape.

Once the steam has died down, remove one of the cans with the aid of a pot holder or kitchen towel. When cool enough to handle, remove the aluminum foil. Run a knife around the edge and unmold. Cut the loaf in half and check to see if it is cooked through to the middle. If not, put both

TIPS & TECHNIQUES

I use cans recycled from Eden-brand organic beans, as they are lead-free and enamel-lined. These cans do not require oiling to facilitate unmolding the cooked breads. If using standard cans, brush the insides lightly with oil before pouring in the batter.

Once cooked, these breads should be unmolded as soon as they are cool enough to handle. Any leftover breads may be thoroughly cooled, then tightly wrapped and refrigerated for up to 1 week (or frozen for up to 3 months). The breads are best when served warm. They can be sliced and reheated in a toaster oven.

To unmold, run a knife around the edge of the can and shake up and down until the bread begins to fall out. Then gently pull it out. In the rare instance that you can't get the bread out, remove the other end of the can and push it out. These breads unmold most easily while still warm.

halves back in the can, cover with foil, and return to the cooker. Cook for an additional 5 minutes under high pressure and again use a natural pressure release.

When the tester loaf is cooked throughout, remove the remaining cans, unmold the breads (see Tips), and serve hot. Allow any leftover loaves to cool to room temperature, then unmold and refrigerate or freeze (see Tips).

ALL-PURPOSE BEAN SALAD

Here's a basic salad recipe that allows you to create a quick entree with leftover beans and ingredients easily kept on hand. Serve the salad on a bed of lettuce or in radicchio cups. *Serves 3 to 4 (may be doubled or tripled)*

For the salad

> 2 cups cooked beans
> 2 cups total of one or more of the following:
>> diced raw carrots, celery, red or green bell pepper
>> cooked corn kernels
>> shredded red cabbage
> 1/3 to 1/2 cup chopped fresh herbs, such as parsley, dill, coriander, or basil

Optional additions

> 1/3 cup chopped scallion greens or red onion
> 1/4 cup chopped olives or oil-packed sun-dried tomatoes
> 2 to 3 tablespoons toasted pumpkin or sunflower seeds
> 1 to 2 tablespoons drained capers

For the dressing

> 2 tablespoons fruity olive oil
> 2 to 3 tablespoons freshly squeezed lemon or lime juice or red wine vinegar
> Salt and freshly ground pepper to taste

Optional garnishes

> Lettuce or radicchio cups
> Sliced avocado (unusually delicious with beans), preferably Haas variety
> Slice of warm goat cheese

In a bowl, combine the ingredients for the salad plus any optional additions. Drizzle the olive oil and lemon juice on top while stirring. Add salt and pepper.

Set the salad on a bed of lettuce or into radicchio cups. Garnish with sliced avocado or goat cheese, if desired.

TIPS & TECHNIQUES

Because beans are rather bland, I find that any accompanying dressing requires an almost equal amount of acid (lemon juice, vinegar, etc.) and oil. Sometimes I even tip the balance in favor of the acid to avoid using excess salt.

Depending upon how many optional additions you use, you may need to use more dressing than is suggested here.

When making up the salad, aim for variety of color.

The salad will quickly absorb the sharp edge of the lemon juice, so the dressing should be added just before serving. Any leftovers will require a bit more lemon juice (or other acid) to perk up the flavors.

VARIATION

Use 1 cup of beans and 1 cup of grains instead of 2 cups of beans.

CRIMSON BEAN SALAD

The brilliant magenta of this salad makes it an attractive candidate for a buffet table. For optimum flavor and appearance, let it marinate for a few hours before serving.
Serves 6

For the dressing

3 tablespoons olive oil

4 to 6 tablespoons freshly squeezed lemon juice

1 to 1½ teaspoons dried oregano leaves (see Tips)

½ teaspoon salt, or to taste

For the salad

1¼ pounds cooked beets, peeled and cut into
½-inch dice

2 to 3 cups cooked white beans, such as navy (pea),
Great Northern, cannellini, or White Runner

1 cup thinly sliced scallion greens

3 tablespoons drained capers or finely chopped sweet
pickle

In a small jar, combine the oil, 4 tablespoons of lemon juice, the oregano, and salt. Shake well to blend.

In a large bowl or storage container, combine the beets, beans, scallion greens, and capers. Pour on the dressing and gently stir. Add salt to taste. Cover and marinate at room temperature for a few hours. Stir in extra lemon juice right before serving, if desired.

Warm White Bean Vinaigrette

3 to 5 minutes high pressure, 10-minute natural pressure release

Food like this transports me to Provence, where I once spent a blessed summer within sniffing distance of lavender fields.

This is an elegant warm bean salad, nice for a luncheon entree any time of year. For an especially dramatic presentation, set individual servings in large radicchio or red cabbage cups. Garnish with cornichons, cherry tomatoes, and Niçoise olives. Steamed green beans and a hearty peasant loaf make good accompaniments.

Leftovers are delicious at room temperature, refreshed with a drizzle of lemon juice. **Serves 5 to 6**

2 cups dried navy (pea), Great Northern, or cannellini
beans, picked over and rinsed, soaked overnight in
ample water to cover or speed-soaked (page 185)
2 tablespoons olive oil
1 cup thinly sliced leeks (white and light green parts) or
coarsely chopped onions
2 teaspoons finely minced garlic
2 teaspoons dried basil leaves
3 cups boiling water
. . . .
1½ cups finely chopped red cabbage
2 to 3 tablespoons drained capers
1 to 2 tablespoons balsamic vinegar or freshly squeezed
lemon juice
Salt to taste

Drain and rinse the beans. Set aside.

Heat 1 tablespoon of the oil in the cooker. Cook the leeks and garlic over medium-high heat, stirring frequently, for 1 minute. Add the basil, water (stand back to avoid sputtering oil), and reserved beans.

Lock the lid in place. Over high heat, bring to high pressure. Lower the heat just enough to maintain high pressure and cook for 3 minutes (navy and Great Northern) or 5 minutes (cannellini). Allow the pressure to come down natu-

rally for 10 minutes. Quick-release any remaining pressure. Remove the lid, tilting it away from you to allow any excess steam to escape. If the beans are not tender, replace (but do not lock) the lid and simmer until they are done. If time permits, allow the beans to sit in the cooker at room temperature with the lid slightly ajar for about 2 hours, during which time they will absorb most of the excess liquid. If serving immediately, lift the beans with a slotted spoon or drain off most of the cooking liquid (save it for stock or for cooking grains) and transfer to a serving bowl.

Stir in the chopped red cabbage and capers. Season the beans with the additional tablespoon of olive oil, vinegar to taste, and salt.

BEAN SALSA

Here's a great recipe for leftover beans. Although pinto, navy, and red kidney beans would all work nicely, I especially like to prepare the salsa with black beans.

Have at least 3 limes on hand, in case the salsa needs an extra dousing. *Makes about 4 cups*

1½ cups cooked beans
⅓ to ½ cup finely chopped red onion
2 cups finely chopped fresh plum tomatoes
1 large yellow or red bell pepper, seeded and diced
1 to 2 jalapeño peppers, seeded and thinly sliced (wear rubber gloves when handling chili peppers)
½ cup tightly packed minced fresh coriander
⅓ cup freshly squeezed orange juice
3 tablespoons freshly squeezed lime juice, approximately
1 teaspoon salt, or to taste
Lettuce or radicchio cups
Sliced or cubed avocado, preferably Haas variety

In a bowl or storage container, combine all the ingredients except the lettuce and avocado. Cover and marinate at room temperature for 2 hours, or refrigerate for up to 4 days. Perk up the flavors by adding more lime juice as needed.

Lift with a slotted spoon and serve in lettuce cups, garnished with avocado.

VARIATIONS

Substitute 1 cup diced jicama or cooked corn kernels for the bell pepper.

Use the salsa as a filling for burritos.

TIPS & TECHNIQUES

Toss leftovers with pasta. Add more lime juice to taste.

Add ½ teaspoon minced garlic to the mixture. (I find the taste of raw garlic harsh and overpowering, but I know that some people like it.)

PICKLES, CHUTNEYS, AND SAUCES

Although you may think of your pressure cooker primarily when it comes time to make soup or rice, the "p.c." also comes in handy for preparing a variety of other foods. Here is a potpourri of enjoyable accompaniments, including recipes for quick pickles, chutneys, and sauces.

PICKLES

Mint-Pickled Beets

3 minutes high pressure

The beets are quickly pickled during their brief sojourn in the cooker. As they marinate in the refrigerator, they become slightly more pickled day by day. These beets make an attractive garnish for bean and grain salads.

Makes about 4 cups

1½ **pounds (4 medium) beets, scrubbed, trimmed,**
   halved, and cut into ¼-inch slices
1 **small red onion, halved, peeled, and thinly sliced**
⅔ **cup water**
⅓ **cup apple cider vinegar**
1 **tablespoon dried mint leaves**
⅛ **teaspoon salt**

Combine all the ingredients in the cooker. Stir to distribute the mint.

Lock the lid in place. Over high heat, bring to high pressure. Lower the heat just enough to maintain high pressure and cook for 3 minutes. Allow the pressure to come down naturally (for more tender beets) or use a quick-release method (for crunchy beets). Remove the lid, tilting it away from you to allow any excess steam to escape. If the beets are not as tender as you'd like, replace (but do not lock) the lid and simmer until they are done.

To serve, lift the beets out of the liquid with a slotted spoon and transfer to individual plates or to a serving bowl. Alternatively, transfer the beets and liquid to a glass container and set aside to cool. Cover tightly and refrigerate for up to 10 days. Turn the container upside down from time to time to distribute the pickling liquid.

TIPS & TECHNIQUES

It's not necessary to peel the beets, but for aesthetic reasons, peel off the hairy or tough spots around the root and stem.

VARIATION

Substitute 1 tablespoon of dried dill for the mint.

QUICK PICKLED BRUSSELS SPROUTS

0–1 minute high pressure

I find this a surprisingly tasty treatment for brussels sprouts. With some sliced carrot added for a splash of color, this pickle is a nice condiment to accompany an Italian or Mediterranean menu. ***Makes about 3 cups***

1 pint (10 ounces) brussels sprouts

⅔ cup water

⅓ cup white wine vinegar

1 teaspoon dried oregano leaves

2 teaspoons minced garlic

⅛ teaspoon salt

Generous pinch of crushed red pepper flakes (optional)

1 medium carrot, halved lengthwise and very thinly
    sliced

6 thin slices lemon

Trim off the stalk ends and cut each sprout into 3 slices (for small to medium sprouts) or 4 (for larger sprouts) from stalk end to top. Set aside.

Bring the water, vinegar, oregano, garlic, salt, and red pepper flakes (if using) to the boil in the cooker. Add the reserved sprouts, the carrot, and lemon.

Lock the lid in place. Over high heat, bring to high pressure. If cooking small to medium sprouts, immediately reduce the pressure using a quick-release method. If cooking large sprouts, lower the heat just enough to maintain high pressure and cook for 1 minute, then reduce the pressure using a quick-release method. Remove the lid, tilting it away from you to allow any excess steam to escape. The sprouts should be crunchy but not hard. If necessary, replace (but do not lock) the lid and let them continue to cook for a minute or two in the residual heat.

Set aside to cool, then transfer the mixture to a wide-mouthed glass jar. Cover tightly and refrigerate for up to 10 days. Turn the container upside down from time to time to distribute the pickling liquid.

JAPANESE DASHI TURNIPS

1 minute high pressure

VARIATION

Substitute peeled rutabagas cut into a ½-inch dice for all or part of the turnips.

This is a wonderful quick way to prepare a lightly salted turnip that works beautifully as a condiment but is mild enough to double as a vegetable side dish. The turnips develop an earthy brown tone from being cooked in the soy sauce; the shiitake add a luscious density of flavor.

Dashi turnips last a week to 10 days in the refrigerator.

Serves 4 to 6

1 cup water

2 tablespoons tamari soy sauce

2 teaspoons mirin (Japanese rice wine; optional)

One 2-inch strip kombu sea vegetable, rinsed (optional)

5 large dried shiitake mushrooms

1 teaspoon sugar (optional)

1½ pounds medium turnips, peeled and cut into 1-inch chunks

Bring the water and soy sauce to the boil in the cooker. Add the remaining ingredients.

Lock the lid in place. Over high heat, bring to high pressure. Lower the heat just enough to maintain high pressure and cook for 1 minute. Reduce the pressure with a quick-release method. Remove the lid, tilting it away from you to allow any excess steam to escape. If the turnips are not quite done—they should be tender-crisp—replace (but do not lock) the lid and let them continue to cook for a few more minutes in the residual heat.

When the turnips are done, remove the shiitakes. Slice off and discard the stems. Cut the caps into thin slivers. Finely chop the kombu (if using). If necessary, lift the turnips out of any remaining cooking liquid with a slotted spoon. Transfer to individual plates or to a serving bowl. Sprinkle the shiitake and kombu over the turnips and serve warm or at room temperature. Refrigerate any leftovers in a tightly covered glass container.

ONION COMPOTE

2 minutes high pressure

This is an irresistible southern French approach to cooking small onions. Served in small portions as a condiment, this chutneylike relish adds a welcome sweet-sour edge. Try it with Curried Quinoa Pilaf or Paella Vegetariana.

It's nice warm, straight out of the pot, but even better after a day's sojourn in the refrigerator. (You can reheat it or serve it at room temperature.) Some of my friends like it so much that they eat it in larger servings, more akin to a vegetable side dish. *Makes about 4 cups*

1½ pounds small white boiling onions (about ¾ ounce each), trimmed, peeled, and halved from root to tip

2 cups coarsely chopped fresh or canned (drained) plum tomatoes

½ cup water

1 to 2 tablespoons balsamic or other red wine vinegar

1 large bay leaf

½ teaspoon dried thyme leaves

⅓ cup dried currants or raisins

½ teaspoon salt

Freshly ground pepper to taste

Place the onions, tomatoes, and water, 1 tablespoon of vinegar, the bay leaf, thyme, currants, salt, and pepper in the cooker.

Lock the lid in place. Over high heat, bring to high pressure. Lower the heat just enough to maintain high pressure and cook for 2 minutes. Reduce the pressure with a quick-release method. Remove the lid, tilting it away from you to allow any excess steam to escape. If the onions are not quite tender, replace (but do not lock) the lid and let them continue to cook for a few more minutes in the residual heat.

Remove the bay leaf. With a slotted spoon, transfer 1 cup of the mixture to a food processor or blender, and purée. Stir the purée back into the onions. Adjust the seasonings and add more vinegar to create a sharper edge, if desired. Serve in small bowls, or transfer with a slotted spoon to a serving dish to use as a condiment. Refrigerate any leftovers in a tightly covered glass container for up to 5 days.

If small white onions are not available, you can substitute larger white or yellow onions (6 to 7 ounces each), peeled and quartered. Alternatively, substitute pearl onions, peeled and left whole.

CHUTNEYS

SUN-DRIED TOMATO CHUTNEY

5 minutes high pressure

This is a memorable chutney to serve with the various Indian dishes in this book. A number of my testers also like to use it as a spread on bagels or crackers, with drained yogurt cheese or tofu cream cheese.

The tomatoes provide an intense, winey flavor, while the fennel and coriander offer aromatic contrast. A dollop of it would go a long way to improve store-bought spaghetti sauce.

The chutney develops more complex flavor as it ages in the refrigerator. ***Makes about 2 cups***

1 tablespoon olive oil
2 teaspoons whole coriander seeds
1 teaspoon whole fennel seeds
1½ cups coarsely chopped onions
2 cups dry-packed sun-dried tomatoes
½ cup raisins
1 cup water
1 tablespoon balsamic vinegar
1 small dried red chili pepper (chipotle preferred), stem removed, seeded and torn into 4 to 5 pieces (wear rubber gloves when handling chili peppers; see Tips)

Heat the oil in the cooker. Sizzle the coriander and fennel seeds over medium-high heat for about 10 seconds; while doing this, pound down on the seeds with the flat tip of a wooden spatula or the handle of a large knife. (Your aim is to crush them slightly.) Add the onions and continue cooking, stirring frequently, for an additional minute. Add the tomatoes, raisins, water (stand back to avoid sputtering oil), vinegar, and chili pepper.

Lock the lid in place. Over high heat, bring to high pressure. Lower the heat just enough to maintain high pressure and cook for 5 minutes. Allow the pressure to come down naturally or use a quick-release method. Remove the lid, tilting it away from you to allow any excess steam to escape.

If you leave in most or all of the chili pepper seeds, this chutney will be fire-alarm hot. If you include 3 or 4 seeds, it will be mildly hot. However, since the heat in chili peppers is quite variable, you might want to err on the side of caution. You can always add a dash of cayenne (ground red pepper) or hot sauce at the end, if the chutney is not potent enough.

I don't find that this chutney needs salt, but you might like to add some.

Stir well and set aside to cool somewhat. Pulse the whole mixture (including any cooking liquid) 8 to 10 times in a food processor to create a coarse purée. Transfer to a glass container and cover tightly. Store in the refrigerator for up to 3 weeks.

FRUITY COCONUT CHUTNEY

5 minutes high pressure

This sweet chutney is a great alternative to the savory one that follows. It goes well with all of the Indian recipes in this book and makes a memorable contribution to Chutney Rice. *Makes about 2 cups*

1½ cups apple juice or 1 cup apple juice and ½ cup
  water (for a less sweet version)
2 tablespoons apple cider vinegar
1 cup chopped pitted prunes
1 cup dried apricots, snipped into bits
1 cup dried, grated, unsweetened coconut
1 to 2 small dried red chili peppers or a generous pinch
  of crushed red pepper flakes
2 teaspoons aniseed
2 teaspoons ground ginger
Pinch of salt

Bring the juice and vinegar to the boil in the cooker. Stir in the remaining ingredients.

Lock the lid in place. Over high heat, bring to high pressure. Lower the heat just enough to maintain high pressure and cook for 5 minutes. Allow the pressure to come down naturally or use a quick-release method. Remove the lid, tilting it away from you to allow any excess steam to escape.

Remove the chili pepper(s), if used. Stir well and set aside to cool. Transfer to a glass container and cover tightly. Store in the refrigerator for up to 3 weeks.

TIPS & TECHNIQUES

This recipe results in a thick chutney. Add ¼ cup more liquid for a thinner condiment.

SAUCES

CRANBERRY-ORANGE SAUCE

5 minutes high pressure

H ere's a terrific alternative to the standard cranberry sauce. It's extremely easy to make and improves with overnight refrigeration, so plan on preparing it a day in advance.

Note: Users of jiggle-top cookers should either avoid this recipe or be on the alert lest a cranberry skin clogs the vent. If the cooker makes any loud hissing sounds, immediately turn off the heat. Once the pressure is down, unlock the lid and finish off the recipe by simmering until done.

Makes about 3 cups

> 2 juice oranges, scrubbed and cut into eighths (discard seeds)
>
> 3 cups whole cranberries (fresh or frozen), picked over and rinsed
>
> ⅓ cup raisins or dried currants
>
> 2 tablespoons finely chopped fresh ginger
>
> ¼ cup maple syrup
>
> ¼ cup water
>
> ¾ teaspoon ground allspice or cinnamon
>
> Pinch of salt

Pulse the unpeeled orange pieces in a food processor until finely chopped. Combine the chopped oranges with the remaining ingredients in the cooker.

Lock the lid in place. If using a jiggle-top cooker, or if your cooker has a thin bottom, set it on a heated Flame Tamer. Over high heat, bring to high pressure. Lower the heat just enough to maintain high pressure and cook for 5 minutes. Quick-release the pressure by running cold water over the lid of the cooker. Remove the lid, tilting it away from you to allow any excess steam to escape.

Stir well and set aside to cool. Transfer to wide-mouthed glass jars and cover tightly. Store in the refrigerator for up to 10 days.

TIPS & TECHNIQUES

The liquid released from the oranges and cranberries should be sufficient to bring the cooker up to pressure with only ¼ cup of added water.

Coconut Squash Sauce

6 minutes high pressure

This quick-and-easy sauce is delicious over rice or steamed vegetables. You can freeze any leftovers for a quick supper down the road. *Makes about 4 cups*

1 tablespoon safflower or canola oil

1½ teaspoons minced garlic

1 jalapeño pepper, seeded and thinly sliced (wear rubber gloves when handling chili peppers)

2 cups coconut milk (page 19)

1½ cups coarsely chopped fresh or canned (drained) plum tomatoes

1 pound butternut or kabocha squash, peeled, seeded, and cut into 1-inch chunks

1 teaspoon salt, or to taste

Heat the oil in the cooker. Cook the garlic over medium-high heat, stirring constantly, until it just begins to brown. Then immediately add the jalapeño, coconut milk (stand back to avoid sputtering oil), tomatoes, squash, and salt.

Lock the lid in place. Over high heat, bring to high pressure. Lower the heat just enough to maintain high pressure and cook for 6 minutes. Allow the pressure to come down naturally or use a quick-release method. Remove the lid, tilting it away from you to allow any excess steam to escape. If the squash is still firm, replace (but do not lock) the lid and continue to steam for a few more minutes in the residual heat.

Stir vigorously to mash the squash and create a thick sauce.

VARIATIONS

For a hotter sauce, add 3 to 4 (or more) of the jalapeño pepper seeds.

Thin leftovers with vegetable stock to make a memorable soup.

HEARTY TOMATO-VEGETABLE SAUCE

10 minutes high pressure

TIPS & TECHNIQUES

The water given off by the tomatoes, mushrooms, and onions should be sufficient to bring the sauce up to pressure. However, if you are experiencing difficulty, stir in ½ cup water or the juice drained from canned tomatoes.

The sugar in tomatoes tends to cause scorching on the bottom of the cooker. Always use a Flame Tamer when preparing recipes that call for tomatoes.

Plum (Roma) tomatoes are ideal for making a thick sauce since they are less watery than other varieties. If you object to the texture of tomato skins or seeds, peel and seed the tomatoes before chopping.

When reheating leftovers, do so over low heat, stirring frequently, to avoid scorching.

The addition of coarse bulgur wheat gives this tomato sauce a hearty appeal and also serves the function of absorbing some of the liquid given off by the tomatoes. It's a nice chunky topping for pasta, grains, or beans. Leftovers freeze beautifully.

Do not attempt this recipe without a Flame Tamer, no matter what type of cooker you are using. *Makes about 6 cups*

1 tablespoon olive oil

2 teaspoons minced garlic

2 cups coarsely chopped onions

2½ pounds fresh plum tomatoes, coarsely chopped (or one 35-ounce can peeled plum tomatoes, drained and chopped)

2 medium carrots, finely chopped

1 large green bell pepper, seeded and diced

½ pound medium fresh mushrooms, trimmed and quartered

½ cup coarse bulgur

2 teaspoons dried oregano leaves

1 teaspoon dried basil leaves

1 teaspoon whole fennel seeds

¼ teaspoon crushed red pepper flakes (optional)

1 teaspoon salt, or to taste

. . . .

2 to 3 teaspoons balsamic vinegar (optional)

Heat the oil in the cooker. Cook the garlic over medium-high heat, stirring constantly, until browned. Immediately add the onions and continue to cook, stirring frequently, for 1 minute.

Stir in the tomatoes (stand back to avoid sputtering oil), carrots, pepper, mushrooms, bulgur, oregano, basil, fennel, red pepper flakes (if using), and salt.

Lock the lid in place. Set the cooker on a heated Flame Tamer. Over high heat, bring to high pressure. (This is likely to take longer than usual.) Lower the heat just enough to maintain high pressure and cook for 10 minutes. Allow the pressure to come down naturally or quick-release the pressure by placing the cooker under cold running water. Remove the lid, tilting it away from you to allow any excess steam to escape.

Stir well. Add a bit of balsamic vinegar to perk up the flavors, if desired.

SQUASH COLOMBO

6 minutes high pressure

Colombo is the name of the currylike spice blend used in the French West Indies. I have combined it with squash to create a thick sauce of complex flavor and luscious texture. It's great over pasta or rice, especially Coconut Rice.
Serves 3 to 4

- 1 cup water
- 1 cup chopped fresh or canned (drained) plum tomatoes
- ½ cup finely chopped onion
- 1 tablespoon finely minced fresh ginger
- 1 to 2 jalapeño or serrano peppers, seeded and thinly sliced (wear rubber gloves when handling chili peppers), or a generous pinch of cayenne pepper (optional)
- 2 teaspoons ground coriander seeds
- 1 teaspoon ground cumin seeds
- 1 teaspoon ground turmeric
- ⅛ teaspoon freshly ground pepper
- 1 teaspoon salt, or to taste
- 1¼ pounds butternut or kabocha squash, peeled, seeded, and cut into 1-inch chunks

Bring the water and tomatoes to the boil in the cooker as you add the remaining ingredients.

Lock the lid in place. Set the cooker on a heated Flame Tamer. Over high heat, bring to high pressure. Lower the heat just enough to maintain high pressure and cook for 6 minutes. Allow the pressure to come down naturally or use a quick-release method. Remove the lid, tilting it away from you to allow any excess steam to escape. If the squash is still firm, replace (but do not lock) the lid and continue to steam for a few more minutes in the residual heat.

Stir well to create a coarse purée. Adjust the seasonings before serving.

VARIATIONS

Add ¼ cup raisins or 3 tablespoons dried currants as you stir the cooked squash.

Thin leftovers with vegetable stock for a tasty soup.

TOFU SPAGHETTI SAUCE

3 minutes high pressure

TIPS & TECHNIQUES

The tofu may be frozen right in the tub it comes in; poke a hole in the top and drain out the water. Then pop it in the freezer overnight. Defrost the tofu about an hour before you need it. (This task can be hastened by soaking the tub of tofu in hot water.)

When squeezing out excess moisture, sandwich the block of tofu between two plates and tip the plates over the sink. Squeeze hard for about 30 seconds.

For an even chewier texture, cut the tofu into ½-inch slices along the short end and lay the slices along the bottom of a shallow plastic container or between two sheets of wax paper. Freeze. After defrosting, cut the tofu into ½-inch cubes. It's not necessary to squeeze out any moisture.

Here's a quick sauce to prepare by doctoring up store-bought spaghetti sauce and using it as the cooking medium for tofu. The tofu is frozen (see Tips) and then defrosted to create a chewier texture. *Do not attempt this recipe without a Flame Tamer.*

Serve Tofu Spaghetti Sauce over pasta, polenta, or steamed grains. My sister, Marian, likes to spoon it over a split-open whole-wheat roll and serve it for lunch (with a knife and fork nearby). A green salad and/or a steamed green vegetable round out the meal nicely. ***Serves 3 to 4***

3 cups prepared spaghetti sauce

1 pound frozen tofu, defrosted, squeezed between two plates to release excess water, and cut into 1-inch chunks (see Tips)

1 cup coarsely chopped onions

1 cup diced green bell pepper

1 teaspoon minced garlic

½ pound medium fresh mushrooms, trimmed and quartered

Salt and freshly ground pepper to taste

. . . .

¼ cup minced fresh parsley, dill, or basil

Begin heating the spaghetti sauce in the cooker as you prepare and add the remaining ingredients except the parsley.

Lock the lid in place. Set the cooker on a heated Flame Tamer. Over high heat, bring to high pressure. Lower the heat just enough to maintain high pressure and cook for 3 minutes. Quick-release the pressure by placing the cooker under cold running water. Remove the lid, tilting it away from you to allow any excess steam to escape.

Stir in the parsley before serving.

Chunky Eggplant Sauce for Pasta

4 minutes high pressure

This welcome alternative to tomato sauce was created by my dear friend Judy Bloom. She likes to serve this sauce with a pasta that has lots of crevices for it to hide out in — such as fusilli or spirals. It's also nice as a topping for grains. This sauce freezes well. ***Makes about 6 cups***

1 tablespoon olive oil

2 cups coarsely chopped onions

1 tablespoon minced garlic

¼ to ½ cup water (see Tip)

2 tablespoons tomato paste

2 pounds eggplant, peeled and cut into ½-inch dice

2 cups coarsely chopped fresh or canned (drained) plum
    tomatoes

1 teaspoon dried basil leaves

¼ teaspoon crushed red pepper flakes

1 teaspoon salt, or to taste

. . . .

½ cup minced fresh coriander or parsley

Heat the oil in the cooker. Cook the onions and garlic over medium-high heat, stirring frequently, for 1 minute. Add the water (stand back to avoid sputtering oil) and stir in the tomato paste until dissolved. Add the eggplant, tomatoes, basil, red pepper flakes, and salt.

Lock the lid in place. Set the cooker on a heated Flame Tamer. Over high heat, bring to high pressure. Lower the heat just enough to maintain high pressure and cook for 4 minutes. Allow the pressure to come down naturally or use a quick-release method. Remove the lid, tilting it away from you to allow any excess steam to escape.

With a slotted spoon, transfer about 2 cups of the vegetables to a food processor or blender, and purée. Stir the purée back into the vegetables to create a thick sauce. Stir in the coriander just before serving.

TIPS & TECHNIQUES

In many cookers, the liquid given off the by eggplant and tomatoes together with a small amount of water will be sufficient to bring up the pressure. Use as little water (or drained tomato juice) as you can get away with.

DESSERTS

If you are one of those people who don't associate dessert with the pressure cooker, this chapter is likely to be full of surprises.

Certainly one of the simplest, healthiest, and easiest desserts you can make is something along the lines of applesauce, which is done in under 15 minutes from start to finish. In addition, the pressure cooker is a great way to bring lightened versions of old-fashioned rice puddings and steamed puddings (I call them pudding-cakes) back into fashion. While such preparations would require 1 to 2 hours in a standard pot, they are cooked under pressure in around 30 minutes. As an added bonus, I can offer you extremely low-fat recipes that bring delicious results.

GINGERED PEAR SAUCE

Up to high pressure, 10-minute natural pressure release

Even if your cooker normally requires 1 cup of liquid to come up to pressure, the pears are likely to release sufficient moisture to reach high pressure with only ½ cup of juice. Add more liquid only if needed.

You can double and triple this recipe, but do not fill the cooker more than two thirds full.

VARIATION

Stir in 1 to 2 tablespoons of port after cooking.

A very pleasing alternative to applesauce, with a zesty edge provided by the fresh ginger.

It's nice to reserve a small uncooked pear for garnish. Just before serving, peel and thinly slice the pear—or dice it—and set it decoratively on top. Add a dollop of whipped cream or tofu whip (page 25), if you like.

If you have a food mill, there's no need to peel and core the pears. *Makes about 4 cups*

> ½ cup pear or apple juice or water
> 2½ to 3 pounds ripe pears, quartered (peeled and cored, if desired)
> 1½ tablespoons finely minced fresh ginger
> ....
> Maple syrup or sugar to taste (optional)

Place the juice, pears, and ginger in the cooker.

Lock the lid in place. If your cooker has a thin bottom, set it on a heated Flame Tamer. Over high heat, bring to high pressure. (This will probably take longer than usual.) Turn off the heat and allow the pressure to come down naturally. Remove the lid, tilting it away from you to allow any excess steam to escape.

Lift the pears from the cooking liquid with a slotted spoon. Pass them through a food mill, or pulse them in a food processor until you achieve the desired texture. Add a sweetener, if you wish. Serve warm or at room temperature in small bowls. Refrigerate leftovers in a tightly covered container for up to 10 days.

CHUNKY CRAN-APPLE SAUCE

Up to high pressure, 10-minute natural pressure release

This variation on the traditional applesauce has a slight edge of tartness and a rosy hue. Dress it up, if you like, with a dollop of whipped cream or tofu whip (page 25). *Makes about 4 cups*

2½ pounds apples, peeled, cored, and cut into quarters
1 cup whole cranberries (fresh or frozen), picked over
   and rinsed
1 cup apple juice
....

2 to 3 teaspoons finely minced orange peel (page 23)
Maple syrup or sugar to taste (optional)

Place the apples, cranberries, and juice in the cooker.

Lock the lid in place. Over high heat, bring to high pressure. Immediately turn off the heat and allow the pressure to come down naturally for 10 minutes. Quick-release any remaining pressure. Remove the lid, tilting it away from you to allow any excess steam to escape.

Stir well to create a coarse purée as you add the orange peel and a sweetener, if desired. Serve warm or at room temperature in small bowls. Refrigerate leftovers in a tightly covered container for up to 10 days.

VARIATIONS

After cooking, stir in Grand Marnier or Curaçao to taste.

Use apple cider instead of juice.

For a smooth sauce, pass the mixture through a food mill.

Apple Granola Jumble

12 minutes high pressure, 10-minute natural pressure release

TIPS & TECHNIQUES

Most of the liquid in this recipe is provided by the apples and the steam.

Here is a quick-and-easy dessert cooked and served in the same casserole. It's a plain-Jane dish that tastes a bit like a brown betty. For optimum taste, serve it warm with some vanilla ice cream or raspberry sorbet on top. Leftovers are great reheated for breakfast.

Feel free to use a low- or no-fat granola, if you like.

Serves 4

1½ pounds Granny Smith apples, peeled and coarsely chopped

⅓ cup raisins

¼ cup coarsely chopped walnuts (use less or omit if granola contains nuts)

3 tablespoons freshly squeezed lemon juice

1½ teaspoons cinnamon (use less or omit if granola is heavily flavored with cinnamon or other spices)

1½ cups granola, preferably maple walnut

½ cup apple juice or water

. . . .

Maple syrup (optional)

Ice cream or sorbet

In a 1½-quart heatproof casserole, toss the apples with the raisins, walnuts (if using), lemon juice, and cinnamon (if using). Stir in the granola and apple juice.

Place the rack and 2 cups of boiling water in the cooker. Lower the uncovered casserole onto the rack with the aid of a foil strip (page 9).

Lock the lid in place. Over high heat, bring to high pressure. Lower the heat just enough to maintain high pressure and cook for 12 minutes. Allow the pressure to come down naturally for 10 minutes. Quick-release any remaining pressure. Remove the lid, tilting it away from you to allow any excess steam to escape. If the apples are not sufficiently soft, return to high pressure for a few more minutes or replace (but do not lock) the lid and let them continue to steam in the residual heat.

Remove the casserole from the cooker with the aid of the foil strip. Stir well before serving. (The mixture is likely to be crumbly.) Add maple syrup to taste, if desired. Top each portion with a scoop of ice cream or sorbet.

DATE-NUT COUSCOUS

5 minutes high pressure, 10-minute natural pressure release

While traveling through Tunisia, I tasted dozens of varieties of couscous, including a number of surprisingly delicious desserts based on this North African staple. Here is my interpretation of a favorite, encountered at a lavish tasting presented by a large couscous factory in Sfax. It is best when served warm. (Reheat leftovers for a tasty breakfast.)

To prepare it, you'll need a 1½-quart casserole or other heatproof dish that will fit into your cooker. **Serves 4**

2 cups vanilla-flavored soy or rice milk (or substitute
    skim or whole milk plus 1 teaspoon vanilla)
1 cup whole-wheat couscous
1 cup finely chopped pitted dates
½ cup finely chopped walnuts

. . . .

1½ to 2 teaspoons rosewater (optional)
Additional ¼ to ½ cup milk (optional)
⅓ cup pomegranate seeds and/or 2 tangerines, peeled
    and divided into segments

VARIATIONS

Use unsalted pistachios instead of walnuts.

Substitute a more refined (white) couscous for the whole-wheat.

In the heatproof casserole, combine the milk, couscous, dates, and walnuts.

Place the rack and 2 cups of boiling water in the cooker. Lower the uncovered casserole onto the rack with the aid of a foil strip (page 9).

Lock the lid in place. Over high heat, bring to high pressure. Lower the heat just enough to maintain high pressure and cook for 5 minutes. Allow the pressure to come down naturally for 10 minutes. Quick-release any remaining pressure. Remove the lid, tilting it away from you to allow any excess steam to escape.

Remove the casserole from the cooker with the aid of the foil strip. Stir the couscous as you add rosewater to taste (if using) and additional milk if the mixture seems dry. Garnish individual portions with pomegranate seeds and/or orange segments.

RICE PUDDINGS

COCONUT RICE PUDDING

*4 minutes high pressure, 10-minute natural
pressure release*

Here's a quick and simple rice pudding with exotic flavor and the crunch of coconut. For a drier rice pudding, use 3½ cups water; 4 cups produces a soupier version. **Serves 4 to 6**

TIPS & TECHNIQUES

To thin the pudding (after cooking or overnight refrigeration), stir in a bit of milk or water while reheating.

For a richer rice pudding, substitute 1 to 1½ cups of milk (soy, rice, or dairy) for an equivalent amount of water.

Some batches of rice absorb more liquid than others. If the cooked pudding seems dry, stir in some milk or water to achieve desired consistency.

3½ to 4 cups water (use higher amount in jiggle-top cookers)

1½ cups extra-long-grain or basmati white rice

1 teaspoon ground cinnamon

¼ teaspoon ground cardamom

½ cup dried, grated, unsweetened coconut

½ cup raisins or dried cherries

⅛ teaspoon salt

2 to 4 tablespoons maple syrup

. . . .

3 to 4 tablespoons finely chopped crystallized ginger

⅓ cup toasted slivered almonds (optional)

Bring the water to the boil in the cooker. Add the rice, cinnamon, cardamom, coconut, raisins, salt, and 2 tablespoons of maple syrup.

Lock the lid in place. Over high heat, bring to high pressure. Lower the heat just enough to maintain high pressure and cook for 4 minutes. Allow the pressure to come down naturally for 10 minutes. Quick-release any remaining pressure. Remove the lid, tilting it away from you to allow any excess steam to escape.

Stir well while adding the crystallized ginger and additional maple syrup, if needed. Garnish with toasted slivered almonds, if desired, and serve warm.

Substitute basmati brown rice for the white rice and add an extra ½ cup water (i.e., 4 to 4½ cups total). Increase the cooking time to 35 minutes under high pressure plus a 10-minute natural pressure release. Owners of jiggle-top cookers should use a Flame Tamer.

BROWN RICE PUDDING WITH APPLES

40 minutes high pressure, 1 to 2 minutes standing

This is an earthy rice pudding that can be dressed up with a scoop of your favorite dairy or nondairy ice cream and an extra grating of fresh nutmeg. The oatmeal adds creaminess to this low-fat, cholesterol-free dessert. Diced raw apple brings some welcome crunch when stirred in at the end.

I like the splash of color supplied by the apple peel; on the other hand, the texture is more mellow when the apples are peeled. Up to you. *Serves 4 to 6*

1 cup long-grain or basmati brown rice
⅓ cup old-fashioned oatmeal
2 to 2½ cups boiling water (use higher amount in jiggle-
    top cookers)
1½ cups apple juice
¾ teaspoon ground cinnamon
¼ teaspoon freshly grated nutmeg
Pinch of salt
¼ cup dried currants or raisins

. . . .

2 large apples, peeled if desired, cored, and cut into ½-
    inch dice
Freshly squeezed lemon juice to taste or 1 tablespoon
    finely minced lemon peel (page 22; optional)

continued

VARIATIONS

Substitute pear juice and fresh pears for the apple juice and apples.

Instead of lemon juice or peel, stir in 1 to 2 tablespoons of orange marmalade.

Place the rice, oatmeal, water, juice, cinnamon, nutmeg, salt, and currants in the cooker.

Lock the lid in place. Set the cooker on a heated Flame Tamer. Over high heat, bring to high pressure. Lower the heat just enough to maintain high pressure and cook for 40 minutes. Allow the pressure to come down naturally or use a quick-release method. Remove the lid, tilting it away from you to allow any excess steam to escape. The pudding is likely to be soupy but will thicken as it sits.

Stir in the apples and cover for a minute or two, just until the apples become warm but do not lose their crunch. Stir in a bit of lemon juice or lemon peel, if desired, to sharpen the flavors. Serve warm.

FIG-HAZELNUT RISOTTO

*7 minutes high pressure, 10-minute natural
pressure release*

Creamy arborio rice creates a welcome addition to the rice
pudding repertoire. I think you'll agree that figs and anise
are fabulous together. For optimum taste, serve warm.
Serves 6

4 cups milk (soy, rice, or dairy), divided

½ cup water

1½ cups arborio rice

1 to 1½ cups chopped dried figs (use the minimum if
you prefer modestly sweetened desserts)

1 teaspoon aniseed

. . . .

½ cup chopped toasted hazelnuts

Bring 3½ cups milk and the water to the boil in the cooker.
Stir in the rice, figs, and aniseed.

Lock the lid in place. If using a jiggle-top cooker, or if your
cooker has a thin bottom, set on a heated Flame Tamer. Over
high heat, bring to high pressure. Lower the heat just enough
to maintain high pressure and cook for 7 minutes. Allow the
pressure to come down naturally for 10 minutes. Quick-release
any remaining pressure. Remove the lid, tilting it away from
you to allow any excess steam to escape.

Stir in the additional ½ cup of milk as you add the hazelnuts. Serve warm.

TIPS & TECHNIQUES

To reheat any leftovers,
stir in a few tablespoons
of water and simmer,
covered, over low heat.
Keep an eye on the pot,
stir frequently, and add
more water as needed.

VARIATION

For a lower-fat version,
use "lite" soy or skim
milk. Alternatively, use
half milk and half water.

STEAMED PUDDING CAKES
AND A BREAD PUDDING

I know that calling these desserts pudding-cakes is the culinary equivalent of sitting on the fence, but there's a certain truth to the description. You see, they are steamed like puddings but often come out with a spongy texture much more akin to cake. Despite every attempt to standardize these recipes, there is still a slight variation of texture from one time to the next.

The way to get the most reliable results is to purchase a 1-quart Bundt pan. It is inexpensive and available by mail from Zabar's (see Mail-Order Sources). Because the Bundt pan is shaped in a ring with a tube in the middle, the batter cooks evenly. It also produces a dessert that's pretty to unmold and serve as you would a cake.

Your other option is to use a 1-quart heatproof casserole or soufflé dish. This often requires adding 5 minutes to cooking time under pressure, and you may still find that the center is slightly undercooked while the outside portion is a bit dry. Perhaps the best approach is to try out a recipe in a heatproof container you already own and then, if you see the potential of these pudding-cakes, invest in a small Bundt pan.

These pudding-cakes are easy to make and quite delicious—especially given the fact that they have none of the butter or oil that usually goes along with such fare.

Despite their delicious taste, these pudding-cakes come out looking a bit plain. You might like to dust them lightly with confectioner's sugar or garnish portions with sliced fresh fruit or a small scoop of sorbet.

BLUEBERRY PUDDING-CAKE

25 to 30 minutes high pressure, 15-minute natural pressure release

The addition of cornmeal gives this pudding-cake an appealing, slightly coarse texture that complements the soft sweetness of the blueberries. **Serves 6 to 8**

½ teaspoon safflower or canola oil and about 2
    teaspoons flour for preparing a 1-quart Bundt pan
    or heatproof casserole
1 cup unbleached white flour
½ cup cornmeal
1 teaspoon baking soda
1 teaspoon baking powder
¾ teaspoon ground cinnamon
¼ teaspoon ground nutmeg
⅛ teaspoon salt
1 tablespoon finely minced lemon peel (page 22)
2 cups blueberries (fresh or frozen)
½ cup berry or apple juice
½ cup maple syrup

Brush oil on the bottom and sides of the Bundt pan or casserole and dust liberally with flour. Tip out any extra flour and set the pan aside.

In a large bowl, combine the flour, cornmeal, baking soda, baking powder, cinnamon, nutmeg, salt, and lemon peel. Gently stir in the blueberries.

In a liquid measuring cup, combine the juice and maple syrup. Stir this mixture into the dry ingredients.

Pour the mixture into the prepared pan, scraping the sides of the bowl with a spatula. Wrap tightly with a sheet of aluminum foil large enough to tuck the ends under the bottom of the pan.

Place the rack and 3 cups of boiling water in the cooker. Lower the pan onto the rack with the aid of a foil strip (page 9).

continued

Lock the lid in place. Over high heat, bring to high pressure. Lower the heat just enough to maintain high pressure and cook for 25 minutes (Bundt pan) or 30 minutes (casserole). Allow the pressure to come down naturally for 15 minutes. Quick-release any remaining pressure. Remove the lid, tilting it away from you to allow any excess steam to escape.

Lift the pan out of the cooker with the aid of the foil strip. Immediately remove the foil covering and set the pan on a rack to cool. You may unmold the pudding-cake by running a knife along the edges, turning the pan upside down, and gently rocking it up and down. Alternatively, slice the pudding-cake right in the Bundt pan or casserole.

Serve warm or at room temperature.

PEAR PUDDING-CAKE

25 to 30 minutes high pressure, 15-minute natural pressure release

This is a personal favorite and gets top ratings from tasters. Choose pears that are ripe but still firm, and you will be pleased to find that they hold their shape quite well. Bartletts work nicely. *Serves 6 to 8*

- ½ teaspoon safflower or canola oil and about 2 teaspoons flour for preparing a 1-quart Bundt pan or heatproof casserole
- ¾ cup whole-wheat pastry flour
- ¾ cup unbleached white flour
- 1 teaspoon baking soda
- 1½ teaspoons ground ginger
- ¼ teaspoon ground cardamom
- ⅛ teaspoon salt
- ⅓ cup dried currants or raisins
- ⅓ cup toasted slivered almonds
- 2 large pears, peeled and cut into ¾-inch dice (about 2 cups)
- ⅔ cup pear or other noncitrus fruit juice
- ⅓ cup maple syrup

Brush oil on the bottom and sides of the Bundt pan or casserole and dust liberally with flour. Tip out any extra flour and set the pan aside.

In a large bowl, combine the flours, baking soda, ginger, cardamom, salt, currants, and almonds. Gently stir in the diced pears.

In a liquid measuring cup, combine the juice and maple syrup. Stir this mixture into the dry ingredients.

Pour the mixture into the prepared pan, scraping the sides of the bowl with a spatula. Wrap tightly with a sheet of aluminum foil large enough to tuck the ends under the bottom of the pan.

Place the rack and 3 cups of boiling water in the cooker. Lower the pan onto the rack with the aid of a foil strip (page 9).

Lock the lid in place. Over high heat, bring to high pressure. Lower the heat just enough to maintain high pressure and cook for 25 minutes (Bundt pan) or 30 minutes (casserole). Allow the pressure to come down naturally for 15 minutes. Quick-release any remaining pressure. Remove the lid, tilting it away from you to allow any excess steam to escape.

Lift the pan out of the cooker with the aid of the foil strip. Immediately remove the foil covering and set the pan on a rack to cool. You may unmold the pudding-cake by running a knife along the edges, turning the pan upside down, and gently rocking it up and down. Alternatively, slice the pudding-cake right in the pan or casserole.

Serve warm or at room temperature.

BANANA PUDDING-CAKE

35 minutes high pressure

This pudding-cake has a strong banana taste and a definite affinity with banana bread. It is good warm as well as at room temperature.

On occasion, a few banana pieces float to the top and turn purple. It looks a bit odd, but I can assure you that the flavor is not affected. *Serves 6 to 8*

VARIATION

Use ½ cup raisins instead of the walnuts.

½ teaspoon safflower or canola oil and about 2
    teaspoons flour for preparing a 1-quart Bundt pan
    or heatproof casserole
¾ cup whole-wheat pastry flour
¾ cup unbleached white flour
1 teaspoon baking soda
1 teaspoon baking powder
⅛ teaspoon salt
½ cup coarsely chopped walnuts
2 large ripe bananas, peeled and cut into ½-inch slices
½ cup apple juice
½ cup maple syrup
2 teaspoons vanilla extract

Brush oil on the bottom and sides of the Bundt pan or casserole and dust liberally with flour. Tip out any extra flour and set the pan aside.

In a large bowl, combine the flours, baking soda, baking powder, salt, and walnuts. Gently stir in the bananas, taking care to separate the slices and coat them with flour.

In a liquid measuring cup, combine the apple juice, maple syrup, and vanilla. Stir this mixture into the dry ingredients.

Pour the mixture into the prepared pan, scraping the sides of the bowl with a spatula. Wrap tightly with a sheet of aluminum foil large enough to tuck the ends under the bottom of the pan.

Place the rack and 3 cups of boiling water in the cooker. Lower the pan onto the rack with the aid of a foil strip (page 9).

Lock the lid in place. Over high heat, bring to high pressure. Lower the heat just enough to maintain high pressure and cook for 35 minutes. Reduce the pressure with a quick-release method. Remove the lid, tilting it away from you to allow any excess steam to escape.

Lift the pan out of the cooker with the aid of the foil strip. Immediately remove the foil covering and set the pan on a rack to cool. You may unmold the pudding-cake by running a knife along the edges, turning the pan upside down, and gently rocking it up and down. Alternatively, slice the pudding-cake right in the pan or casserole.

Serve warm or at room temperature.

Pumpkin Bread Pudding

20 minutes high pressure, 10-minute natural pressure release

For this luscious recipe, you will need a 2-quart heatproof casserole that will fit into the cooker with at least ½ inch to spare around the edges. After it is steamed and cut into wedges for serving, this bread pudding has an uncanny resemblance to a layer cake. You may also scoop it out for a less formal presentation.

Good for Thanksgiving or any fall-winter menu. Serve it hot, perhaps with a scoop of vanilla ice cream on top. A real winner! *Serves 8*

2 cups milk (soy, rice, or dairy)
One 16-ounce can solid-pack unseasoned pumpkin purée
    (2 cups)
⅓ cup maple syrup
2½ teaspoons ground cinnamon
1 to 1¼ teaspoons ground ginger
½ teaspoon freshly grated nutmeg
⅛ teaspoon salt
10 to 12 slices (about ½ inch thick) Italian or French
    bread, preferably whole-wheat, stale or air-dried for
    12 to 14 hours (see Tips)
⅔ cup raisins

continued

TIPS & TECHNIQUES

The number of bread slices you need will vary according to the shape of your casserole and the size of the loaf. If you want to air-dry just enough for this use, create three sample layers in the casserole as you slice.

For an impromptu preparation of this pudding, you can dry out the bread slices on the rack of a toaster oven set to 400 degrees. Remove the bread as soon as it begins to turn light brown.

If not serving immediately, let the pudding sit in the cooker with the lid ajar. If it sits for a short while after cooking, the pudding will hold its shape better when sliced.

In a food processor or blender, combine the milk, pumpkin, maple syrup, spices, and salt until well blended. Pour about one quarter of the mixture into the bottom of a 2-quart heatproof casserole. Arrange a layer of bread on the pumpkin mixture, breaking slices in half as needed to fit. Distribute one third of the raisins on top of the bread. Then pour on another one quarter of the pumpkin mixture and spread it more or less evenly over the bread and raisins with a knife. Repeat, layering the bread, raisins, and pumpkin mixture twice more. (You will have three bread layers in all and should end with the pumpkin mixture on top.) Wrap the casserole tightly with a sheet of aluminum foil large enough to tuck the ends under the bottom.

Place the rack and 2 cups of boiling water in the cooker. Lower the casserole onto the rack with the aid of a foil strip (page 9).

Lock the lid in place. Over high heat, bring to high pressure. Lower the heat just enough to maintain high pressure and cook for 20 minutes. Allow the pressure to come down naturally for 10 minutes. Quick-release any remaining pressure. Remove the lid, tilting it away from you to allow any excess steam to escape.

Lift the casserole out of the cooker with the aid of the foil strip. Just before serving, remove the foil covering. Serve warm, cutting wedge-shaped portions or scooping out with a serving spoon.

APPENDIX

TROUBLE SHOOTING

Until you get well acquainted with the pressure cooker, from time to time its behavior may puzzle you. It's a good idea to read the manufacturer's instruction booklet thoroughly. In addition, here are some explanations for things that may happen.

Always turn off the heat and release all pressure before attempting to remove the lid to check on what's happening.

JT= jiggle-top cooker **SG**= second-generation cooker

The cooker is taking a long time to come up to pressure.	You are cooking a larger quantity of food than usual. Be patient.
	There is insufficient liquid. Add an additional ¼ to ½ cup as needed.
	The cooker is filled well beyond the recommended capacity and there is not sufficient space for the steam pressure to gather. Cook the ingredients in two batches.
	You may need a new rubber gasket. Try lightly coating it with vegetable oil.
	SG: The pressure regulator is not screwed in tightly. Quick-release the pressure and check under the lid.
	JT: The vent is clogged with a particle of food. Quick-release the pressure, then remove the lid and clean thoroughly.
Water is dripping down the sides of the cooker.	You may need a new rubber gasket. First try lightly coating it with vegetable oil.
	SG: You have forgotten to lower the heat after reaching high pressure. The gasket has extruded. Quick-release the pressure. Set the gasket in place and return to high pressure. Lower the heat to maintain high pressure and proceed as directed in the recipe.
Liquid is spouting from the vent.	Immediately turn off the heat. Do not attempt to move the cooker until the pressure comes down naturally. Consider the following possibilities:
	You forgot to turn down the heat after reaching high pressure. Or, you did not lower the heat sufficiently and pressure kept building. Return to high pressure and then immediately lower the heat.
	The cooker is too full. Cook the ingredients in two batches.
	The food inside (probably beans or grains) is creating foam. After releasing the pressure, stir in a tablespoon of oil. Make certain that the vent is clean, and resume cooking.

Wash and thoroughly dry the gasket. Coat it lightly with vegetable oil. If this doesn't help, replace the gasket.

It's difficult to get the lid to lock in place.

A vacuum has been created inside the cooker. Either wait until the cooker cools entirely or bring it back up to pressure and quick-release. The lid should come off easily.

I can't get the lid off after the pressure has been released.

Use a Flame Tamer (page 6).

Increase the liquid slightly the next time you cook this recipe.

If you've done an initial browning, be sure that no ingredients (such as onions or garlic) are sticking to the bottom.

Food either forms a crust or burns on the bottom of the cooker.

FURTHER RESOURCES: VEGETARIAN NUTRITION

Books

The New Laurel's Kitchen, A Handbook for Vegetarian Cookery & Nutrition by Laurel Robertson, Carol Flinders, and Brian Ruppenthal (Berkeley: Ten Speed Press, 1986).

Vegan Nutrition: Pure and Simple by Michael Klaper, M.D. (Alachua, FL: Gentle World, 1987).
Can be mail-ordered from Gentle World, Inc., P.O. Box 1418, Umatilla, FL 32784. $10.95 postpaid.

Magazines

All of these magazines frequently run articles on the latest research findings.

Vegetarian Times, P.O. Box 446, Mt. Morris, IL 61054-8081. Subscriptions are $24.95 per year.

Natural Health, P.O. Box 57320, Boulder, CO 80322-7320. Subscriptions are $24 per year.

Vegetarian Journal, P.O. Box 1463, Baltimore, MD 21203. Subscriptions are $20 per year.

Organizations

North American Vegetarian Society, P.O. Box 72, Dolgeville, NY 13329. Members receive an informative quarterly magazine, *Vegetarian Voice;* the society holds an annual summer conference with excellent cooking classes and speakers on nutrition. Membership is $18 per year.

The American Vegan Association, P.O. Box H, Malaga, NJ 08328. An excellent mail-order source of books on vegan nutrition.

MAIL-ORDER SOURCES

Most of the companies listed below send free catalogs upon request. For additional sources, consult:

Green Groceries: A Mail-Order Guide to Organic Foods by Jeanne Heifetz (New York: HarperCollins, 1992).

An exciting annotated compendium of sources for a wide variety of fresh and dried ingredients.

General

GOLD MINE NATURAL FOOD CO.
1947 30th Street
San Diego, CA 92102
800-475-FOOD
An excellent source of high-quality organic foods, including grains, beans, and sea vegetables (including sea palm). They also sell the New Ohsawa Pot (page 117) for cooking rice under pressure.

Beans, etc.

BEAN BAG
818 Jefferson Street
Oakland, CA 94607
800-845-BEAN
The largest variety of boutique beans I've seen anywhere, most harvested within the last year. Bean Bag also carries a good range of organic beans.

DEAN & DELUCA
560 Broadway
New York, NY 10012
800-221-7714
A nice variety of high-quality boutique beans as well as gourmet products of all kinds, including arborio rice for risotto.

Chili Peppers

LOS CHILEROS DE NUEVO MEXICO
P.O. Box 6215
Santa Fe, NM 87502
505-471-6967
An excellent source, including the best chipotles I've found.

Dried Fruit

TIMBER CREST FARMS
4791 Dry Creek Road
Healdsburg, CA 95448
707-433-8251
Also sells dried tomatoes.

Herbs and Spices

FRONTIER COOPERATIVE HERBS
P.O. Box 299
Norway, IA 52318
800-669-3275
Fine-quality herbs and a good, reliable (not too hot) chili
powder.

SPICE HOUSE
P.O. Box 1633
Milwaukee, WI 53201
414-768-8799
Spice House prides itself on selling the best and freshest; it
also offers lots of house special blends.

Instant Stock

VOGUE VEGE BASE
888-236-4144
If you have trouble finding this product in your local health
food store, you can call this number for a local distributor or
to order directly.

Pressure Cookers

ZABAR'S
2245 Broadway
New York, NY 10024
212-787-2000
A good selection of cookers sold at discount prices and shipped
out promptly.

For background and purchasing information, you may wish to
contact the following manufacturers directly:

CUISINARTS
150 Milford Road
East Windsor, NJ 08520
800-726-0190

KUHN-RIKON DUROMATIC
Swiss Kitchen
228 Bonnair Center
Greenbrae, CA 94904
800-662-5882

MAGEFESA USA
P.O. Box 328
Prospect Heights, IL 60070
800-923-8700

T-FAL CORPORATION
25 Riverside Drive
Pine Brook, NJ 07058
201-575-1060

INDEX

Grain Cooking Times at a Glance

For basic cooking instructions, see pages 115 – 119 and check Index under individual listings.

Grain (1 Cup)	Cups Liquid	Teaspoons Optional Salt	Minutes Under High Pressure	Yield in Cups
Amaranth	1½–1¾**	½–1*	4 plus 10-minute npr[§]	2
Barley (hulled)	3[†]	½–1	35–45	3½–4
Barley (pearl)	3[†]	½–1	18–20	3½
Buckwheat	1¾[†]	½–1	3 plus 7-minute npr[§]	2
Bulgur	1½	½–1	5 plus 10-minute npr[§]	3
Job's Tears[‡]	2½	½–1	16 plus 10-minute npr[§]	3
Kamut	3[†]	½–1*	35–45	2¾
Millet[‡]	1¾–2**	½–1	10 plus 10-minute npr[§]	3½–4
Oats (whole groats)	3[†]	½–1	25–30	2–2½
Quinoa	1½	½–1	1 plus 10-minute npr[§]	3–3½
Rye berries	3	½–1	25–30	2½
Spelt	3	½–1*	35–45	2¼
Triticale	3	½–1*	35–45	2–2½
Wheat berries	3	½–1*	35–45	2¼
Wild rice	3	¼	22–28	2½–3

*To ensure proper absorption of water, add salt after cooking.
[†]Add 1 tablespoon oil to control foaming action.
[‡]Toast before boiling (page 167).
[§]npr = natural pressure release
**Use higher amount in jiggle-top cookers.

Brown Rice Cooking Chart at a Glance

For basic cooking instructions, see page 122.

For a dry rice, use the smaller amount of liquid.
For a moist rice and in jiggle-top cookers, use the maximum.

Cups Brown Rice	Cups Boiling Liquid	Teaspoons Optional Salt	Tablespoons Optional Oil	Approximate Yield in Cups
1	1¾–2	½	1	2¼
1½	2½–2¾	¾	1	3½
2	3½–4	1	1½	5
3	5–5½	1½	2	7

NOTE: Do not fill the cooker more than halfway.